Untangling the Mayhem: Crises and Prospects of the Middle East

INTERNATIONAL RELATIONS IN ASIA, AFRICA AND THE AMERICAS

Edited by Andrzej Mania & Marcin Grabowski

VOL. 3

PETER LANG

Radka Havlová (ed.)

Untangling the Mayhem: Crises and Prospects of the Middle East

PETER LANG

Bibliographic Information published by the Deutsche Nationalbibliothek
The Deutsche Nationalbibliothek lists this publication in the Deutsche Nationalbibliografie; detailed bibliographic data is available in the internet at http://dnb.d-nb.de.

Library of Congress Cataloging-in-Publication Data A CIP catalog record for this book has been applied for at the Library of Congress

ISSN 2511-588X
ISBN 978-3-631-74092-7 (Print)
E-ISBN 978-3-631-76265-3 (E-PDF)
E-ISBN 978-3-631-76266-0 (EPUB)
E-ISBN 978-3-631-76267-7 (MOBI)
DOI 10.3726/b14442

Peter Lang – Berlin · Bern · Bruxelles · New York · Oxford · Warszawa · Wien

This publication has been peer reviewed.

www.peterlang.com

Table of Contents

Acknowledgements

The authors wish to thank the Faculty of International Relations of the University of Economics, Prague, for its financial support of this publication by the internal grant No. IG212016 "Crises in MENA and southwest Asia: democratisation, militancy and security". A special thanks also belongs to Dr. Jeremy Alan Garlick for his helpful comments. The authors are also grateful to all colleagues who provided help and their comments to the presented text as well as to all those who supported the authors during the process of writing.

Foreword

Current events taking place in the Middle East and North Africa (MENA) are not only reshaping (political) orders in the region but are also having a deep impact on the existing international order. The current situation in the MENA region has led to political and military interventions as well as increased security measures. Furthermore, certain militant groups have emerged in the MENA region, namely, the Islamic State (IS) in Iraq and Syria, and affiliated groups in Egypt, Algeria and Libya which have complicated the situation in the region further by challenging state authority, forming parallel state-like apparatuses and carrying out transnational attacks in different parts of the region as well as in Europe. Deteriorating living conditions have forced millions of people to flee and take refuge in neighbouring states such as Turkey, Lebanon and Jordan. Consequently, the study of changes in the MENA region as well as southwest Asia has an enormous importance not only in terms of adding value to the existing literature but also in terms of exploring the new and broad horizons of understanding the complexities and consequences of the recent events in the region.

This book focuses on the region of the MENA in its wider perception. The World Bank defines the MENA region as the area of Algeria, Bahrain, Djibouti, Egypt, Iran, Israel, Iraq, Jordan, Kuwait, Lebanon, Libya, Morocco, Oman, Qatar, Saudi Arabia, Syria, Tunisia, the United Arab Emirates, the West Bank and Gaza (Palestine), and Yemen. In order to illustrate the recent development and democratization in this region, Turkey has here been added as one of the substantial players in the region. With the exception of Israel, all the above-mentioned countries are characterized by the strong role of Islam in the majority of citizens' religious life. Hence, this book focuses on the recent development and the (de-)democratization processes in Egypt, Iraq, Lebanon, Libya, Palestine, Syria, Yemen and Turkey.

We discuss the recent developments in the region with the objective of providing a complex analysis of the factors which have influenced these developments. The book captures the situation in the respective countries as of the spring 2017, and therefore further development in the individual countries is no longer reflected and explained in the individual case studies. The book presents the current developments in each of the respective countries in their complexity, and it pays attention to internal as well as external factors shaping the countries. It also uses the democratization process as an analytical framework, without the normativity attributed to it by some of the Western literature. Our primary objective is to provide a comprehensive discourse about the recent development in the selected countries of the Middle East. However, as many of the countries are deeply influenced by historic roots of the conflicts, some analyses such as Yemen or Iraq also discuss the historic roots of the conflicts.

The first chapter is devoted to the theoretical and methodological framework of the book. Based on a wide range of literature, the chapter aims to provide the reader with important information about the MENA region and the theory of democratization. We propose three groups of factors, which may have a strong influence on democracy.

The case studies which are included in this book follow the structure outlined in the theoretical chapter. Looking at the selected Arab countries of the MENA region and Turkey, the authors focus in particular on the recent developments in the selected countries. Many of these countries have gone through the democratization process, yet the outcomes are rather unclear and vary significantly in the individual states.

The countries selected for analysis represent the variety of the MENA region. Geographically North Africa is represented by Libya and Egypt while the other case studies reflect the situation in the Levant. The authors have also tried to capture the development in countries with different religions, and although in the majority of the analysed countries Islam is a dominant religion, there are also significant Christian minorities, for instance in Lebanon, Syria, Palestine or Egypt. Although the majority of analysed countries are Arab countries, Turkey stands out as a non-Arab country of the region. In addition, the authors have attempted to capture the recent development in countries which have gone through a foreign intervention, such as Iraq or Libya, as well as those without an outside intervention. Finally, the authors present the different outcomes of the recent developments ranging from states which are in fact in a state of war, such as Yemen, Syria or Iraq, to countries in which the development has been relatively more peaceful (Palestine, Turkey, Egypt and Lebanon).

The chapter on Egypt deals with the massive protests of the Arab Spring in 2011, which brought an end to the almost thirty years long rule of the regime of Hosni Mubarak, promising a path towards more freedom and democratic reforms. However, the following development has showed that the transition to democracy in Egypt is rather problematic due to various factors, which are often deeply rooted in the preceding regimes.

Concerning Iraq, the chapter presents the case study in a broader historical context as the Arab Spring did not significantly alter the course of the recent developments; in fact, the structural and political roots of the current disintegration of the country go quite far back in history. Unfortunately, the country did not enjoy many peaceful years in its modern history and the state of its society and economy illustrates well the mistakes the international community as well as its own governments committed in the past.

The chapter on Lebanon deals with its unique political system that is constructed according to the religious mosaic of the country. However, the question of that diversity being a curse or a blessing remains unanswered as it is, simultaneously, at the base of the Lebanese multicultural society and its daily struggles. Lebanon was not directly affected by the Arab Spring itself but by the overall situation in the region, which hit the Lebanese political, economic and civil reality.

Libya is an example of a foreign imposed regime change hidden within the stream of the Arab Spring that led to chaos and destabilization in the country. Western countries led by France and Great Britain succeeded in overthrowing the dictator, but did not think about what would follow after Gaddafi was gone. Democratization in this case led to destabilization that is continuing even six years after the regime change. The chapter on Libya focuses on the causes of this chaos and analyses the potential future development in Libya.

Palestine represents a special case in which the very existence of Palestine as an independent state is challenged by some members of the international community. The chapter analyses the recent developments linked to the Arab Spring which did not really lead to major changes in Palestine as more significant changes have been occurring within Palestinian society itself.

As for Syria, it is in the spotlight of the international community as well as the battlefield of superpowers and different major players in the game of the region's geopolitics. The internal frustration that flourished in 2011 within the Arab Spring quickly escalated and turned into a civil war giving space to terrorism and extremism. The chapter focuses mainly on the political and religious background to the current situation, in addition to the international dimension of the conflict.

When analysing the MENA region, it is also necessary to mention Turkey, to which we have devoted a chapter analysing the recent development in this country. Turkey under the rule of incumbent Adalet ve Kalkınma Partisi (AKP) was presented by some as a model country for Islamic states. Economically on the rise, seemingly combining moderate Islam with democratic reforms and aspiration for EU accession, Turkey seemed an ideal partner. Nevertheless, recent developments show in a clear light that the reforms undertaken turned from democratization to de-democratization and that steps towards authoritarianism could be, even if more secretly, detected in Turkey years before.

The concluding case study of Yemen's recent developments unfortunately does not finish the book on a positive note. Yemen, similar to Syria, because of its internal developments, became a scene of a proxy war between regional and international players and is currently suffering from a grave humanitarian crisis. In this case, discussion of democratization efforts needs to make way for conflict resolution as well as the possible post-conflict reconstruction.

The authors are aware of the fact that Middle East is a very popular region in academic literature, and there is a wide range of literature discussing the situation in the states we analyse in this volume. In the chapter dealing with Egypt, a variety of sources have been used, such as academic books, analyses and articles published in professional journals, data and reports from non-governmental organizations (Freedom House, Transparency International, etc.) as well as data from the World Bank or the UN. Some of the most used volumes and analyses include the works of Esposito, Sonn, and Voll (2016), El Medni (2013), Laub (2014) or Trager (2015, 2016, 2017).

Iraq's chapter draws on the existing academic literature as well as World Bank or UN data. When analysing the 1990s humanitarian crisis, extensive studies by Geoff (1998) and Shehabaldin and Laughlin (1999) are used, the current political disintegration of the country is illustrated through authors such as Gerges (2016) and Baxter and Akbarzadeh (2008).

The chapters about Lebanon and Syria use all sorts of literature in several languages, particularly in English, French and Arabic, which provides a large scale of information from different points of view. For Syria, reports by the Carnegie Middle East Center, studies by Fabrice Balanche, and monographies by Baron (2014) and Erlich (2014) were used. As for the Lebanese history and political system, they were illustrated in the literature of Corm (2003) and Messara (1994, 1997). In addition, data about the refugees were found mainly on United Nations High Commissioner for Refugees (UNHCR) websites. Finally, information about the civil society and media were drawn from different analyses and articles from several local and international sources such as the Washington Institute, the EU and Naharnet.

As for Palestine there have been several analyses published mostly online and in professional journals dealing with the recent development in the territory, such as the ones of Aronson (2011), Baroud (2012), Dessi (2012) or Finkelstein, Mounin and Stern-Weiner (2013); however, a comprehensive analysis of the situation in Palestine based on the complex criteria defined in our volume has been so far missing. Regime change in Libya is mostly studied from the perspective of causes and process (Landen, 2012; Terrill, 2015) and in terms of contrast between Gaddafi's regime and chaos that which has evolved since his fall (Hamid, 2016; Mattes, 2016). For explanation of the regime change it is necessary to work with online resources, such as news portals (Al Jazeera, BBC, Reuters), statistics (World Bank, IMF) and also with quotations and evaluations of politicians on the international scene (Barack Obama, Tony Blair, David Cameron, Nicolas Sarkozy).

There is a growing body of literature on recent developments in Turkey, such as Rodriguez et al. (2013), yet rarely are those put into complex relations and/or comparison with the developments in the rest of the MENA region, which should be the contribution of the presented publication. The very recent affairs, such as the attempted July 2016 coup, are presented mostly in online analysis and, with the rare exception of Cağaptay (2017) lack deeper explanation regarding the roots of the present developments and the similarities and differences to happenings in the neighbouring MENA region.

Yemen's chapter is quite specific as its history and development have been well-documented in the literature. However, the country is currently in a state of war and undergoing a serious humanitarian crisis. Hence, the works by Phillips (2011), Lewis (2015) and Carapico (1998) have been employed, as well as various news feeds, in order to analyse the current on-the-ground situation.

The authors nevertheless feel that a detailed analysis of the recent developments in the selected MENA countries based on a set of the same criteria applied to all the states is currently missing. The authors thus hope that after reading this edited volume the reader will have a better understanding of the current development in selected countries of the MENA region. And although the analysis in the book is not very encouraging on the whole, it is, the authors believe, necessary in order to give the reader a sense of the immensity of the problems facing the region and what would be required to solve them. The authors hope that by analysing the issues in depth the reader can understand the variety and complexity of the development within the MENA region and the main challenges the countries are currently facing.

Kristýna Stejskalová and Karolína Najmanová

Factors influencing democratization in the MENA region

Democracy and the Middle East are two terms that were for many centuries hardly related to each other. At the end of the 20th century, two controversial experts, Samuel Huntington and Francis Fukuyama, stood out of the crowd and called attention to the fact that the 21st century could bring a new perception of international order and conflicts. Huntington believed that after the end of the Cold War, conflicts would appear not just between states, but rather between different cultural and religious identities that would clash.[1] His strongest opponent, Francis Fukuyama, claimed that history was coming to the end as the Western liberal democracy had become the final form of government, and this marked the endpoint of the sociocultural evolution of mankind.[2]

An increasing number of countries have transformed their form of government into democracies since the end of the Cold War.[3] From 2010 to 2012, Middle East and North Africa (MENA) region experienced the so-called Arab Spring, which has the analogy of a clash between Islamic religion and the Western system of values with democracy as its highest good. The problematic process of democratization in the MENA region could therefore be understood as a clash between the theories of Fukuyama and Huntington. Nevertheless, both these theories have been challenged over time and we are reflecting on these challenges in this chapter. As this book demonstrates, the process of democratization in the MENA region is a complex issue that needs to be analysed from several points of view.

Although the theoretical discussion starts with the well-known work of Samuel Huntington and Francis Fukuyama, it then devotes substantial attention to challenges to both these approaches. The specifics of the MENA region applied to theoretical approaches are also taken into account in this debate. The result of this approach is a set of factors which are perceived as influencing the democratization processes, although to a varying degree. These factors then serve as a framework to be applied to the case studies presented further on in the book. As a result, the

---

1 Huntington, *The Clash of Civilizations and the Remaking of World Order*.

2 Fukuyama, *The End of History and the Last Man*.

3 Gates et al., "Institutional Inconsistency and Political Instability: Polity Duration, 1800–2000".

book presents the reader with a complex analysis of contemporary development in the MENA region.

Democratization in a particular country may have its individual course influenced by a variety of aspects. Nevertheless, it is possible to study the common features of democratization that have an impact on the process of transition to democracy globally as well as specifically in the MENA region. These features are analysed in this chapter and allow us to explain the causes, process and consequences of the transitions taking place in the MENA region. In the following case studies, each author decides which factors of democratization are crucial for understanding of the democratization process and the recent development in the particular country. Analytical attention is devoted to the recent processes in the countries as seen through the prism of (de)democratization.

1. Characteristics of the MENA region

This book focuses on the region of the Middle East and North Africa in its wider perception as explained in the introduction. In order to create a good basis for future analysis, it is important to provide the reader with the characteristics of the region. Information on economic, social, political and security conditions will be given throughout the case study chapters. However, this part defines the concept of a state and how it is perceived in MENA countries. The state concept in the Arab world is based on two important elements – religion and language; both are shared by the countries and create a sense of collective identity. In fact, considering the stated preconditions, all MENA countries, with the exception of Israel, Turkey and Iran, could be taken as one nation-state; by 'nation' is meant the Arab nation called umma.[4] This term refers to people who have at least one common characteristic, such as religion, place, or time.[5] Egypt, which pioneered secularization and Europeanization in the 18th and 19th century,[6] has a constitution declaring that its *"system [is] based on ... the country's historical heritage and the spirit of Islam. The Egyptian people are part of the Arab nation and work toward total Arab unity..."*.[7] This example clearly shows that the meaning of 'state' in the Arab world is interconnected with Islam and the only existing nation is the Arab nation. In contrast, Western civilizations understand the term 'state' as a secular

4 Luciani, *The Arab State*, 2.

5 Khalaf Allāh, *Al-Qur'ān Wa-Al-Dawlah*.

6 Salame, *The Foundations of the Arab State*, 51.

7 Egypt's government, "Egypt Constitution: Chapter One: The State".

unit, which is based always on an individual nation. This different point of view causes many misunderstandings, as this book will demonstrate.

At this context, the great debate between wataniyya and qawmiyya concepts has to be mentioned. Wataniyya means loyalty of people to their national territory (homeland, native country) called Watan. It basically refers to state-based nationalism, for which one could also use term patriotism. In countries such as Egypt, Syria and Turkey can be found political parties, which use Watan in their names.[8] On the other hand, qawmiyya means ethnic based nationalism. The world Qawm could be translated as a tribe or ethnic nationality. This term has been also used for pan-Arab nationalism, which is a reason why it is often connected with calls for creation of revolutionary Arab unity, represented for example by Gamal Abdel Nasser.[9]

There is no consensus on how to define and measure democracy. Lacking consensus is not only a matter of academic debates, but the definition remains unclear for US policy makers who promote this regime type around the world.[10] As aptly noted by Horowitz [11] "*the world's only superpower is rhetorically and militarily promoting a political system that remains undefined — and it is staking its credibility and treasure on that pursuit*". Generally, the definitions of democracy can be divided into two groups according to a 'thin' or minimalist concept and a 'thick' or wider concept.[12] The 'thin' concept includes the immensely influential academic definition of democracy referring to Robert Dahl's concept of polyarchy. According to Dahl, [13] "*polyarchy is based on eight institutional requirements: all adult citizens have the right to vote (1) and are eligible for public office (2), political leaders have the right to compete (3), elections are free and fair (4), citizens can form and join political parties and other organisations (5) and are free to express themselves on all political issues (6), diverse sources of information exist and are protected by law (7) and government policies depend on votes and expressions of preference (8)*".

Definitions based on the 'thick' concept also work with the dimension of political rights and civil liberties, but are broadened by the aspect of society and political culture.[14] For the purpose of this book we use a definition of democracy as a "*...form of governance with limited power of executives who are controlled by*

8 Sela, *The Continuum Political Encyclopedia of the Middle East*, 153.
9 Sela, 154–55.
10 Kekic, "Democracy Index".
11 Horowitz, "The Struggle for Democracy".
12 Coppedge et al., "Conceptualizing and Measuring Democracy: A New Approach".
13 Dahl, *Polyarchy*.
14 Kekic, "Democracy Index".

other institutions. Governments are selected directly or indirectly through competitive elections with open entry for candidates".[15]

A comprehensive list of factors for measuring democracy is provided within the concept of the *Democracy Index* published by the Economist Intelligence Unit. These factors are focused on measuring pluralism, civil liberties and political culture and are based on Dahl's concept of polyarchy.[16] The *Democracy Index* is based on five categories: electoral process and pluralism; civil liberties; the functioning of government; political participation; and political culture. Each category has a rating on a 0 to 10 scale, and the overall index of democracy is the simple average of the five category indexes. The methodology is based on a combination of a dichotomous and a three-point scoring system for the 60 indicators. According to the overall index outcome, countries are then divided into four categories. The *Democracy Index* offers four categories of regimes: full democracies, flawed democracies, hybrid regimes, and authoritarian regimes.[17]

Full democracies (scoring 8–10) respect civil liberties and basic political freedoms, governmental checks are functioning, while the judiciary is independent with enforceable decisions, and the media is diverse and independent.[18] Within the MENA region, there is no regime ranked as a full democracy.[19] Flawed democracies (scoring 6–7.9) have, in comparison with full democracy, an underdeveloped political culture with a low level of political participation, and sometimes problems with the functioning of governance.[20] Within the MENA region, Tunisia and Israel are the only countries ranked as flawed democracies.[21] Hybrid regimes (scoring 4–5.9) face problems with the fairness of elections, accompanied by governmental pressure on political opponents, non-independent judiciaries and a very high level of corruption.[22] Within the MENA region, there are four countries ranked as hybrid regimes: Lebanon, Morocco, Palestine and Iraq, and Turkey as one of the studied cases.[23] Authoritarian regimes (scoring below 4) are typical for dictatorships, with limited political pluralism, abuse of civil liberties, and nonexistent or unfair elections. Media are often state-owned and controlled by the

15 Gleditsch and Ward, "Diffusion and the International Context of Democratization".
16 Kekic, "Democracy Index".
17 "Democracy Index 2015".
18 "Democracy Index 2015".
19 "Democracy Index 2016: A Year of Political Stagnation in MENA".
20 "Democracy Index 2015".
21 "Democracy Index 2016: A Year of Political Stagnation in MENA".
22 "Democracy Index 2015".
23 "Democracy Index 2016: A Year of Political Stagnation in MENA".

ruling regime, judiciaries are not independent and censorship is very common.[24] Authoritarian regimes are most common in the MENA region, and are currently present in Jordan, Kuwait, Algeria, Egypt, Qatar, Oman, Bahrain, the United Arab Emirates, Sudan, Iran, Libya, Yemen, Saudi Arabia and Syria.

Since the first publication of the *Democracy Index* in 2006, average scores in the MENA region recorded only a modest improvement. In 2016, the MENA region experienced political stagnation and similar was expected in 2017 due to social unrest, war, terrorism and the impact of low oil prices. States with long-established autocratic policies, such as the Gulf Arab states, have stable scores on a long-term basis. Exceptionally, Saudi Arabia and Oman, typically ranked low, improved their global ranking. Nevertheless, this improvement is caused more through setbacks in other regions than by positive improvements within their own region. Since the Arab Spring, surprisingly, countries in the MENA region have not achieved much progress in the democracy ranking. The only exception is Tunisia, which graduated into a 'flawed democracy' in 2014. However, Tunisia's transition to democracy did not go hand in hand with improvements in economic performance as expected by young Tunisians.[25]

In this book is also mentioned the *Fragile State Index,* which was introduced by the United States think tank, The Fund for Peace in 2005. The index is created to *"highlight not only the normal pressures that all states experience, but also to identify when those pressures are outweighing a states' capacity to manage those pressures"*.[26] The ranking is composed by the sum of score for 12 indicators, divided into three categories – social, economic and political. Based on the result of the index four categories of states are defined ranging from very stable to less stable – sustainable, stable, warning and alert. Considering the states, which are analysed in the book, only two categories could be used. Egypt, Turkey and Palestine are ranked as countries with warning status, whilst Yemen, Syria, Iraq, Lebanon and Libya have alert status. The data are not provided for Palestine, as it is not recognised by the United States.[27]

24 "Democracy Index 2015".
25 "Democracy Index 2016: A Year of Political Stagnation in MENA".
26 "Fragile State Index".
27 "Fragile State Index".

2. Theory of democratization

Democratization has become a phenomenon that is being studied by many experts [28, 29, 30] in the field of political science and international relations. One of the most significant theories concerning the process of democratization was proposed at the end of the 20th century by Samuel Huntington.[31] According to him, the process of democratization is developing in three waves. Huntington has measured the proportion of democratic regimes over time and proposed his findings as *global patterns of democratization*. According to his theory, the first wave of democratization started in the early 19th century and persisted until 1920. The second wave came with World War II when many countries reversed to autocracy in the 1950s. The third wave began in the mid-1970s and continued through the 1990s with the end of the Cold War.

Why does the pattern of democratization proceed in waves? Huntington explains waves of democratization as "*a group of transitions from nondemocratic to democratic regimes that occur within a specified period and that significantly outnumber transitions in the opposite direction during that period of time*". According to his theory, in most cases a wave happens as a process that includes liberalization together with non-democratic elements, therefore democratization during a wave is only partial.[32]

Despite criticisms concerning several aspects of Huntington's theory, such as his definition of democracy[33] or the operationalization of the research,[34] the theory has been widely accepted.[35] Nevertheless, Huntington's theory has opened the floor for academic debates concerning questions such as what are the factors causing democratic waves or how could it be measured whether the transition was successful or not.

---

28 Huntington, *The Third Wave*.

29 Gill, *Globalization, Democratization and Multilateralism*.

30 Stepan and Linz, "Democratization Theory and the 'Arab Spring'".

31 Huntington, *The Third Wave*.

32 Huntington, "Democracy's Third Wave", 15.

33 Przeworski, *Democracy and Development*.

34 Doorenspleet, "Development and Democracy: Power and Problems of Empirical Research".

35 Jaggers and Gurr, "Transitions to Democracy: Tracking Democracy's Third Wave with the Polity III Data".

Many scholars [36, 37, 38] have been influenced by Huntington's research. In the context of democratization and Arab Spring there might be also mentioned the relatively recent and currently discussed theory of the fourth wave of democratization. According to Muhamad Olimat, this latter wave began with the regime change policy in the MENA countries adopted by the G. W. Bush administration after 9/11 and eventually led to the process known as the Arab Spring. However, due to the nature of the Arab world as well as the unpreparedness of the Americans, the success of US regime change policy is questionable. After any change of regime in the region there is a possibility of violence and revolutions, thus creating even more instability.[39]

The term Arab Spring refers to "*a series of anti-government uprisings affecting Arab countries of North Africa and the Middle East beginning in 2010*".[40] Since 2010, plenty of publications [41, 42, 43, 44] have been written on the topic of the Arab Spring, giving reasons for the causes of the uprisings, explanations of the process, or expectations for the future. Some of the case studies in this book present democratization processes in countries that are reasonably housed under the concept of the Arab Spring (Egypt). Other studies present different processes of democratization, forced by external entities (Iraq, Libya).

The transition process can be influenced by three categories of factors: internal non-institutional factors, institutional factors and external factors.[45] Within these categories crucial factors that may or may not influence the process of democratization in particular countries are mentioned. If there are other typical features having a significant impact on a country's transition to democracy, then they will be further specified in the case studies.

---

36 Olimat, "The Fourth Wave: Revolution and Democratization in the Arab Middle East".
37 Fawcett, *International Relations of the Middle East.*
38 Saikal and Acharya, *Democracy and Reform in the Middle East and Asia.*
39 Olimat, "The Fourth Wave: Revolution and Democratization in the Arab Middle East", 2–3.
40 Merriam – Webster Dictionary, "Merriam – Webster Dictionary: Arab Spring".
41 Inbar, *The Arab Spring, Democracy and Security.*
42 Yusuf, "Middle Eeast Transitions: A Long, Hard Road".
43 Altomonte and Ferrara, *The Economic and Political Aftermath of the Arab Spring.*
44 Danahar, *The New Middle East.*
45 Strand et al., "Democratic Waves? Global Patterns of Democratization, 1816–2008".

3. Internal non-institutional factors

Democratization is not a one-time event, but a process influenced by long-term and short-term factors. Moreover, these factors vary throughout the countries where the process of democratization takes place. Considering the idea that the most significant players in international relations are states, one could divide the factors influencing the democratization into ones that are internal and external to the state. Internal factors are aspects referring to a state's inner environment, its economy, politics, form of government, population and rule of law. Some of these factors are institutional, such as form of government or rule of law, while others are non-institutional, such as civil society or extremism.

Authors studying internal non-institutional factors have given the most significant attention to economic factors. Several authors [46, 47] emphasize the strong relationship between socio-economic development and democratization.

3.1 Economic factors

A group of economic variables such as gross domestic product, level of employment, inflation, poverty rate, balance of trade and investments can without any hesitation help in identifying signs of democratization. However, the relation between the level of economic development and democracy is not as easy to understand as it might appear at first glance. Although economic factors surely have a substantial impact on the development of democracy, they are not determinative. According to a number of studies [48, 49, 50], it is known that a strong correlation between the level of economic development and democracy exists; however, sometimes it is not enough to bring about democracy.[51]

Basically, economic factors could be divided into two groups. The first one is known as internal economic factors, which include factors such as GDP, institutional environment and cultural tradition. Nowadays, however, much more attention is dedicated to the second group – external factors, such as trade, economic cooperation and transnational corporations. It has obtained greater significance

46 Lipset, "Some Social Requisites of Democracy: Economic Development and Political Legitimacy".
47 Vanhanen, *Prospects of Democracy*.
48 Huntington, *The Third Wave*.
49 Przeworski, *Democracy and Development*.
50 Lipset, "Some Social Requisites of Democracy: Economic Development and Political Legitimacy".
51 Huntington, *The Third Wave*, 59.

due to the trend of economic globalization, which could be defined as a process of integration of national scale economies in the global network via trade, investments and finance.[52] Because national economies are de facto units of the global one, this part will be dedicated mainly to aspects of the domestic economy which are influenced by external factors.

Scholars are not aligned in their approach to the influence of economic factors. In fact, there are three different approaches. A minor number of scholars [53, 54] claim that economic factors have a negligible impact on democracy. Their main argument is that the factors are overestimated and the process of democratization in different countries cannot be compared due to different conditions.[55]

A second group of scholars [56, 57, 58] posits that redistribution of incoming foreign capital, decision-making situated outside the nation borders combined with low competitiveness of the local market and different economic interests have a negative impact on democracy. In their eyes, economic globalization causes the weakening of mechanisms supporting the domestic market; low competitiveness then leads to bankruptcy; and deepening public debt and increasing inequalities in society are solved by repressions, and of course weakening democracy.[59] A further reference for this exists in the viewpoint of Immanuel Wallerstein, whose theory of core and periphery shows that increasing cooperation between rich and developing countries leads to significant inequalities in society and in consequence the suppression of democracy.[60]

The biggest and most influential group suggests quite the opposite to the other two groups.[61, 62] Samuel Huntington was a strong advocate of this approach. In his opinion, "*The future of democracy depends on the future of economic development. Obstacles to economic development are obstacles to the expansion of democracy*".[63]

52 Shangquan, "Economic Globalization: Trends, Risks and Risk Prevention", 1.
53 Hirst, *From Statism to Pluralism.*
54 Li and Reuveny, "Economic Globalization and Democracy: An Empirical Analysis".
55 Hirst, *From Statism to Pluralism.*
56 Rodrik, *Has Globalization Gone Too Far?*
57 Wallerstein, *Capitalist Agriculture and the Origins of the European World-Economy in the Sixteenth Century.*
58 Gill, "Globalisation, Market Civilisation, and Disciplinary Neoliberalism".
59 Rodrik, *Has Globalization Gone Too Far?*
60 Wallerstein, *Capitalist Agriculture and the Origins of the European World-Economy in the Sixteenth Century.*
61 Edwards, *Crisis and Reform in Latin America.*
62 Huntington, "Democracy's Third Wave".
63 Huntington, 31.

The third wave started in 1950s, when economic growth led to the economic rise of many countries connected with democratizing tendencies. From the 1970s until the 1990s, democracy accelerated around the world, however with various intensity among regions. Whilst East and South Asia have shown significant economic growth connected with deeper democratic thoughts, the Middle East, North Africa, Latin America and Caribbean developed in the opposite position.[64] Based on Huntington's empirical research the three kinds of economic factors that affect democracy could be defined.[65]

The first factor is sufficient economic level. Poor countries are dealing with their own problems such as hunger and poverty. In this case the transition to democracy is unlikely. On the other hand, in the most developed countries democracy already exists. This statement could be demonstrated by the values in the *Democracy Index* – there is a significant correlation between the economic (GDP) and democratic levels, which demonstrates the interdependence of variables.[66] Countries known as 'mid-developed' are the most likely to promote the democratization process. This group tends to strengthen liberalization of market and trade, improve social conditions and empower bilateral and multilateral relations with other players. These interactions help the country to get into the so-called political transition zone, which basically means the first step to a full democratic regime.[67]

Rapid economic growth stirs changes in economic structures, in beliefs and cultures.[68] Practically, any extreme economic fluctuation may cause the weakening of an authoritarian regime. As an example, one could mention the collapse of the Soviet Union, whose economic growth between 1960 and 1989 was one of the worst in the world.[69] Once dissatisfaction with the existing conditions appears inside the society, the need for regime change seems to be inevitable.[70] Moreover, rapid growth is the basis for future economic development, which tends to raise expectations, exacerbates inequalities and creates stress. Finally, thanks to all these processes, greater political mobilization and participation are created.[71]

Last, but not at least, is the oil price development, which is particularly important in the MENA region. Based on empirical facts, deviations in oil prices cause

64 Huntington, 32.
65 Huntington, "Democracy's Third Wave".
66 Kekic, "Democracy Index".
67 Huntington, "Democracy's Third Wave", 31.
68 Huntington, 31.
69 Easterly and Fischer, "The Soviet Economic Decline: Historical and Republican Data".
70 Huntington, *The Third Wave*, 60.
71 Huntington, 68–70.

greater discontent with the regime. Depending on conditions, the regime has to either liberalize and become more democratic or increase repressions.[72]

Economic level, economic growth and oil price development are the most discussed economic factors of the democratization process; however, one has to take into account also other possibilities. For instance, during the 1980s and 1990s high debts and economic problems led to the increased need for loans. The World Bank and the International Monetary Fund were able to provide them, but under conditions of greater liberalization and democratization.[73] Economic sanctions imposed by states or international organizations such as the UN or EU also have a significant impact on the economic situation and development towards democracy. Cox and Cooper Drury claim that democracies tend to impose more sanctions on non-democratic countries to enforce democratization and greater respect for human rights.[74]

The influence of economic factors on democratization is very tricky. In some cases, democracy has a positive impact on the economy, since it is the key point for liberalization, openness and greater economic development. On the other hand, democratization could lead to the collapse of economy. These trends are heavily influenced by conditions inside the specific country.

3.2 Civil society

The term civil society was created by ancient Greek philosophers and frequently used by the Romans. However, at that time, the civil society was equated with the state. The modern meaning emerged in the late 18th century – civil society was separated from the state and its meaning was based on promotion of citizens' wishes and interests. The term was renewed once again after the World War II, when Antonio Gramsci named it as a crucial aspect in the fight against tyranny.[75]

Nowadays the term civil society has become a 'mantra' for various interest groups and politicians. Thanks to the increasing number of democracies around the world, the space to create civil societies has opened. However, the understanding of the term is very weak, mostly because the definition is very complicated and questionable.[76]

---

72 Huntington, 70.

73 Limpach and Michaelowa, "The Impact of World Bank and IMF Programs on Democratization in Developing Countries".

74 Cox and Drury, "Democratic Sanctions".

75 Carothers and Barndt, "Civil Society", 18–19.

76 Carothers and Barndt, 19.

The problem of defining civil society derives from the fact that the term has different meanings for different people. In particular, this book has to differentiate between the Western approach and the way civil society is understood in the MENA countries. As an example of the Western understanding, civil society can be defined *"as the realm of spontaneously created social structures separate from the state that underlie democratic political institutions"*.[77] It could be clearly seen that the definition incorporates various institutions and interest groups, which could be for example foundations, trade unions, support groups, NGOs, NPOs, clubs or charities. However, different kinds of organization mean different relations to the state – some segments could be democratic, anti-democratic, undemocratic or even non-political. These organizations are often called the 'agents of democratization'. They must embody three characteristics: democratic operation; their agenda must contain some demand for democracy; and they must gain enough power to play an influential role in the democratic process.[78]

The understanding of civil society in the MENA countries is rather different. Most of the definitions created in the Arab world deal with two questions. Firstly, is civil society a secular sphere (Western approach) or could religious organizations and movements be considered as central parts of civil society? Secondly, does civil society consist of groups which only mediate relations between citizens and state without aspiring to political power, or may organizations have political capacities? Arab scholars are not unified in their answers. For example, at-Tahir Labib, Ali al- Kinz and Abd al- Qadir deny the existence of a civil society in the Arab world at all, because of the expansion of fundamentalist structures, absence of a culture of democracy or a dialog between state and citizens.[79] Another definition of as-Sayyid Yassine points out that civil society is the *"democratic, secular sphere between the authoritarian Arab states and the movements of political Islam"*.[80] It is evident when discussing civil society in the context of the Arab world, religion cannot be omitted as it plays an important role and creates a strong contrast with the Western understanding. On the other hand, democratization is based on Western ideals and understanding of democracy – for this reason, the Western concept is examined here more deeply in order to specify the ways in which Arab countries could improve their civil society to stimulate a democratization process.

---

77 Fukuyama, "I. The Primacy of Culture".

78 Boose, "Democratization and Civil Society", 311.

79 Hamzawy, *Civil Society in the Middle East*, 32.

80 Yassin, *The Future of Civil Society: The Cultural Crisis and the Future of Civil Society*, 792.

Relations between civil society and the state are often blurred, because the state may play an important role in shaping civil society as well as vice-versa. Every part of the civil society is shaped by distribution of interests, social norms and power resources which are created by the society itself. An important interlink in the relation between state and civil society are political parties that have the role of mediator and transmitter of ideas.[81]

Civil society is often mentioned as a foundation for successful democratization, but the relation is not so easy. A weak civil society leads to a lack of civil engagement and social trust. On the other hand, a too strong civil society could reflect dangerous political weakness.[82] In order to push the democratic process in the right direction, civil society might be active, diverse, and represent and reflect the ideas and demands of society.

Civil society has a very wide spectrum of tools and ways to promote democracy. The most important of them are the following. Civil society shifts the balance of power between state and society in favour of the latter, because it has the capability to weaken the capabilities of states. However, in every country it has different intensity. In the authoritarian regimes of Latin America and East Asia, the power of states is extensive, but certain organised forces in the society exist and have the power to influence affairs. On the other hand, in the majority of African countries the state is a dominant player, but very weak and eroded by the invasions of particularistic social pressures.[83] Civil society also has a disciplinary role in relation to the state – it enforces standards of public morality and performance, and improves the accountability of both politicians and administrators.[84] Moreover, it performs an intermediary role between state and society, because it is capable of promoting political communication and transmits the demands and interests of various sectors of the population in order to improve democratic policies. Last, but not at least, civil society fulfils a constitutive role by redefining the rules of the political engagement along democratic lines – its power to create and sustain a set of new norms and rules which regulate the behaviour of the state and the relations between state and public.

All the above mentioned aspects were present during the period of the Arab Spring. As an example, in Egypt the army, supported by civil society, weakened the state power by overthrowing the regime of Hosni Mubarak.[85] However, civil

81 White, "Civil Society, Democratization and Development (I)", 381.

82 Carothers and Barndt, "Civil Society", 21.

83 White, "Civil Society, Democratization and Development (I)". 383.

84 White, 383.

85 Anderson, "Demystifying the Arab Spring", 4.

society in MENA countries was and still is relatively weak from the Western perspective, which is evidenced in low literacy levels, weak market-driven economies and insufficient political participation in comparison to Western standards.[86] Moreover, even scholars from the region question the existence of civil society due to authoritarian regimes, the marginality of the middle classes, increasing fundamentalism and absence of democratic culture.[87]

3.3 Media

The media are a very specific factor influencing the process of democratization. The media belong to both institutional internal factors and external factors. We decided to put the media into the group of internal factors due to the specifics of democratization in the MENA region. In many countries (mainly during the Arab Spring), the media have played the role of catalyst of the processes. In some of these countries (Tunisia, Egypt, Syria), the media were a source of inspiration for uprisings as people saw events unfolding in their neighbourhood. In some countries (Libya, Syria), the media took the role of witness of the violent repression of demonstrations. On the other hand, in some cases (Iraq, Syria) the media played a manipulative role in picking up certain information and thus creating an incomplete picture of the situation, leading to manipulation of both the domestic and international public. The specific role of the media in helping with recruitment was used by Islamic State when gaining strength and spreading fear through a video campaign, not just in the MENA region, but also in Europe.

Nevertheless, in all countries the media (and specifically the state-owned media), play a crucial role in the political transition processes. Access to the state-owned media is usually given only to the official government, and therefore this political representation has an advantage against the opposition. For the opposition, the media is one of the institutions they must overcome in order to get respect and attention from the public. In the following case studies, the media will be studied from both perspectives – as an external factor influencing the international public and domestic public, and as an internal factor working for the party that has superiority in the process of democratization.

While studying the role of the media in the democratization process in the MENA region it is crucial to understand the specifics related to the media in different MENA countries. It is necessary to examine which role the state media have and how much they are influenced by the government. Moreover, it is necessary

86 Boose, "Democratization and Civil Society", 312.
87 Hamzawy, *Civil Society in the Middle East*, 32.

to study the approach of Western and international media to the democratization process in MENA countries, which might have an impact on the speed and fluency of the process as well as on the broader picture the international public creates concerning the democratization process. These analyses will be included in the following case studies.

Whilst studying democratization processes in the MENA region, it is crucial to realise that appearance of social networks or internet broadcasting is quite recent in comparison with other parts of the world. Therefore, these media can be referred to as new Arab media. The media reached the Arab world through Europe after the invention of satellite-based newspaper distribution and editing in the 1980s and satellite-based Arab broadcasting in the 1990s. The highest importance is given to three London-based newspapers: *Ash-Sharq al-Awsat* from Saudi Arabia, *al-Hayat* from Lebanon and *as-Quds al-Arabi* from Palestine. The mass media phenomenon has reshaped the Arab world with the advent of satellite TV. [88] Academic debates on the topic of the new Arab media emerged with the appearance of Al-Jazeera in the region in 1996. The story of Al-Jazeera is interesting and gives a broader picture of what specific role the media have in the Arab world.[89] Jon Alterman[90] claims that the new Arab media can lead to a new relationship between the state and the media, producing less efficiency of old modes of censorship.

The new Arab media can have democratic potential in several aspects. They are decreasing the strength of authoritarian regimes, because people are more willing to watch and even discuss politics. New media also weaken the image of the infallible ruler, because people can notice that their rules are not infallible and that their decisions and direction can be challenged. Thanks to the new media opposition movements and personalities have the chance to appear on TV and gain more popularity. New media are also teaching a new culture of debate. People can see that there is an alternative to just passively accepting the politics of the ruler, and learn how to constructively debate and create their own opinions. From the commercial point of view, new Arab media follow the needs of the citizens, watch trends and the needs of the population and adjust their programme to these trends in order to be able to keep up with their competitors.[91]

88 Jung, *Democratization and Development.*
89 Miles, *Al Jazeera: How Arab TV News Challenged the World.*
90 Alterman, *New Media, New Politics?*
91 Jung, *Democratization and Development.*

On the other hand, there are critics who emphasise the anti-democratization features of the new Arab media.[92] Owners of the new media are often related to Arab regimes. Therefore, instead of weakening authoritarian regimes, the new media are given the opportunity to expand their power into new areas, as the owners of the new media are often personal allies with representatives of the regime.[93] The media can raise issues, but cannot pursue them. Even though the media bring issues to the light, in the end they just function as an instrument for venting anger. Political culture is not used to reacting to the things brought up by the media and just ignore them, and therefore people are even more dissatisfied as they recognize the problem but can see no political action against it. New Arab media also have an elite character. Not every citizen in the MENA region can afford to have electronic devices or TV. Moreover, the new media usually broadcast in modern standard Arabic which is not understandable to non-educated citizens. Therefore, the satellite channels are only affordable for the rich, and clearly directed towards well-educated citizens.[94] Media workers are not politically neutral. Staff working for the media tend to project their political opinions into the articles and reports they prepare. Therefore, the media often present only one point of view concerning a situation. Moreover, journalists often focus more on criticism of political action instead of high-quality investigation as they are under time pressure to release their articles as fast as possible to appear on new Arab media networks.

3.4 Extremism and religion

The relation between democracy and extremism is very difficult to pin down. Extremism is defined as *"a tendency towards extreme measures and views in politics and as an attempt to solve problems with radical methods, including by means of violence and terror"*.[95] Extremism has many faces, such as religious extremism, right and left-wing extremism, nationalist extremism, and so on. Nowadays, scholars as well as media devote the largest part of their attention to radical Islamic extremism as well as terrorism.[96, 97]

92 Jung.
93 Sakr, *Satellite Realms: Transnational Television, Globalization and the Middle East.*
94 Jung, *Democratization and Development.*
95 Mustafayev, *Terrorism (Definition, Awareness and Prognostication)*, 67.
96 Kepel, *The War for Muslim Minds.*
97 Mamdani, *Good Muslim, Bad Muslim.*

In general extremism and its values have been understood as running counter to democracy.[98] However, thinking about it more deeply, the relation is not so straightforward. Development of radical thoughts could prove the vitality of democracy and bolster it.[99] In countries where the democratization process is still ongoing, greater space for expressing opinions as well as radical thoughts could create dangerous situations, which could lead to an increase of extremism and insecurity. Moreover, extremists are also able to use democratic tools to gain more powers – for example Hamas, a Palestinian Sunni-Islamic fundamentalist organization, won parliamentary elections in the Palestinian territories in 2006 and gained complete control of the Gaza Strip.[100]

The causes of extremism could be diverse – poverty, a rigid political system, non-democratic rule, political persecution and terror, weak civil society, non-existing independent media, etc. However, every country is different, so the causes differ too. Taking poverty as an example, some scholars [101, 102] claim that extremism derives from poverty. In case of Hamas, bad living conditions and poverty have caused the radicalization of many young Palestinians.[103]

Lack of democracy often leads to dissatisfaction and the creation of extremist groups. On the other hand, the democratization process itself could create an atmosphere of radicalization and the establishment of extremist movements inside the society. At the same time, it might help to undermine the foundation of existing extremism.[104]

Authoritarian political systems, military regimes and theocracies create good conditions for the rise of extremism, violence and terrorism. Democracy, thanks to all its characteristics and features is a good way to combat these problems.[105] On the other hand, they resist all aspects of democracy, and give power to government institutions and officials. Due to authoritarianism, coercive methods and brutal repressions in the MENA region are ideal for extremist movements. Conversely democratic thought and compromise are often doomed from the beginning. The region is afflicted with high unemployment, declining productivity and a growing crisis of legitimacy, which leads many educated and unemployed young people to

---

98 Mudde, *On Extremism and Democracy in Europe.*
99 Breton, *Political Extremism and Rationality*, 131.
100 Milton-Edwards, "The Ascendance of Political Islam", 301.
101 Windsor, "Promoting Democratization Can Combat Terrorism", 44.
102 Mason and James, *Religious Extremism*, 16.
103 Windsor, "Promoting Democratization Can Combat Terrorism", 44–45.
104 Windsor, 43.
105 Olimat, "The Fourth Wave: Revolution and Democratization in the Arab Middle East".

even more frustration. Moreover, the population is often uninformed or discouraged by the lack of political and economic opportunities.[106] Due to that they try to find the cause of all their problems outside their own borders.

However, at this point one might take into account the role of the Arab Spring which profoundly changed the access to information and opportunities. Before the Arab Spring, service providers as well as information flows were heavily supervised by governments, and loss of access to the Internet was normal in Egypt or Tunis.[107] With the attention of the rest of the world after the Arab Spring the situation improved, as it will be seen from the case studies in this book.

At this point, one has to examine terms connected with extremism and Islam in greater depth. According to Adeeb Khalid, Islam cannot be clearly defined because it is determined by Muslims; the debate about Islam itself is an ongoing phenomenon and followers could decide to use many positions and arguments.[108] In short, Islam is a very complex phenomenon, which has many dimensions and forms in time as well as in space, ranging from religious, ethical, theological, social and economic to legal and political spheres. Another term frequently used by politicians and journalists worldwide after 9/11 is Islamism.[109] Pipes perceives Islamism as an *"ideology that demands man's complete adherence to the sacred law of Islam and rejects as much as possible outside influence, with some exceptions (such as access to military and medical technology)"*.[110] This term is very often confused with Islamic extremism, which is defined as a *"militant and very violent expression and practice of Islam by Muslims who have fundamentalist view of their religion"*. Islamic extremists are people *"who employ violent means to spread their fundamental beliefs"*[111] and who are convinced that their behaviour is right.

Last, but not at least, democracy could be used as a tool for undermining existing extremist groups: *"Democratic institutions and procedures, by enabling the peaceful reconciliation of grievances and providing channels for participation in policymaking, can help to address those underlying conditions that have fuelled the rise of extremism"*.[112] This strategy was used after 9/11 by the United States

106 Windsor, "Promoting Democratization Can Combat Terrorism", 46.

107 Wagner, European Parliament, and DG for External Policies, *After the Arab Spring*, 8–10.

108 Khalid, *Islam after Communism*, 202–3.

109 Mozaffari, "What Is Islamism?", 18.

110 Pipes, "Distinguishing between Islam and Islamism".

111 Scheina, "Lessons Learned from Attacks on Mass Transit".

112 Windsor, "Promoting Democratization Can Combat Terrorism", 43.

as regime change policy, which was one of several parts of the Bush doctrine.[113] However, democracy imposed by force by foreign actors hardly ever survives, which is the case in Iraq.[114]

4. Internal institutional factors

Internal institutional factors are series of factors emerging from activities of different institutions. Three main institutions have been chosen as they are considered as the most significant aspects of democratization: security and defence structures (army, police and intelligence agencies), political institutions (government, parliament) and the rule of law (courts, prisons). Other studied institutions are the health service, welfare, education, religious and cultural institutions. Institutions can support waves of democratization under two circumstances: if there is a 'stickiness' that prevents changes, and in case there exists dependence between events and situations in different entities.[115]

4.1 Security factors

Security can be perceived as the "*provision of private services in the protection of people, information and assets for individual safety or community wellness*". [116] A definition of security applicable to the state or nation was published by Fischer and Green [117] claiming that "*security implies a stable, relatively predictable environment in which an individual or group may pursue its ends without disruption or harm and without fear of such disturbance or injury*".

The security of the state is determined by external security, given by the situation on the international scene and by the relationship with neighbouring countries. These factors are described below under external factors such as international shocks, systemic wars, new states and political neighbourhood.

Internal state security is provided by the armed and police forces by the will of citizens to protect their territory, and by the rule of law, judiciary system and equal system of government. Full and flawed democracies share institutional features, most importantly transparency, constitutionalism and public consent. Transparency gives access to information to citizens, other government officials

---

113 "The National Security Strategy of the United States of America", 3.

114 Windsor, "Promoting Democratization Can Combat Terrorism", 50.

115 Strand et al., "Democratic Waves? Global Patterns of Democratization, 1816–2008", 12.

116 Craighead, *High-Rise Security and Fire Life Safety*.

117 Fischer and Green, *Introduction to Security*.

and societal groups. Based on information about policy they can be aware of the possible choices and they are capable of informed judgments about these choices.[118] Constitutionalism defines and limits the power of government, ensuring the existence of a range of policy inputs and predictable processes subject to contestation.[119] Public consent refers to "*institutions for making government policies depend on votes and other expressions of preference*".[120]

The idea that democracy may be connected to military service was developed by Niccolo Machiavelli. He made a strong claim about the importance of a conscript army for a republic and the peril associated with mercenaries.[121] The idea that citizenship may be connected with military service is common for both republican and liberal theories of democracy. The arguments about the ideal form of military service and the way it may affect democracy vary. Nevertheless, the range of mobilization policies recommended for democracies is fairly narrow and focuses mainly on conscripts or volunteers.[122] Stanislav Andreski suggests that the relationship between the citizen and the state and the citizen and the military service can be associated with arguments about the rise of democratic states. According to Andreski, the higher the military participation ratio in military services, the more democratic a state is.[123] The Arab Spring has influenced the introduction of compulsory military service in Qatar and United Arab Emirates, and a re-introduction in Kuwait. Conscription is compulsory also in Algeria, Tunisia, Egypt, Syria, Jordan and Israel.

Whilst studying the internal security aspects of democratization focus is put on several markers given by the abilities and capacity of armed and police forces, and by citizens' participation in the military service. Another important marker is the composition of security structures, mainly through the participation of minorities and different religious groups. These aspects might play a crucial role in the process of democratization in particular countries.

---

118 Henderson, "The Public and Peace: The Consequences for Citizenship of the Democratic Peace Literature".

119 Avant and Sigelman, "Private Security and Democracy: Lessons from the US in Iraq".

120 Henderson, "The Public and Peace: The Consequences for Citizenship of the Democratic Peace Literature".

121 McCormick, "Machiavellian Democracy: Controlling Elites with Ferocious Populism".

122 Avant and Sigelman, "Private Security and Democracy: Lessons from the US in Iraq".

123 Andreski and Radcliffe-Brown, *Military Organization and Society*.

4.2 Political factors

Describing factors of democratization, it is impossible to leave out political aspects. The majority of transitions to democracy [124, 125] are preceded by military regimes, one party systems, personal dictatorships, etc. Due to changes in the mindset of society, economic shifts or other factors, the regime becomes weaker and the democratization process starts.

The means by which a regime will be quickly and effectively changed depends on a large group of factors. One can basically divide them into external/international and internal/domestic. External factors provide the impetus for change by giving the country in question some needed ideas and models. Then it is the turn of the internal players to internalize them and create the desired change.[126]

First, causes of regime change inside an existing country have to be analysed. In the Western part of the world democracy is generally understood as the ideal type of regime.[127] Due to the predominance of Western structures, this conviction is also seen desirable for Middle Eastern countries. Moreover, without taking into account cultural or other differences, society gradually requires greater levels of Western values to be more respected and used also in their countries. Due to this trend, authoritarian countries have to deal with deepening problems of legitimacy, because values desired by society are unfamiliar to them, so they are forced to back their power by nationalism.[128]

However, the ideal scenario of transition to democracy does not necessarily have to come true – the MENA countries attempts to reach democracy often end up with the creation of another non-democratic regime. Different sources of change come from external players such as the United States. The United States is able to help countries with the solution of their problems but only on condition of democratization.[129] The reason why the United States is involved in democratization is based on the essential values of American culture. This idea is called 'Manifest Destiny' and was created in the 19th century when the United States expanded its territory. Because of the latter, Americans see their mission in

124 Stoner and McFaul, *Transitions to Democracy.*

125 Snyder, *Transitions to Democracy and the Rise of Nationalist Conflict.*

126 Schmitz and Sell, "International Factors in the Processes of Political Democratization", 33.

127 Norris, *Critical Citizens*, 45.

128 Huntington, *The Third Wave*, 46.

129 Caryl, "The Democracy Boondoggle in Iraq".

promoting and defending democracy throughout the world.[130] This behaviour led to the establishment of several democratic regimes in the Middle East; nevertheless, their stability is questionable.

There are many internal factors – the level of political polarization, the state of extremism in society, tolerance, the strength of the middle class, consensus on political and social values, respect for human rights, political history, and openness of the economy and level of education. External aspects are also very diverse thanks to the increasing level of globalization – influence by a prodemocracy foreign power, the proportion of democratic states amongst neighbouring countries, international organizations, etc.[131]

The political dimension of democratization represents a very complicated process influenced by many factors. The democratic regime needs to be backed not only by elites, but also by the middle class. Arab society is quite complicated in this regard – traditionally according to Islam all people are equal, however in reality the distribution of wealth significantly divides society. Starting from the top, members of elites are the richest people in the countries, often have ties with ruling governments, and use their position to gain even more financial resources and power. They are frequently the ones who decide about the country's direction. The biggest part of society is represented by the middle class, which is educated and productive, but dependent on state resources and elites. Finally, the opinions and needs of the poor are often overlooked.[132] This division clearly shows the dependence of the middle class on elites and the reason for their low political activity.

4.3 Rule of law – judiciary system

Observing internal institutional factors, this chapter is going to examine briefly also the rule of law. This concept, created in the 16th century in Britain, is based on three important preconditions – the policy has to be governed by general rules created in advance; rules must be applied and enforced; and disputes must be resolved effectively and fairly. The rule of law is defined as: "*The authority and influence of law in society, esp. when viewed as a constraint on individual and institutional behaviour; (hence) the principle whereby all members of a society (including those in government) are considered equally subject to publicly disclosed legal codes and processes*".[133]

---

130 Stephanson, *Manifest Destiny*.

131 Huntington, *The Third Wave*, 37–38.

132 Churchill and Lutfiyya, *Readings in Arab Middle Eastern Societies and Cultures*, 40–43.

133 Oxford English Dictionary, "Rule of Law".

For the Western world it is natural to function according to the rule of law. Institutions such as comprehensive laws or a constitution based on popular consent, a functioning judicial system, and established law enforcement agencies with professional officers are present in every state. To explain it simply – laws based on long term practice must be accepted by society in general; the system, which enforces them, is based on principles of equality and democracy; the enforcing of laws is done by educated and trained officers. An important feature of Western system is secularism.

In contrast, the rule of law in Islamic countries is perceived differently. Most countries in the MENA region base their legal system on the civil law using elements of the French legal system or the common law, which is a British legal tradition. Those systems are mixed with Islamic law. The connection to religion creates a big difference between Western and Islamic civilizations – Sharia law is the cornerstone of the legal system in Arab countries. The sense of justice and equality is influenced by religion, so the approach of governments is also different. Nowadays, one can discern greater pressure of the Western world on Arab countries to bring their systems of laws closer to Western models, for example by question punishments imposed by Sharia, position of women, working ethics, etc. in order to create a more suitable environment for foreign investors.[134]

From this brief observation, it is evident that the rule of law is understood differently in the MENA countries and the Western world, which is also the cause of problems in the democratization process. The key difference is caused by the role of religion – Islam creates the basis for the legal system called Sharia; on the other hand, Western society has based its systems on the principle of secularism.

5. External factors

The state is always influenced by its surroundings, and therefore external factors play a crucial role during the process of democratization. These factors are given by neighbouring countries, by international shocks, and also by media that has a role in triggering uprisings spilling over from one country to another. Significant effects on democratization in one state can cause an international shock such as global war, or the formation of new states with unstable institutions. External factors are mostly interconnected and influenced by current situations on the international scene. The spill-over effect causes the process of democratization spilling over from one country in the region to another, as happened in the MENA region.

134 Panara and Wilson, *The Arab Spring*, 97.

In extreme cases of the coercive external influence of the transition regime change is imposed from the outside.[135] This transition happened fully for example in Iraq where foreign-imposed regime changes were led by the United States. Partially, it is the case of Libya, where military intervention was a reaction to suppression of anti-government demonstrations and led directly to regime change.

Autocracies are less likely to endure in a region with more democratic states, especially when a neighbouring country experiences a transition to democracy. Gleditsch and Ward built a model investigating how much the transition in neighbouring countries influences democratization in another country. Their results have shown that when more than half the neighbouring states undergo a transition to democracy, the chances that an autocratic regime endures dramatically decrease.[136] On the other hand, democracies surrounded by countries with autocratic regimes are more likely to fail, especially when the democracy is new and newly established institutions are still fragile. Moreover, in some cases autocratic neighbours may cause security threats to newly established democracies.[137] Generally, the stability of political systems depends, among other factors, on the form of governance in their neighbourhood; hence, they tend to change in the direction of the regime type that prevails in the region.[138]

International shocks have an important role in the trends of political transitions, and thus explain the form of waves in which democratization occurs. International shocks are unpredictable events of an economic character that emerge in one place and can spread into other parts of the world. Examples of international shocks are financial crises, inflation episodes, depreciation of a currency, recessions and changes in world market conditions for commodities.[139] These shocks are influencing MENA region mainly in a form of oil prices divergences (Libya, Iraq) or as spill-over effect of financial crisis (Tunis).

War is another crucial factor that can influence the change of regime in the country where it happens and in neighbouring countries as well. In the case of systemic war, its results can even influence the change of regimes in countries that did not directly take part in the war, but are somehow influenced by its results. The relationship between the regime type and conflict has been examined on three main levels: monadic (nation-state), dyadic (relational) and systemic. The monadic level examines the question whether democracies are generally more

135 Gleditsch and Ward, "Diffusion and the International Context of Democratization".
136 Gleditsch and Ward.
137 Thompson, "Democracy and Peace: Putting the Cart before the Horse?"
138 Strand et al., "Democratic Waves? Global Patterns of Democratization, 1816–2008".
139 Frankel, "Economic Shocks and International Politics".

likely to maintain peace and focuses on the relationship between a state's regime type and its foreign policy.[140] The dyadic level focuses on the bilateral relationships between states and examines whether democracies are more likely to maintain peaceful relations with each other. On a dyadic level, many authors have concluded that democracies do not fight each other.[141, 142, 143] The systemic level focuses on the question of whether a higher proportion of democracies on the international scene increases the probability of peace.[144]

One of the possible explanations of a relationship between war and democratization came from Mitchell, Gates and Hegre.[145] They argue that up to a certain threshold level, democratization could support a number of wars in the system. On the other hand, war again increases the rate of democratization in the international system. This idea explains the tendency of democracies to win wars and their ability to promote democratic regimes in the aftermath of war.[146] This idea has been further developed by Kadera et al.[147] claiming that the survival of democracies is dependent on the capabilities of the democratic group allied to other political systems on the international scene.

Mesquita, Siverson and Woller present evidence that regime changes happen almost twice as often during wars and immediately after wars than in peacetime. Moreover, most of these after-war regime changes affect autocracies.[148] The idea that war is associated with greater democratization [149] is supported by evidence from the history of the 20th century. After World War I and World War II, democracies which won the war promoted their form of government to the defeated countries.[150]

Another consequence of systemic war is the break-up of the empire or the state and the formation of new states. This evidence has been proven by history.

---

140 Mitchell, Gates and Hegre, "Evolution in Democracy-War Dynamics".
141 Bremer, "Dangerous Dyads: Conditions Affecting the Likelihood of Interstate War, 1816–1965".
142 Weede, "Some Simple Calculations on Democracy and War Involvement".
143 Russett et al., *Grasping the Democratic Peace.*
144 Gleditsch and Hegre, "Peace and Democracy: Three Levels of Analysis".
145 Mitchell, Gates, and Hegre, "Evolution in Democracy-War Dynamics".
146 Reiter, *Foreign-Imposed Regime Change.*
147 K.M, M.J.C, and M.L, "Democratic Survival, Peace, and War in the International System".
148 de Mesquita, Siverson, and Woller, "War and the Fate of Regimes: A Comparative Analysis".
149 Stam, *Win, Lose, or Draw.*
150 Strand et al., "Democratic Waves? Global Patterns of Democratization, 1816–2008".

In the case of World War I, the Ottoman Empire and the Austro-Hungarian Empire broke up, and their territory disintegrated into smaller, independent states. A similar effect happened after World War II and led to decolonization, when former colonies gained their independence. Further evidence came with the end of the Cold War, when former states of the Soviet Union gained their independence. Strand[151] claims that new states generally tend to establish their first political systems as mostly democratic. On the other hand, new states tend to experience a so-called reversed wave as their democratic institutions are very fragile and easily overpowered. Therefore, new states are more likely to experience regime change and it is even possible that due to unstable institutions this regime change can move in the direction of an authoritarian regime.

The amount of time necessary to strengthen the democratic institutions built into new states differs from country to country. There are factors that have an impact on the duration of the process, for example experience with democracy from the past, political neighbourhood, the size of the population and its composition, and the abilities and popularity of the leading politicians. Most countries in the MENA region emerged as new states after the mandate for administration terminated. These states differ in their history with their mandate administrator and their post-decolonization relationships. In some of them, the process of democratization is difficult due to the composition of their population – numerous minorities differ by their religion and sometimes even by the language they speak (Libya, Lebanon).

6. Conclusion

Democratization is a phenomenon appearing in the MENA region in recent years. The process itself has short-term and long-term factors that contribute to the final transition. The probability of a fluent and successful transition depends on crucial factors that were introduced in this chapter. The most significant role is played by the nature of the region in which the democratization wave happens. Specifically, for the MENA region, religion, history and political culture play a substantial role.

Factors having an impact on the process of democratization can be divided into internal (institutional and non-institutional) and external. Non-institutional internal factors are the economy, civil society, extremism and religion. Internal institutional factors related to the transition to democracy are politics, security and rule of law. External factors that play a key role in the democratization process

---

151 Strand et al.

in the MENA region are characterized as neighbouring countries, international shocks, systemic wars, new countries and spill-over effect of media.

The aim of this chapter was to provide the reader with the key features of the democratization process in general, while picking up the factors that are most significant for democratization in the MENA region specifically. It is necessary to point out that even though countries in the MENA region have many things in common, it is impossible to generalize the process of democratization without studying individual countries. For this reason, the next chapters are dedicated to case studies of crucial countries necessary for the recent development of a comprehensive framework of democratization in the MENA region.

References

Alterman, Jon B. *New Media, New Politics?: From Satellite Television to the Internet in the Arab World*. Policy Paper, no. 48. Washington, DC: Washington Institute for Near East Policy, 1998.

Altomonte, Carlo, and Massimiliano Ferrara, eds. *The Economic and Political Aftermath of the Arab Spring: Perspectives from Middle East and North African Countries*. Cheltenham, UK: Edward Elgar, 2014.

Anderson, Lisa. "Demystifying the Arab Spring." *Foreign Affairs*. 90, no. 3 (2011): 2–7.

Andreski, Stanislav, and A. R Radcliffe-Brown. *Military Organization and Society*. Berckley; Los Angeles: University of California Press, 1971.

Avant, Deborah, and Lee Sigelman. "Private Security and Democracy: Lessons from the US in Iraq." *Security Studies* 19, no. 2 (2010): 230–65. https://doi.org/10.1080/09636412.2010.480906 (Accessed June 30, 2017 as well as all forthcoming).

Boose, Jason William. "Democratization and Civil Society: Libya, Tunisia and the Arab Spring." *International Journal of Social Science and Humanity*, no. 2 (2013): 310–15. https://doi.org/10.7763/IJSSH.2012.V2.116.

Bremer, Stuart A. "Dangerous Dyads: Conditions Affecting the Likelihood of Interstate War, 1816–1965." *The Journal of Conflict Resolution* 36, no. 2 (1992): 309–41. https://doi.org/10.1177/0022002792036002005.

Breton, Albert, ed. *Political Extremism and Rationality*. Cambridge; New York: Cambridge University Press, 2002.

Carothers, Thomas, and William Barndt. "Civil Society." *Foreign Policy*, no. 117 (1999): 18–24+26–29. https://doi.org/10.2307/1149558.

Caryl, Christian. "The Democracy Boondoggle in Iraq," June 3, 2013. http://foreignpolicy.com/2013/03/06/the-democracy-boondoggle-in-iraq/.

Churchill, Charles W, and Abdulla M Lutfiyya. *Readings in Arab Middle Eastern Societies and Cultures*, 2012. https://doi.org/10.1515/9783110815740.

Coppedge, Michael, John Gerring, David Altman, Michael Bernhard, Steven Fish, Allen Hicken, Matthew Kroenig, et al. "Conceptualizing and Measuring Democracy: A New Approach." *Perspectives on Politics* 9, no. 2 (2011): 247–67. https://doi.org/10.1017/S1537592711000880.

Cox, Dan G, and A Cooper Drury. "Democratic Sanctions: Connecting the Democratic Peace and Economic Sanctions." *Journal of Peace Research* 43, no. 6 (November 2006): 709–22. https://doi.org/10.1177/0022343306068104.

Craighead, Geoff. *High-Rise Security and Fire Life Safety*. 3rd ed. Amsterdam; Boston: Butterworth-Heinemann/Elsevier, 2009.

Dahl, Robert Alan. *Polyarchy: Participation and Opposition*. 26. print. New Haven: Yale Univ. Press, 1998.

Danahar, Paul. *The New Middle East: The World after the Arab Spring*. Rev. paperback ed. London: Bloomsbury, 2015.

"Democracy Index 2015." Accessed June 30, 2017. https://www.eiu.com/public/topical_report.aspx?campaignid=DemocracyIndex2015.

"Democracy Index 2016: A Year of Political Stagnation in MENA," January 27, 2017. http://country.eiu.com/article.aspx?articleid=755057259&Country=Lebanon&topic=Politics&subtopic=Forecast&subsubtopic=Democracy+index.

Doorenspleet, Renske. "Development and Democracy: Power and Problems of Empirical Research." European Consortium on Political Research Joint Sessions of Workshops. Copenhagen, 2000.

Easterly, William, and Stanley Fischer. "The Soviet Economic Decline: Historical and Republican Data." World Bank, April 30, 1994. http://documents.worldbank.org/curated/en/452851468768730480/The-Soviet-economic-decline-historical-and-republican-data.

Edwards, Sebastian. *Crisis and Reform in Latin America: From Despair to Hope*. Oxford; New York: Published for the World Bank [by] Oxford University Press, 1995.

Egypt's government. "Egypt Constitution: Chapter One: The State.," 1980. Available at: http://www.egypt.gov.eg/english/laws/constitution/chp_one/part_one.aspx.

Fawcett, Louise L'Estrange, ed. *International Relations of the Middle East*. 3rd ed. Oxford: Oxford University Press, 2013.

Fischer, Robert J, and Gion Green. *Introduction to Security*. Amsterdam; Boston: Butterworth-Heinemann, 2004. http://site.ebrary.com/id/10166959. The Fund For Peace. "Fragile State Index.", n.d. http://fundforpeace.org/fsi/.

Frankel, Jeffrey. "Economic Shocks and International Politics." *Survival* 54, no. 3 (2012): 29–46. https://doi.org/10.1080/00396338.2012.690977.

Fukuyama, Francis. "I. The Primacy of Culture." *Journal of Democracy* 6, no. 1 (1995): 7–14. https://doi.org/10.1353/jod.1995.0007.

–. *The End of History and the Last Man*. Book, Whole. New York: Avon, 1993. http://vse.summon.serialssolutions.com/2.0.0/link/0/eLvHCXMwdV07CwIxDA6ii5ui4hMKzh69h_Y6iyK4iAiii_Su6aYOiqC_3uRORUXHdkhbGvLql68AYeDJwZdNkNYOlQlHsY2V0SkmDFaIMWT3TllShqlZ6u1cLdbc1q0_Kxne5YReevu29p__ZkiOLJj20ycXzEq-eeVBGdclBdL5a61UDExQD_ad55g5R2iZN-cyrUCRGw6qUEhPNejTvQk8WHF0IucCvgpK9gXFaYIC3bPYm0MdutPJajwbkKTdo_6ye-0taECRcnpsgtBR6luH6IweRgoTExsMokRGPvojp5IW1H-KaP-Z70A5R-JxbaALJUe6i73sRHduMGfl.

Gates, Scott, Håvard Hegre, Mark P Jones, and Håvard Strand. "Institutional Inconsistency and Political Instability: Polity Duration, 1800–2000." *American Journal of Political Science* 50, no. 4 (2006): 893–908. https://doi.org/10.1111/j.1540–5907.2006.00222.x.

Gill, Stephen. "Globalisation, Market Civilisation, and Disciplinary Neoliberalism." *Millennium* 24, no. 3 (December 1995): 399–423. https://doi.org/10.1177/03058298950240030801.

–. *Globalization, Democratization and Multilateralism*. Book, Whole. Houndmills; Tokyo: Macmillan, 1997. http://vse.summon.serialssolutions.com/2.0.0/link/0/eLvHCXMwY2AwNtIz0EUrE5ITU1MsDZLMUswtklKBdW5qmgUwYaSZmBqbGaYlmYG2EjsGWUZ5mweEg7Z1W6KOZOiVFafqJVehl_ao92YA6zoTcD_IEFgFgxJ5pCd4dtbYGFgeAztiSBwTM-jROzBJND5oCw8z0E6kmsZNkIEFtPtAiIEpuViEwQhyIj90q6SOQkpqbn4yKMogAgqJeSkK4BWBOYmgjcQ5mcW5ogwybq4hzh66QIPjoWMz8XB3G4kxsAD7–6kSDAqmwLLQzCA5BbzH1cQk1dIizdAoxcw4xdA4DchKkmQQxWqEFA5xaQYuyJmroHEDGQbWNGC6TpUFexAAWXJwFw.

Gleditsch, Kristian Skrede, and Michael D. Ward. "Diffusion and the International Context of Democratization." *International Organization* 60, no. 4 (2006): 911–33. https://doi.org/10.1017/S0020818306060309.

Gleditsch, Nils Petter, and Havard Hegre. "Peace and Democracy: Three Levels of Analysis." *The Journal of Conflict Resolution* 41, no. 2 (1997): 283–310. https://doi.org/10.1177/0022002797041002004.

Hamzawy, Amr, ed. *Civil Society in the Middle East*. Erstausg., 1. Aufl. Nahost-Studien 4. Berlin: Schiler, 2003.

Henderson, Gordon P. "The Public and Peace: The Consequences for Citizenship of the Democratic Peace Literature." *International Studies Review* 8, no. 2 (2006): 199–224. https://doi.org/10.1111/j.1468–2486.2006.00571.x.

Hirst, Paul Q. *From Statism to Pluralism: Democracy, Civil Society, and Global Politics*. London; Bristol, Penn: UCL Press, 1997.

Horowitz, Irving Louis. "The Struggle for Democracy." *The National Interest*, no. 83 (2006): 114–20.

Huntington, Samuel P. "Democracy's Third Wave." *Journal of Democracy* 2, no. 2 (1991): 12–34. https://doi.org/10.1353/jod.1991.0016.

Huntington, Samuel P. *The Clash of Civilizations and the Remaking of World Order*. Book, Whole. New York: Touchstone Book, 1997. http://vse.summon.serialssolutions.com/2.0.0/link/0/eLvHCXMwY2AwNtIz0EUrE8wSQVsajU0N04AVfGJiKrAeSjNMSTFINDM2NzJOA0W8Y5BllLd5QDhoW7cl6kiGXllxql5yFXppj3pvBmjOyQh09rYhsAoGJfJIeD8I2OQ3RJ7uMjIFlQGIdgeUD7q_z8AMdL48sA9hBOOYABsMltCjepAk4XyQvCGwZgK6EalmchNkYAHtVhBiYEouFmGwAka6QjKwPZyhkJ-mkJxZlpkD22apkJiXogBs7CkUpeaCL6ACqQAfl6oAPn1TlEHGzTXE2UMXaEE8dEwnHu5fIzEGlrz8vFQJBgVLcwOTpGSjZCPT1BQTk2RLC0tgaywl2cAUGPCpZkaJkgyiWI2QwiEuzcAFOasVNN4gw8CaBswPqbJgjwIAstp7Yg.

–. *The Third Wave: Democratization in the Late Twentieth Century*. The Julian J. Rothbaum Distinguished Lecture Series, v. 4. Norman: University of Oklahoma Press, 1991.

Inbar, Efraim. *The Arab Spring, Democracy and Security: Domestic and International Ramifications*, 2014. Routledge; BESA Studies in International Security.

Jaggers, Keith, and Ted R Gurr. "Transitions to Democracy: Tracking Democracy's Third Wave with the Polity III Data." *Journal of Peace Research* 32, no. 4 (1995): 469–82.

Jung, Dietrich. *Democratization and Development: New Political Strategies for the Middle East*. New York, N.Y.: Palgrave Macmillan, 2006. http://www.SLQ.eblib.com.au/patron/FullRecord.aspx?p=307743.

Kekic, Laza. "The Economist Intelligence Unit's Index of Democracy." Economist, 2007. http://www.economist.com/media/pdf/DEMOCRACY_INDEX_2007_v3.pdf.

Kepel, Gilles. *The War for Muslim Minds: Islam and the West*. Cambridge, Mass.: The Belknap Press of Harvard Univ. Press, 2006.

Khalaf Allāh, Muḥammad Aḥmad. *Al-Qur'ān Wa-Al-Dawlah*. Vol. 1981, Bayrūt: al-Mu'assasah al-'arabīyah lil dirāsāt wa-al-nashr.

Khalid, Adeeb. *Islam after Communism: Religion and Politics in Central Asia*. With a new afterword. Berkeley, Calif.: Univ. of California Press, 2014.

K M, Kadera, Crescenzi M J C, and Shannon M L. "Democratic Survival, Peace, and War in the International System." *American Journal of Political Science* 47, no. 2 (2003): 234–47. https://doi.org/10.1111/1540–5907.00016.

Li, Quan, and Rafael Reuveny. "Economic Globalization and Democracy: An Empirical Analysis." *British Journal of Political Science* 33, no. 1 (September 12, 2002): 29–54. https://doi.org/10.1017/S0007123403000024.

Limpach, Sophia, and Katharina Michaelowa. "The Impact of World Bank and IMF Programs on Democratization in Developing Countries." *Center for Comparative and International Studies (ETH Zurich and University of Zurich)*, no. 62 (2010). https://www.ethz.ch/content/dam/ethz/special-interest/gess/cis/cis-dam/Research/Working_Papers/WP_2010/2010_WP62_Limpach_Michaelowa.pdf.

Lipset, Seymour Martin. "Some Social Requisites of Democracy: Economic Development and Political Legitimacy." *The American Political Science Review* 53, no. 1 (1959): 69–105. https://doi.org/10.2307/1951731.

Luciani, Giacomo, ed. *The Arab State*. London: Routledge, 1990.

Mamdani, Mahmood. *Good Muslim, Bad Muslim: America, the Cold War, and the Roots of Terror*. 1st ed. New York: Pantheon Books, 2004.

Mason, Paul, and Otto James. *Religious Extremism*. London: Evans, 2010.

McCormick, John P. "Machiavellian Democracy: Controlling Elites with Ferocious Populism." *American Political Science Review* 95, no. 2 (2001): 297–313. https://doi.org/10.1017/S0003055401002027.

Merriam - Webster Dictionary. "Merriam - Webster Dictionary: Arab Spring," 2017. https://www.merriam-webster.com/dictionary/Arab%20Spring.

Mesquita, Bruce Bueno de, Randolph M. Siverson, and Gary Woller. "War and the Fate of Regimes: A Comparative Analysis." *The American Political Science Review* 86, no. 3 (1992): 638–46. https://doi.org/10.2307/1964127.

Miles, H. *Al Jazeera: How Arab TV News Challenged the World*. Little, Brown Book Group, 2010. https://books.google.cz/books?id=EFt3RiYWcA4C.

Milton-Edwards, Beverley. "The Ascendance of Political Islam: Hamas and Consolidation in the Gaza Strip." *Third World Quarterly* 29, no. 8 (December 2008): 1585–99. https://doi.org/10.1080/01436590802528739.

Mitchell, Sara McLaughlin, Scott Gates, and Håvard Hegre. "Evolution in Democracy-War Dynamics." *The Journal of Conflict Resolution* 43, no. 6 (1999): 771–92. https://doi.org/10.1177/0022002799043006005.

Mozaffari, Mehdi. "What Is Islamism? History and Definition of a Concept." *Totalitarian Movements and Political Religions* 8, no. 1 (March 2007): 17–33. https://doi.org/10.1080/14690760601121622.

Mudde, Cas. *On Extremism and Democracy in Europe*. Routledge Studies in Extremism and Democracy 34. London New York: Routledge, 2016.

Mustafayev, Chingiz Feyruz oglu. *Terrorism (Definition, Awareness and Prognostication)*. Baku: CINAR-CAP printing house, 2005.

Norris, Pippa. *Critical Citizens: Global Support for Democratic Government*. Oxford; New York: Oxford Univ. Press, 1999. http://site.ebrary.com/id/10283643.

Olimat, Muhamad. "The Fourth Wave: Revolution and Democratization in the Arab Middle East." *Journal of International Women's Studies* 12, no. 3 (2011): 1–6.

Oxford English Dictionary. "Rule of Law," 2017. http://www.oed.com/.

Panara, Carlo, and Gary Wilson, eds. *The Arab Spring: New Patterns for Democracy and International Law*. Nijhoff Law Specials 82. Leiden; Boston: Martinus Nijhoff Publishers, 2013.

Pipes, Daniel. "Distinguishing between Islam and Islamism," June 30, 1998. http://www.danielpipes.org/954/distinguishing-between-islam-and-islamism.

Przeworski, Adam, ed. *Democracy and Development: Political Institutions and Well-Being in the World, 1950–1990*. Cambridge Studies in the Theory of Democracy. Cambridge: Cambridge University Press, 2000.

Reiter, Dan. *Foreign-Imposed Regime Change*. Oxford University Press, n.d. // politics.oxfordre.com/10.1093/acrefore/9780190228637.001.0001/acrefore-9780190228637-e-335.

Rodrik, Dani. *Has Globalization Gone Too Far?* Washington, D.C: Institute for International Economics, 1997.

Russett, Bruce, William Antholis, Carol R. Ember, Melvin Ember, and Zeev Maoz. *Grasping the Democratic Peace*. Princeton University Press, 1993. http://www.jstor.org/stable/j.ctt7rqf6.

Saikal, Amin, and Amitav Acharya, eds. *Democracy and Reform in the Middle East and Asia: Social Protest and Authoritarian Rule after the Arab Spring*. London: Tauris, 2014.

Sakr, Naomi. *Satellite Realms: Transnational Television, Globalization and the Middle East*. London: IB Tauris, 2001.

Salame, Ghassan. *The Foundations of the Arab State*. London: Routledge, 2013.

Scheina, Robert. "Lessons Learned from Attacks on Mass Transit." presented at the Lecture presented at the Maryland Transit Administration Police Terrorism Training, Baltimore, 2008.

Schmitz, Hans P, and Katrin Sell. "International Factors in the Processes of Political Democratization." In *Democracy Without Borders: Transnationalisation and Conditionality in New Democracies*, 23–41. London: Routledge, 2002.

Sela, Avraham, ed. *The Continuum Political Encyclopedia of the Middle East*. Rev. and updated ed. New York: Continuum, 2002.

Shangquan, Gao. "Economic Globalization: Trends, Risks and Risk Prevention." United Nations, Development Policy and Analysis Division, 2000. http://www.un.org/en/development/desa/policy/cdp/cdp_background_papers/bp2000_1.pdf.

Snyder, Jack L. *Transitions to Democracy and the Rise of Nationalist Conflict*. Vol. 2000. Hebrew University of Jerusalem: LeonarDavis Institute for International Relations, n.d.

Stam, Allan C. *Win, Lose, or Draw: Domestic Politics and the Crucible of War*. Ann Arbor: University of Michigan Press, 1999.

Stepan, Alfred, and Juan J. Linz. "Democratization Theory and the 'Arab Spring,'" Number 2, April 2013, no. Volume 24 (n.d.). http://www.journalofdemocracy.org/sites/default/files/Stepan-24-2.pdf.

Stephanson, Anders. *Manifest Destiny: American Expansionism and the Empire of Right*. New York: Hill and Wang a division of Farra, Straus and Giroux, 2005.

Stoner, Kathryn, and Michael McFaul, eds. *Transitions to Democracy: A Comparative Perspective*. Baltimore: Johns Hopkins University Press, 2013.

Strand, Havard, Havard Hegre, Scott Gates, and Marianne Dahl. "Democratic Waves? Global Patterns of Democratization, 1816–2008," 12–13, 2012. Paper prepared for the 3rd International Conference on Democracy as Idea and Practice, Oslo, 12–13 January 2012. The paper has been funded by the Polarization and Conflict Project CIT-2-CT-2004-506084 funded by the European Commission-DG Research Sixth Framework Program and the Research Council of Norway project V-204454. We thank Mark Crescenzi, Ewan Harrison, Tim McKeown, Michael MacKuen, John MacMillan and Zeev Maoz for their comments on previous versions of this paper http://www.uio.no/english/research/interfaculty-research-areas/democracy/news-and-events/events/conferences/2012/papers-2012/Strand-Hegre-Gates-Dahl-wshop7.pdf

The White House "The National Security Strategy of the United States of America." Washington D.C.: The White House, 2002. http://nssarchive.us/NSSR/2002.pdf.

Thompson, William R. "Democracy and Peace: Putting the Cart before the Horse?" *International Organization* 50, no. 1 (1996): 141–74. https://doi.org/10.1017/S0020818300001697.

Vanhanen, Tatu. *Prospects of Democracy: A Study of 172 Countries*. New York: Routledge, 1997.

Wagner, Ben, European Parliament, and DG for External Policies. *After the Arab Spring: New Paths for Human Rights and the Internet in European Foreign Policy*. Luxembourg: EUR-OP, 2012.

Wallerstein, Immanuel. *Capitalist Agriculture and the Origins of the European World-Economy in the Sixteenth Century: With a New Prologue*. The Modern World-System, Immanuel Wallerstein. Berkeley, Calif.: Univ. of California Press, 2011.

Weede, Erich. "Some Simple Calculations on Democracy and War Involvement." *Journal of Peace Research* 29, no. 4 (1992): 377–83. https://doi.org/10.1177/0022343392029004002.

White, Gordon. "Civil Society, Democratization and Development (I): Clearing the Analytical Ground." *Democratization* 1, no. 2 (June 1994): 375–90. https://doi.org/10.1080/13510349408403399.

Windsor, Jennifer L. "Promoting Democratization Can Combat Terrorism." *The Washington Quarterly* 26, no. 3 (June 2003): 43–58. https://doi.org/10.1162/016366003765609561.

Yassin, As-Sayyid. *The Future of Civil Society: The Cultural Crisis and the Future of Civil Society*. Beirut: The Centre of Arabic Union Studies, 1992.

Yusuf, Shahid. "Middle Eeast Transitions: A Long, Hard Road." IMF Working Paper, 2014. https://www.imf.org/external/pubs/ft/wp/2014/wp14135.pdf.

Jan Chudoba

Egypt

In 2011, millions of Egyptians united with the aim of achieving their ultimate goal – to overthrow the regime of Hosni Mubarak, who had served as the president of Egypt for nearly 30 years. The main reasons for discontent were corruption, the lack of rule of law and freedom, the growing gap between the minority of wealthy elites and the impoverished majority, high unemployment rates, the lack of opportunity and the bad economic situation. The revolution promised a path towards more freedom and democratic reforms; however, six years after the revolution, many Egyptians are disillusioned and many say that today's situation closely resembles the Mubarak era, or is even worse. [1]

In order to better understand the context, it is necessary to mention key historical events. From the establishment of the Republic of Egypt in 1953, which followed Egyptian independence from the United Kingdom, to 2011, there were three main regimes – the regime of Gamal Abdel Nasser (1956–1970), the regime of Anwar Sadat (1970–1981) and the regime of Hosni Mubarak (1981–2011). Although these regimes differed in many ways, all of them were based on top-down rule, with security forces playing an important role.[2]

The last two decades of Mubarak's rule were marked by a continuous effort to suppress Islamists, particularly the Muslim Brotherhood (MB), which was the most important non-governmental movement and opposition. It was officially banned, but its members still took part in the parliamentary elections process as independents.[3]

It should be noted that although Mubarak was toppled in the revolution in 2011, most of the important people in the military, judiciary and the bureaucratic apparatus remained the same, their power uncontested. After the revolution, the military body – the Supreme Council of Armed Forces (SCAF) – assumed power before the new election took place.[4]

Although the revolution was not an Islamic revolution, but rather broad-based protests supported by all different classes, the MB eventually came to the forefront.

1 Trager, "Stuck With Sisi."

2 Esposito, Sonn, and Voll, *Islam and Democracy after the Arab Spring*. p.202

3 Laub, "Egypt's Muslim Brotherhood."

4 Brown and El-Shimy, "Did Sisi Save Egypt?"

In the parliamentary election in 2012, the Freedom and Justice Party established by the MB gained 47% of all votes, and another Islamist party, al-Nour, which was even more conservative, gained 25%.[5] Ultimately, the MB candidate, Mohammed Morsi, won the presidential election in 2012.[6]

However, there was growing discontent with and opposition to the Morsi government, which was trying to gain more power and limit the power of the judiciary and military. Some considered his actions to be justified, fearing the potential for military rule and supporting Morsi's efforts to curb the power of those connected to the old regime. Yet others perceived Morsi's actions as a path towards authoritarianism with Islamic law. Moreover, most of his promises regarding a range of issues, including the economy or equal rights for women or Christians, were not fulfilled in his one year in office, and he was seen as highly incompetent. Gradually, millions began to protest against Morsi, and in July 2013, the military, led by the minister of defence General Abdel-Fattah al-Sisi, ousted Morsi.[7]

Al-Sisi appointed a new interim president, Adly Mansour. The new interim government banned the MB, prosecuted many of its members, limited freedom of assembly and took other steps towards limiting freedom and consolidating its power with the strong support of the military. In May 2014, al-Sisi was elected president of Egypt, in an election where he had no serious opponent and which was marked by a low turnout, illustrating the disillusionment of Egyptians.[8]

As of May 2017, al-Sisi is still the president of Egypt and democracy in Egypt faces serious challenges – according to the Economist Intelligence Unit's Democracy Index, the level of democracy was at its highest level in 2012, whereas since 2013 the index has been similar or even lower than in the last years of the Mubarak era.[9] There are good reasons to claim that al-Sisi's regime is even more repressive than the regime of Hosni Mubarak, which illustrates the return to authoritarian rule.[10]

The aim of this chapter is to elaborate on the main factors that contributed both to the outbreak of the revolution in 2011 and to the failure of the democratic process, and to examine the current democratic potential in Egypt with the help of these factors.

---

5 Martini and Worman, "Voting Patterns in Post-Mubarak Egypt."

6 The Carter Center, *Presidential Election in Egypt: Final Report*.

7 Esposito, Sonn, and Voll, *Islam and Democracy after the Arab Spring*. pp.224–227

8 Cunningham, "In Egypt Election, Low Turnout Undercuts Sisi's Goal of Sweeping Mandate."

9 EIU Democracy Index, "EIU Democracy Index 2016."

10 Perra, "Between Expectations and Reality."

1. Internal non-institutional factors

In order to understand this chapter, it is necessary to explain in more detail what the MB is, as this organization played a great role in Egypt for many years (particularly after the revolution), not only as a religious group, but also as a part of civil society and as a political factor, most notably after the revolution in 2011.

The MB is a Sunni Islamist movement founded in Egypt in 1928 with a strong transnational character, having supporters or strong political parties throughout the Islamic world,[11] with ties to other Islamist organizations or political parties, such as Palestinian Hamas (Hamas was founded as a wing of the MB)[12] and the Turkish ruling party, the Justice and Development party.[13] Rejecting the Western model of secular government, the MB was established as an organization with the aim of promoting Islamic law and values in society. At the same time, it gradually became active in other areas, such as social welfare and political activism.[14] It developed a high degree of organization with a pyramid-shaped hierarchy and sophisticated recruitment system, trying to ensure that the exact goals set on the national level could be executed on local levels, which partly explains their success in Egypt after the Arab Spring.[15] The role of the MB in Egyptian society will be further explained within specific sections.

1.1 Economic factors

When considering economic factors, it is important to look not only at GDP, but, more importantly, at how the GDP is distributed among the population; moreover, the unemployment rate is a significant indicator. These represent more important reasons why people revolt.

According to data from the World Bank, GDP growth was almost always positive during the rule of Mubarak.[16] From 2000 to 2010, GDP growth was, on average, around 5%, and a year before the revolution, in 2010, it was 5.15%. GDP per capita was also on the rise in this period – the annual growth rate of GDP per capita was on average around 3%.[17]

---

11 Laub, "Egypt's Muslim Brotherhood."
12 Hamas Covenant 1998, "Hamas Covenant 1988."
13 Schanzer and Tahiroglu, "Ankara's Failure."
14 Laub, "Egypt's Muslim Brotherhood."
15 Trager, "The Unbreakable Muslim Brotherhood."
16 The World Bank, "GDP Growth (Annual %) | Data."
17 UNCTADstat, "UNCTADstat – Table View – Gross Domestic Product: Total and per Capita, Current and Constant (2005) Prices, Annual, 1970–2015."

However, as noted previously, it is important to examine who mostly benefitted from the GDP growth. The development of the poverty rate did not correlate with the development of GDP; in fact, the number of people living under the poverty line (which is $2 per day per person according to the World Bank) increased from 2000 to 2009 by around 5%, reaching more than 20% in 2009.[18]

It is also important to examine food prices, as food expenditures account for a large part of the total expenditures of Egyptians. Food prices in Egypt increased rapidly throughout the 2000s, which was, taking into consideration the high poverty rate, a huge burden for the population. In the year 2010 alone, food prices rose by 30%.[19]

Apart from figures, the perceptions of people are of great significance, as not hard data, but rather how people feel, determine their actions. According to Gallup polls in 2010, only one-fifth of the Egyptian population believed that the economic situation was getting any better, and only around 16% of Egyptians believed that the economic situation was good. At the same time, 88% of Egyptians believed that democracy would help progress.[20] In addition, similar to other Middle Eastern countries, high unemployment combined with an extensive population growth (Egypt's population is approximately 93 million and the population growth is 2–3% per year) and with the fact that people under 30 constitute around two-thirds of the total population[21] result in a high unemployment rate among young people (reaching between 25–30% in 2010 and 2011),[22] who were the driving force of the revolution.

However, the economic situation did not improve after Mubarak had been ousted; in fact, it even deteriorated in many respects. The unemployment rate increased after the revolution, reaching more than 12%, and it has remained that high ever since.[23] Food prices continued to rise, the Egyptian pound was devaluating and many young people still felt there was a lack of opportunity.[24] It should be noted that the fact that economic conditions were worsening during the Morsi's

18 Akcesme, "Poverty and Economic Inequality as the Leading Causes of the 2011 Egypt Revolution."

19 Maher, "The Political Economy of the Egyptian Uprising – ProQuest."

20 Gallup, "Egypt."

21 Abdel-Tawab and Roushdy, "Survey of Young People in Egypt | Population Council."

22 The World Bank, "Unemployment, Youth Total (% of Total Labor Force Ages 15–24) (Modeled ILO Estimate) | Data."

23 Trading economics, "Egypt Unemployment Rate | 1993–2017 | Data | Chart | Calendar | Forecast."

24 Trager, *Arab Fall*. p.212

presidency, as he was not able to tackle the economic challenges, was one of the factors that led to ousting him.[25]

Almost four years after Morsi was ousted, the economic prospects are not positive, as the inflation or unemployment rates remain very high and the economy faces similar challenges as it did before and after the revolution.[26] In the first quarter of 2017, the inflation rate was the highest in the last 30 years, reaching above 30%.[27] The decision to free float the Egyptian pound diminished the currency's value by more than 50% against the dollar, which made the imports much more expensive; taking into consideration that food in Egypt remains mostly imported, the prices of food skyrocketed – this year food price inflation reached 41% [28]. The public debt is rising and important economic reforms have not been carried out; instead of that, much money has been spent on other areas, such as megaprojects with uncertain returns like the costly widening of the Suez Canal in 2014–2015 (which was, in the main, massively used for propagandist purposes) or an increase in arms imports.[29]

To sum up, it can be stated that economic factors, such as deteriorating standards of living, unemployment (particularly youth unemployment) connected with the lack of opportunity, high inequality, rising food prices and increasing poverty, were among the important catalysts of the Egyptian revolution, meaning that they contributed to the striving for democracy. Despite GDP growth, the economic situation of most people worsened. Although economic factors played a significant role in the revolution, they paradoxically also contributed to the fact that the democratic process eventually failed; people felt that their demands, including economic ones, were not met. It is a question whether a further deterioration of the economic situation will not encourage people to massively protest again in the near future; however, it is obvious that although economic problems may contribute to ousting an authoritarian regime, they can hardly ensure a successful transition to democracy.

25 Trager, "Egypt Two Years After Morsi."

26 The Economist, "State of Denial; Egypt's Economy."

27 El-Behary, "Egypt Annual Inflation Rates Hits the Highest Records since 30 Years, CAPMAS."

28 ICG, "Keeping Egypt's Politics on the Agenda."

29 Ibid.

1.2 Civil society and media

1.2.1 Civil society

As in many countries from the Middle East and North Africa (MENA) region, civil society activities have been widely restricted by the government; as a result, civil society has not developed sufficiently. The Mubarak regime curbed civil society organizations (CSOs) severely. CSOs were required to register with the Ministry of Social Solidarity (MOSS), which exercised control over them.[30] This was exacerbated by Law 84, passed in 2002, restricting non-governmental organizations (NGOs) and increasing governmental power to deny licenses and control funding.[31] Apart from the official laws, CSOs were often harassed or threatened by the State Security Investigations Service.[32]

In general, freedom of expression, which is important for civil society to develop, was very limited in the Mubarak era. The Freedom House rated Egypt as "not free" throughout the 2000s before the revolution, the Economist Intelligence Unit's Democracy Index classified Egypt as an "authoritarian regime."[33] Freedom House reports informed annually about laws and state activities that severely oppressed journalists and opposition parties, absence of independent media, discrimination of Christians and other minorities, etc. From 2000 to 2010, there was practically no improvement in the level of freedom according to Freedom House.[34]

However, even in such an environment, civil society was existent and active to a limited degree, although mostly focusing on issues such as education, health, or family welfare, avoiding political topics, human rights concerns or other issues that could be perceived as criticism of the government.[35]

The most important organization that participated in civil society activities was the MB, which was officially banned but often tolerated (in contrast to the regime of al-Sisi, which declared them a terrorist organization). It dominated some CSOs, as it was able to combine religious, educational, charitable and other activities, while being active politically.[36] It also ran many social services, which the state

30 Herrold, "NGO Policy in Pre- and Post-Mubarak Egypt."

31 Monitor, "Egyptian Human Rights Take a Hit with Tough New Law; Activists Are Watching the Implementation of 2002 Law on Nongovernmental Groups."

32 Herrold, "NGO Policy in Pre- and Post-Mubarak Egypt."

33 EIU Democracy Index, "EIU Democracy Index 2016."

34 Freedom House, "Egypt | Country Report | Freedom in the World | 2001"; Freedom House, "Egypt | Country Report | Freedom in the World | 2011."

35 McInerney, "SCAF's Assault on Egypt's Civil Society."

36 Weber, "Modernity, Civil Society, and Sectarianism." p. 521

was not able to do sufficiently, and therefore gained much popularity. Although there was much scepticism about the MB and much criticism of its Islamist goals, particularly in the West, it became an important part of Egyptian civil society, as its members were involved in a wide range of activities – they established evening schools, committees for charitable and welfare work, hospitals, etc.[37] As a result of these activities and its sophisticated organization, the MB became the largest opposition force in Egypt.[38] During the revolution, the MB did not play a significant role, and although some of its members joined the protests, they did so on their own, and the MB did not initiate them.

Apart from NGOs and the MB, there were other important civil society groups in the Mubarak era. One of the most significant ones was the April 6 Youth Movement, which was formed in 2008 and organized several protests and strikes between 2008 and 2011, and had to face the government's strong opposition. Gradually, it became a significant movement with several other branches. Eventually, using social media and being well-organized, the April 6 Youth Movement became one of the key players in initiating and organizing the revolution in 2011.[39] Given the high percentage of young people in the Egyptian population, a youth movement has the potential to attract many Egyptians.[40]

Another civil movement, the National Association for Change (established in February 2010), played an significant role in the revolution.[41] Last but not least, the Cairo Institute for Human Rights Studies was also important – it enabled people to (legally) participate in public life through organizing seminars, conferences and other public events, as it was an official organization permitted by the state; however, that is also why its influence was limited.[42]

Before toppling Mubarak, Egyptian civil society had been united in pursuing one ultimate goal – Mubarak must step down. However, the interests of various groups of people (ranging from Islamists, including the MB and its supporters, to more secular liberals or leftists) differed after the revolution, and unity was weakened. Immediately after the revolution, CSOs had significantly more freedom than before, and there was a willingness among them to reconstruct the country into a

37 Ibid.
38 Trager, "The Unbreakable Muslim Brotherhood."
39 Ibrahim, "6 April."
40 EL Medni, "Civil Society and Democratic Transformation in Contemporary Egypt: Premise and Promises."
41 Ibid.
42 Ibid.

civil state, with independent NGOs playing the role of agents of democracy.[43] Civil society activists also wanted the government to draft a new law in order to promote freedom and strengthen civil society (instead of the restrictive law from 2002). Nevertheless, these goals could not be achieved in the short term, as the power was in the hands of the army. Gradually, the environment for civil society was becoming more restrictive again, as the military body SCAF, which was ruling the country, was trying to undermine the civil society activities (e.g. by claiming that the NGOs work on behalf of foreign agendas) or to gain more control over the NGOs.[44]

The MB appeared to be best organized of all organizations and movements after the revolution, succeeding both in parliamentary and presidential elections and ruling the country until Morsi was ousted (for more information, see section 2.2). After that, there was a crackdown on civil society on all fronts. The MB was banned and its members were detained and thousands sentenced to death in massive death trials. Moreover, many important CSOs were gradually banned, and their members persecuted. For instance, some of the funding members of the April 6 Movement were sent to prison (for disobeying an anti-protest law issued after the coup in 2013) for three years, and the movement was outlawed by court in 2014.[45]

This trend further continued after al-Sisi was elected president. Today, civil society activities are monitored, any public expressions of protests are punished and media are not free (for more information, see the following section).[46] In addition, Egyptians often do not want to join any protest for which the MB declares support because they do not want to be associated with them. As a result of a lack of opposition, most people still do not see any alternative between the MB and the regime.[47]

As for freedom of speech and other freedoms, Egypt saw improvement in 2012, being rated by Freedom House as "partly free."[48] However, due to the military coup in 2013 and the comeback of military rule, this index worsened and the situation even deteriorated in some respects compared to the Mubarak era. Opposed to the civil society, the power of the army has risen significantly since the coup (for more details, see section 2.1), whereas liberal and other civil forces have been targeted.[49]

---

43 Herrold, "NGO Policy in Pre- and Post-Mubarak Egypt."
44 McInerney, "SCAF's Assault on Egypt's Civil Society."
45 Al-Ahram Gate, "April 6."
46 Freedom House, "Egypt | Country Report | Freedom of the Press | 2017."
47 Trager, "Stuck With Sisi."
48 Freedom House, "Egypt | Country Report | Freedom in the World | 2013."
49 al-Anani, "Extremism Under Sisi."

1.2.2 *Media*

In the Mubarak era, the media was mostly owned or influenced by the state, there was little room for opposition and most media served as a tool for regime propaganda, with some exceptions regarding privately owned newspapers.[50] The propaganda can be illustrated by the fact that during the revolution, a few days before Mubarak was ousted, the main headline of the state media *Al Ahram* had been: "Millions March to Support Mubarak Nationwide."[51]

However, similar to other Arab countries where the Arab Spring took place, the crucial role in the revolution was played by social media, as the government did not succeed in restricting them and they were gaining popularity, particularly among young people, who were the driving force of the revolution. Facebook and Twitter in particular became essential tools in organizing the protests and raising awareness among the citizens about the atrocities committed by the regime; for instance, after a young man Khaled Said had been beaten to death by the police, the photos of his disfigured corpse and his story spread over the internet, and the Facebook group "We are all Khaled Said" became one of the important platforms for mobilizing people to join the protests.[52] The government tried to fight back by shutting down the internet in the first days of the revolution, which did not prove successful.[53]

Following the revolution in 2011, various new private media channels appeared, and there was much optimism among the citizens that the environment was finally changing, as the plurality of voices and opinions increased. However, this atmosphere lasted for only a very short period – the military rulers started cracking down heavily on media freedoms, putting on trial people who criticized military rule and using violence against journalists who were trying to cover any protests. The state media glorified the military and private ones were expected to do the same. As a result, the much-needed reform of media did not take place.[54]

However, when Morsi assumed power, the intimidation of journalists only intensified. Many journalists were charged with insulting the president or Islam, and more private channels were shut down.[55]

---

50 Hammond, "Egyptians Fight to Retool State Media."

51 Abdulla, "Egypt's Media in the Midst of Revolution."

52 Chebib and Sohail, "The Reasons Social Media Contributed To The 2011 Egyptian Revolution."

53 Abdulla, "Egypt's Media in the Midst of Revolution."

54 Ibid.

55 Ibid.

Despite the significant role of the social media in the revolution in 2011, they arguably did not contribute positively to the attempted democratic transition; on the contrary, they might have impeded the process. According to the analysis conducted by the non-profit organization PeaceTech Lab, social media encouraged segregation into communities of the like-minded, while contributing to the growing disagreement and grievances between the groups through spread of fear or rumours, instead of enhancing dialogue and understanding between them.[56]

After Morsi had been ousted, the state-owned media changed their tone again, in favour of the military and against Morsi and the MB. Islamist media were closed, and the Egyptian media environment became more restrictive. According to "Reporters without borders", Egypt is, in 2017, among 20 countries with the worst state of media freedom, being ranked 161st out of 180 countries in the Press Freedom Index,[57] compared to 127th place (out of 173) during the Mubarak era. In 2012 and 2013, it was ranked 158th of 178 countries.[58] In addition to that, in the Freedom House report on freedom of the press in Egypt in 2016 it was stated that "Egypt was the world's third-worst jailer of journalists in 2016."[59] Today, all major TV channels, press and much of the internet media deliver the same narratives, which are in accordance with the government's approach.[60]

Although the internet offers a platform which is not as restricted as others, it also has been targeted with censorship; for example, in May and June 2017, the government reportedly blocked access to at least 64 news websites (for instance Al-Jazeera, Huffington post (in Arabic), Mada Masr).[61]

In sum, the level of media freedom is probably the lowest in history, which has deep roots in the Mubarak regime, and is further deteriorating. Needless to say, this fact poses a serious challenge to potential democratization.

1.3 Extremism and religion

In Egypt, almost 90% of the population are Muslims (mostly Sunnis, Shia constitutes around 1%), whereas around 10% (approximately 9 million) are Christians (mostly Copts), who constitute the largest Christian community in the Middle

56 Lynch, Freelon, and Aday, "How Social Media Undermines Transitions to Democracy."
57 RSF, "Egypt."
58 RSF, "Egypt Falls Again in World Press Freedom Index, Now Ranked 159th | Reporters without Borders," 0.
59 Freedom House, "Egypt | Country Report | Freedom of the Press | 2017."
60 Ibid.
61 CPJ, "Egyptian Human Rights Group Reports 64 Websites Blocked."

East.[62] Islam is the state religion of Egypt, which is explicitly stated in the constitution to the present day.[63] The religious tensions between Christians and Muslims have been posing a problem in Egypt during the last few decades and although Muslims and Christians fought together against Mubarak in 2011, the grievances did not disappear.[64]

As mentioned before, the parliamentary and presidential elections in 2011–2012 were marked by the success of Islamists. The Morsi government drafted a new constitution, promoting a strong role for Sharia law in the society [65] (for more details, see section 2.2). Morsi was also accused of being incapable of preventing sectarian violence, as the number of sectarian attacks on Egyptian Copts increased.[66]

Nevertheless, the toppling of Morsi further provoked sectarian grievances, while the police and army often ignored such incidents, which resulted in the further spread of attacks.[67] According to Eshhad, a project under the auspices of the non-profit organization "The Tahrir Institute for Middle East Policy," around 400 incidents of sectarian violence occurred between August 2013 and June 2016, most of which targeted Egyptian Copts, while the largest number of the attacks occurred after Morsi.[68] From December 2016 to the end of May 2017, there were four large terrorist attacks against Christians in Egypt, killing more than 100 Christians.[69]

In the wake of the removal of Morsi and the ban on the MB, there was a rising number of attacks against government forces in the Sinai Peninsula, which evolved into a violent insurgency and a war between the Egyptian army and the Islamist insurgents.[70] This is still in progress in June 2017. With the spread of the so-called Islamic state since 2014 and its violent ideology, many Sinai insurgents have pledged allegiance to this organization. As a result, extremism has been on the rise in Egypt.[71]

---

62 Halpern, "Egypt Has Figured Out How to Defeat ISIS."
63 McRobie, "Egypt: A Tale of Two Constitutions – ProQuest."
64 Brownlee, "Violence Against Copts in Egypt."
65 McRobie, "Egypt: A Tale of Two Constitutions – ProQuest."
66 Brownlee, "Violence Against Copts in Egypt."
67 Ibid.
68 Eshhad, "Eshhad Quarterly Report."
69 Sanchez and Samaan, "Dozens Dead as Gunmen Attack Bus of Coptic Christians in Egypt."
70 Hauslohner, "An Insurgency Is Taking Root in Egypt's Restive Sinai Peninsula Following the July Coup."
71 al-Anani, "Extremism Under Sisi."

In his speech at al-Azhar[72] university in December 2014, al-Sisi expressed the necessity to fight extremist ideologies and stressed "the need to revolutionize Islam," emphasizing the role of al-Azhar in this process.[73] Counterterrorism became one of the priorities of al-Sisi's government and many measures have been taken – the supervision of a large number of mosques by the regime, a military campaign against Islamic State of Iraq and the Levant (ISIL) in Sinai, a crackdown against the MB, but also the above-mentioned restrictions against NGOs, tightening control over press and other measures curbing freedom not only of Islamists, but also of liberals and other advocates of freedom.[74] In the name of counterterrorism, the regime also combats moderate ideas of democracy, freedom and justice.[75]

On the other hand, even though many people have been jailed or oppressed under the pretext of counterterrorism measures, al-Sisi portrays himself as the one who can bring security to Egypt, implying that there are only two choices – either him, or extremism and chaos.[76] As a result, due to terrorism, more people feel that extraordinary measures and restrictions of freedom are more justifiable, and many Egyptians think there is no alternative. Thus, extremism represents a serious obstacle to democracy in Egypt.

2. Internal institutional factors

2.1 Security factors

Security forces have had a crucial role in Egypt for all the regimes since Nasser's government, who staged a military coup against British rule. However, its power increased especially during the Mubarak era, when the Egyptian military started to acquire more economic and political power. The military established many companies and high military officers occupied important administrative positions.[77] In addition, following the Camp David peace treaty between Egypt and

---

72 Al-Azhar is designated as the most prominent Islamic university not only in Egypt, but also in the whole Sunni Islamic world, being a significant actor in propagating Islam and shaping Islamic thought. Al-Azhar has been a pillar of the Egyptian state for over 1,000 years Barak, "The Al-Azhar Institute – A Key Player in Shaping the Religious and Political Discourse in Egypt."

73 Lappin, "Peace with Islam Now Possible."

74 Linn and Linn, "Sisi's Islam."

75 The Economist, "Worse than Mubarak; Repression in Egypt."

76 Trager, "Stuck With Sisi."

77 Abul-Magd, "The Egyptian Military in Politics and the Economy: Recent History and Current Transition Status."

Israel in 1979, the USA started providing Egypt with military aid of $1.3 billion annually,[78] which Egypt has been provided to the present with a partial suspension after the coup in 2013 until March 2015.[79] In addition, economic liberalisation in the 1990s and 2000s resulted in a competition between civilian and military enterprises, while the military managed to succeed in expanding their businesses.[80] As a result, the army's influence in Egypt rose significantly, although mainly in the economic sphere.

Paradoxically, the role of the army even increased after the revolution in 2011. Although the army did not initiate the revolution, it eventually joined the protesters and enabled the ousting of Mubarak, and the Egyptian people placed their trust in the army. In the aftermath of the revolution, the military body SCAF, mentioned before, took the lead and ran the country in the transitional period. Following the revolution, thousands of people were arrested, and parliamentary elections, planned for September 2011, were postponed by the SCAF.[81]

The military did not give up on its power even in the period of Morsi's presidency, maintaining its economic and even political influence to a certain degree. Before Morsi was elected president, the SCAF had issued a constitutional declaration that limited the powers of the presidential office and increased the powers of the army. Morsi did not manage to limit its role and strength.[82] In the coup in June 2013, the crucial role was played, again, by the military and then minister of defence general al-Sisi, although it was the Egyptian people who gave them the mandate.

Since al-Sisi was elected president in 2014, the power of the army has been on the rise. Many people compare his regime to the regime of Mubarak; however, there is a striking difference between the two regimes with regard to the military. Whereas Mubarak's rule was backed by the dominant party National Democratic Party (NDP), which served as a source of his political legitimacy, al-Sisi has to rely entirely on the army. In the Mubarak era, the military was favoured by him, having much power; nevertheless, it was not the driving political force, as this role was secured by the NDP. The army was privileged as long as it supported Mubarak.[83] In contrast, al-Sisi's legitimacy stems from the military. Therefore, he

78 Ibid.
79 Sharp, "Egypt: Background and U.S. Relations."
80 Noll, "Egypt's Armed Forces Cement Economic Power."
81 Esposito, Sonn, and Voll, *Islam and Democracy after the Arab Spring*. p.213
82 Brown and El-Shimy, "Did Sisi Save Egypt?"
83 Linn, "The Army And Its President."

has made a great effort to, so to say, keep the army satisfied, by granting it much political and economic power.

Since Morsi was ousted, the army has also significantly expanded its economic activities, including sectors such as food, energy or construction. It is difficult to find out what the proportion of the economy controlled by the army is, as there is no reliable hard data. While President al-Sisi claims that the army accounts for less than 2% of GDP, some experts estimate that the figure may be about ten times higher,[84] while others estimate as much as 40%.[85]

A specific example of the military's power in the Egyptian economy is its influence on food supplies, which are crucial in Egypt, as there have been sharp increases in the price of food (for instance, in November 2016); as a consequence, there is a need for food subsidies, on which a significant portion of the population is dependent, and which are controlled by the army.[86] Potentially, there is a danger of misusing this privilege, as the military can basically decide who is eligible. Moreover, it often proves to be difficult for private companies to win public contracts due to their inability to compete with large military enterprises. The growing influence of the army in the Egyptian economy is not likely to change, as the president is heavily dependent on its backing because of a lack of democratic legitimacy.[87]

The military remains a significant actor in Egypt. It played a crucial role in the revolution in 2011 and since then its strength has been increasing. Although the military made the revolution in 2011 possible, it also, in turn, slowed down the democratization process, and in 2013, the military put an end to it. Given the seriousness of the situation at the end of Morsi's presidency, it is hard to judge whether the ousting of Morsi was a necessary step or the right thing to do; nevertheless, the result is the strengthening of the army's positions accompanied by restrictions of freedom and democracy. It is certain that the army would play a significant role in any potential democratization process, and it is a question whether the army would make such a process possible. In general, a military with sweeping powers, which has a high degree of autonomy and which is not under civilian control, constitutes an obstacle to a democratic transformation.

84 Noll, "Egypt's Armed Forces Cement Economic Power."
85 Hamama, "Sisi Says Military Economy Is 1.5% of Egypt's GDP, but How Accurate Is This?"
86 Noll, "Egypt's Armed Forces Cement Economic Power."
87 Ibid.

2.2 Political factors

As is obvious from the previous sections, a fully democratic political culture has never developed in Egypt. In the Mubarak era, there was one strong party, the NDP, of which Mubarak was a member. Although the first parliamentary election took place in 1987 and then elections were held regularly, they were mostly rigged, marked by oppression of political opponents, and left little space for any opposition.[88] The only exceptions were the presidential and parliamentary elections in 2005, both of which were, despite some drawbacks, considered freer and fairer than any elections before (the MB members, running as independents, won almost 20% of seats in the parliament).[89] However, the following crackdown against the MB and other opposition and the highly rigged elections in 2010 were a big disappointment for Egyptians, many of whom ceased to believe in any possible change and democratization of the regime, which was one of the reasons for the outbreak of the revolution in 2011.[90]

Parliamentary elections that took place in 2011–2012 were regarded as the first relatively free elections in the history of Egypt – it was very easy to form a party and participate, unlike in the Mubarak regime, and voters were mostly able to participate in the process without hindrances from the state. On the other hand, there were some drawbacks as well, including a crackdown on peaceful protests, prosecution of prominent public figures for insulting the state or religion, and prosecution of CSOs. In addition, the emergency law which started in 1981 (following the assassination of the then president Anwar Sadat) and has been implemented continuously since then, giving the state sweeping powers, was in effect during the process of the election, impeding the rule of law. Consequently, thousands of civilians were brought before military tribunals.[91]

After Morsi had assumed office in 2012, a new constitution was drafted and approved in a referendum; however, many criticized it as undemocratic and promoting political Islam, as it was seen as strengthening the position of Sharia law in Egypt, while opening doors for stricter interpretations of it.[92] This constitution was replaced by a new one drafted under the military rule in 2013, having a

88 Mumtaz, "The Fall of Mubarak."

89 Ibid.

90 Hamzawy, "From Too Much Egyptian Opposition to Too Little—and Legal Worries Besides."

91 The Carter Center, *Final Report of the Carter Center Mission to Witness the 2011–2012 Parliamentary Elections in Egypt.*

92 McRobie, "Egypt: A Tale of Two Constitutions – ProQuest."

less Islamic tone than the previous one, providing more freedoms, condemning discrimination and giving more powers to the military (such as the right to appoint the defence minister for eight years).[93] The new constitution, which is still in effect today, was approved in January 2014 in a referendum by 98% Egyptians while the MB boycotted the referendum.[94]

In 2014, al-Sisi was elected president, and parliamentary elections finally took place, after a long delay, between October and December 2015, meaning that Egypt had effectively been without a parliament for over three years. Both presidential and parliamentary elections were marked by extremely low turnouts, a lack of genuine competition, vote-buying, non-transparent spending and forbidden propaganda around the electoral posts. As for the parliamentary elections, the turnout was almost twice as low as in the previous ones (around 28%), showing Egyptians' loss of faith in elections.[95] The parliament is hardly a counterbalance to the executive and judicial branches, as it is mostly composed of al-Sisi's allies, people with strong business ties to the regime or figures from the Mubarak regime.[96]

A serious problem, occurring at all levels of the society, is corruption. Transparency International ranked Egypt as the 108th out of 175 countries in the Corruption Perceptions Index[97] (CPI) in 2016, compared to 88th position out of 168 in 2015.[98]

One example that illustrates the current state of corruption in Egypt is the case of Hisham Geneina, a former head of the Central Auditing Organisation, Egypt's main oversight body. He was removed from office by presidential decree issued by al-Sisi in 2016 and sentenced to one year in prison, after he stated in an interview that the amount of corruption in Egypt had exceeded EGP 600bn.[99] This power to fire the heads of watchdog agencies, which are supposed to be independent,

---

93 Rizk and El Sharnoubi, "Egypt's Constitution 2013 vs. 2012: A Comparison."

94 Ibid.

95 Aly and Essaila, "Egypt's 2015 Parliamentary Elections: A Prelude to Stability?"

96 Al-Arian, "Egypt's Hollow Parliament."

97 The CPI captures "the informed views of analysts, businesspeople and experts in countries around the world", while the low score shows that institutions like police or judiciary are untrustworthy and do not function properly Transparency International, "Research – CPI – Overview."

98 Transparency International, "Transparency International – Egypt."

99 El-Fekki, "'I Don't Hope for Restoration, Rather Admission of Legal Violation in Presidential Decision': Hisham Geneina – ProQuest."

was given to the president by the legislative amendment passed by parliament before this incident.[100]

An extreme level of corruption, present under Mubarak as well, was one of the reasons why Egyptians toppled his regime. The persistence of corruption after the revolution has undermined Egyptians' belief in the possibility for change, resulting in their disengagement from the political process altogether.

With regard to democratization, education is crucial. In Egypt, education faces serious challenges – according to UNESCO, the literacy rate is almost 75.84%, meaning that almost 25% (around 16 mil.) Egyptians older than 15 years cannot read and write.[101] There is a shortage of teachers and the study system is mostly flawed and ineffective. As the population is increasing exponentially, it is likely that the shortage of teachers will continue to beleaguer Egyptian schools.[102] In the last few years, public spending on education has risen, and there is an improving trend – the literacy rate of youth (15–24 years) is 93%.[103] Nevertheless, the problem with education in Egypt persists, and it will take many years to tackle.

Needless to say, poor education severely impedes the democratization process, as uneducated people are often easier to manipulate, and they are less likely to organize and be active in politics. Educated people generally understand better the importance and principles of democracy and they engage more in political movements[104] – the April 6 Movement, mentioned before, was also founded and organized mostly by well-educated people.

2.3 Rule of law – judiciary system

Despite the fact that principles such as "separation of powers" or ensuring equal rights by the state are embodied in the constitution, they are often violated. In the previous sections, the situation regarding freedoms (such as freedom of speech or assembly), environment for CSOs or violations of human rights were discussed. As of today, the state of the rule of law is critical, which can be illustrated by violations of human rights, discrimination against religious groups or women, often ignored by the state. In 2016, the Global Gender Gap Report, which measures inequalities

100 Abdel Salam, "The Limits of Fighting Corruption in Egypt."
101 UNESCO, "Country Profile: Egypt."
102 Sewilam et al., "Introducing Education for Sustainable Development into Egyptian Schools." pp.222–223
103 UNESCO, "Country Profile: Egypt."
104 Glaeser, Ponzetto, and Shleifer, "Why Does Democracy Need Education?" p.31

between men and women, ranked Egypt at 132 out of 145 countries worldwide.[105] However, this is not only the fault of the government, but also of the society as a whole, as it remains mostly conservative. When talking about rule of law, it is also necessary to mention the extensive violence used by the state against protesters, most notable of which is the Rabaa massacre in August 14, where around 1,000 Morsi supporters were killed, which was described as one of the largest killings of demonstrators in a single day in modern history.[106]

There has been a whole range of laws passed since Morsi was ousted that threaten the rule of law and give more powers to the military-security establishment at the expense of civilian institutions. Some examples of these laws are the Military Facilities Law from October 2014, which greatly expanded the jurisdiction of military courts,[107] the counterterrorism law from February 2015, which enables the authorities to impose heavy sentences for crimes under the definition of terrorism (which is very broadly defined and easily misused), and the newest Judicial Bodies Law from April 2017, giving the president more power over the judiciary through allowing him to appoint key judges of four judicial bodies (the Administrative Prosecution Authority, the State Lawsuits Authority, the Judiciary Law and the State Council Law), lowering the independence of the judiciary.[108]

As for the Egyptian judiciary, some rulings showing that the judiciary has not been non-partisan should be mentioned. In 2012, the first democratically elected parliament (controlled by Islamists) was dissolved by the Supreme Constitutional Court SCC, and in general, the judiciary made it difficult for Morsi to rule. After his ousting, the judiciary helped the new regime to fight against the MB members and other opposition, sentencing more than 1,200 MB members to death (including Morsi himself) in 2014. The trials lasted just a few hours and did not allow for defence testimony.[109] Other mass death trials continued in 2015. In addition, the courts have rehabilitated many officials from the Mubarak era, including Mubarak himself.[110] These and other events show that Egyptian courts have been deeply biased and dependent on the regime, which dates back to the Mubarak era, showing how deep this dependency is. An independent judiciary is crucial to every democratic country and if the courts are biased and work mostly for the regime, it represents a huge obstacle to democratization.

105 World Economic Forum, "Global Gender Gap Report 2016. Egypt."
106 Dunne and Hamzawy, "Egypt's Secular Political Parties."
107 HRW, "Egypt: Unprecedented Expansion of Military Courts."
108 Hamzawy, "How Sisi Is Using the Law as a Tool to Restore Tyranny."
109 Elmasry, "Al Jazeera, Doha, Qatar, Mohamad Elmasry Column."
110 Walsh, "Egypt Roared as Mubarak Fell. It's Mute as He's Freed."

3. External factors

There is no doubt that the revolution in Tunisia, which toppled the regime of Zine El Abidine Ben Ali on January 14, 2011, became a catalyst for the Egyptian revolution, as it inspired Egyptians and showed them it is possible to change the authoritarian regime.[111] The protests soon spread across other Arab nations (although in each of these countries, there was a different development) – Libya, Syria, Yemen and Bahrain. However, the situations in Libya, Syria and Yemen dramatically worsened after 2011 as these countries faced civil wars and, particularly Syria and Yemen, humanitarian catastrophes (see the chapters about Syria, Yemen and Libya). Moreover, the main challenge in the Middle East became ISIL, whose ideology spread throughout the Middle East, including Egypt – particularly in Sinai, as discussed previously.

Towards the end of Morsi's presidency, extremism was on the rise, and many people feared that Egypt could be on the brink of collapse, and that it might evolve into chaos as in some other countries of the region after 2011. Therefore, the situation in these countries also influenced the Egyptian support for military rule and crackdown on extremism, as people saw it as a better alternative than chaos (see section 1.3).

For Egypt, the relationship with the USA has been of much importance for several decades. Cooperation between the two countries began when Sadat sought peace with Israel in the 1970s and relations with the USA were improving. After the peace treaty in Camp David in 1979, the USA started providing Egypt with economic and military aid, which continued during the Mubarak era and has been continuing until the present. Between 1948 and 2016, the USA provided Egypt with $77.4 billion in foreign aid; in this manner, the aid also helped entrench the Mubarak regime,[112] and bolster the extensive power of the Egyptian military.

During the anti-Mubarak protests, the USA changed its approach, seeing the huge opposition against him, and started supporting his demission and the democratic process, although there was a fear that Islamists might come to power.[113] After Morsi was ousted, there was a short period when some of the aid was suspended by the USA amid fears of violation of human rights by the military regime, but was then restored.[114] Today, annual economic aid, including military aid, is

111 Esposito, Sonn, and Voll, *Islam and Democracy after the Arab Spring*. p.209

112 Sharp, "Egypt: Background and U.S. Relations."

113 Sharp, "Egypt: Background and U.S. Relations."

114 Ibid.

provided to Egypt, which is not likely to change under President Trump, who supports al-Sisi more than his predecessor.[115]

The approach of most EU states to the revolution was similar to that of the USA – first, they were very cautious, but in the end they supported the resignation of Mubarak.[116] As for the EU-Egypt relations under al-Sisi, most EU states also maintain close ties with his regime, and some states (Germany, the UK) also provide Egypt with economic aid, even though there are many concerns about human rights in Egypt. However, given the situation in some other countries in the region and the massive wave of migration from the Middle East to Europe, most EU governments promote the stability of Egypt, considering al-Sisi a partner in curbing illegal migration and in the fight against terrorism.[117]

The influence of the Gulf states on Egypt also should not be omitted, as some of them provide Egypt with huge economic support; since al-Sisi assumed office in 2014, Saudi Arabia, the United Arab Emirates and Kuwait have given billions of dollars of aid (around $4 billion a year) to Egypt, with more billions in investments, helping Egypt to pay for its $12 billion loan from the International Monetary Fund IMF.[118] However, the relationship between Egypt and Saudi Arabia faces many problems, particularly because of different views on the Syrian conflict (al-Sisi supports the Syrian president al-Assad, whereas Saudi Arabia is staunchly against him, as the Saudis perceive that any support for Assad is also support for Iran); apart from that, Saudi Arabia has expressed many concerns about how the Egyptian government manages aid.[119] Despite these and other disputes, Saudi Arabia and the above-mentioned Gulf states continue supporting Egypt, as it is an important ally in the region and its collapse would bring many problems.

While the support of the USA, some key EU states, the above-mentioned Gulf states and Russia (which also developed good relations with al-Sisi) is important for the undemocratic al-Sisi regime, it is difficult to say whether their potential resentment of the regime would change anything. Moreover, even if there was, hypothetically, strong opposition to the regime, leading eventually to its collapse, it does not mean that it would contribute to more democracy, as the main preconditions for democracy must be created primarily at the domestic level.

---

115 Benaim, "What Does Trump Really Want From Sisi?"

116 Metawe, "How and Why the West Reacted to the Arab Spring: An Arab Perspective – ProQuest."

117 Albaraa, "The Real Reason behind Thaw in EU-Egypt Tensions."

118 Aly and Ibish, "Egypt-GCC Partnership: Bedrock of Regional Security Despite Fissures."

119 Ibish, "Egypt and Saudi Arabia."

Apart from Saudi Arabia and other Arab Gulf states, it is important to mention Egyptian relations with other neighbouring countries, such as Libya and Israel/Palestine, and their impact on the stability of Egypt.

Libya has been facing violence and extremism since the former Libyan leader, Muammar Gaddafi, was toppled, which has evolved into a full scale civil war. Moreover, Islamist militants, many of whom pledged allegiance to ISIL, control chunks of Libyan territory.[120] The Egyptian border with Libya, which is more than 1,100 km long, is highly unsecured and porous, and cross-border terrorist attacks and arms proliferation are an everyday reality. Consequently, the instability of Libya has a negative influence on the stability of Egypt, increasing the threat of extremism[121] (for more information, see the chapter about Libya).

Israel, on the other hand, had good relations with Egypt before the Arab Spring, as Israel endorsed the Egyptian president Mubarak and his willingness to cooperate with Israel. During the revolution, the Israelis were still supporting Mubarak, fearing that his ousting might bring instability in the region, including Israel.[122] After a time of deterioration in relations between the two countries during the Morsi presidency, relations have been improving since al-Sisi assumed office. The improvement in relations concerns not only the area of security, where the ties are very strong due to the fight against terrorism (particularly in the Sinai Peninsula, where Israel approved the Egyptian deployment of additional forces beyond the number stated in the peace treaty from 1979), but also the economic and political areas. After three years, Egypt appointed an ambassador to Israel and in 2016 there was a visit by an Egyptian foreign minister (after nearly a decade). As described by some analysts, the relations between the two countries have reached "the highest level in history."[123]

In contrast to that, al-Sisi's government left the borders between Gaza and Egypt closed, as it considers Hamas, which governs the Gaza strip (for more information, see the chapter about Palestine) to be linked with the MB, and therefore a terrorist organization. In addition, it has been reported that Hamas cooperates with the Islamic state affiliate "Sinai Province."[124] Taking into consideration the sensitivity of the Palestinian issue, there is a potential for the al-Sisi government to alienate Egyptians by cooperating more with Israel in the future. Moreover, if Palestinians get the impression that the Egyptian government prefers Israel to

---

120 Morajea and Cunningham, "Militants Fill Void in Libya 'S Civil War – ProQuest."
121 Wenig, "Egypt's Security and the Libyan Civil War."
122 Muhareb, "Israel and the Egyptian Revolution."
123 Tahhan, "Egypt-Israel Relations 'at Highest Level' in History."
124 Jones and El-Ghobashy, "World News."

Hamas, it might result in more support from Palestinians for Sinai insurgents, creating a bigger threat to Egypt. All in all, it is difficult to say with certainty what final effect on potential democratization a stronger relationship with Israel and alienation of Palestine may have, if any.

With the exception of Israel, Egypt is surrounded by unstable countries or territories (Libya, Gaza, Sudan) and by Saudi Arabia, which is one of the most repressive countries in the world. These countries are unlikely to have any positive impact on the democratization process, but rather the opposite.

4. Conclusion

In 2011, many believed Egypt was on the path to becoming more democratic. However, toppling an authoritarian regime does not ensure democracy, and Egypt is a case in point. After the revolution, some necessary reforms (such as freedom the of press, independence of the judiciary) were carried out insufficiently or not at all, and most importantly, the military, which the people saw as an ally during and after the revolution, reverted to Mubarak-style rule after it seized power. The structures of the "deep state," consisting of a complex system of the military, the judiciary and bureaucracy, have hardly changed, and the attempt at democratic parliamentary and presidential elections ended up with the rule of Islamists, who were commonly considered to be incompetent and were believed to lead the country towards an Islamic state. The popular resentment of Morsi and his government was heard, but also exacerbated and misused, by the military and judiciary structures, which took power once again, with an even firmer grip than before.

The regime of al-Sisi is based on suppressing opposition, sweeping powers of the security apparatus, a biased judiciary and misuse of fear of extremism and terrorist attacks for further curbing freedoms and extending powers of the president and the military, which is exacerbated by propaganda in the media. In addition, the regime has support not only from some important states in the region, but also from the world powers.

However, the problems are much deeper – even if this regime fell, it would not mean the country would become democratic, as the experience of Egyptians shows. Furthermore, if the president is changed, it does not impact the "deep state." On top of that, there is less will among the people to radically change anything after 2011, as the largest opposition power at that time, the MB, has been harshly suppressed, and people are also highly demoralized by the failure of the transition after the revolution.

The underlying problems lie in the lack of education, high polarisation of the society, extensive power of the military and judiciary, high corruption rate and undeveloped civil society. All of these are very deep-rooted in Egyptian society, and therefore require much time to improve, which is difficult to achieve in a repressive environment. In addition, extremism and wars in the region intensify all problems and strengthen authoritarian rule. Therefore, the situation regarding democracy in Egypt should not be expected to significantly improve any time soon.

References

Abdel Salam, Mohamed. "The Limits of Fighting Corruption in Egypt." *Carnegie Endowment for International Peace*, October 13, 2016. http://carnegieendowment.org/sada/?fa=64852.

Abdel-Tawab, Nahla G., and Rania Roushdy. "Survey of Young People in Egypt | Population Council," 2015. http://www.popcouncil.org/research/survey-of-young-people-in-egypt (accessed June 15, 2017).

Abdulla, Rasha. "Egypt's Media in the Midst of Revolution." *Carnegie Endowment for International Peace*, July 16, 2014. http://carnegieendowment.org/2014/07/16/egypt-s-media-in-midst-of-revolution-pub-56164 (accessed June 15, 2017).

Abul-Magd, Zeinab. "The Egyptian Military in Politics and the Economy: Recent History and Current Transition Status." *CMI – Chr. Michelsen Institute*, no. 2 (2013): 1–6 https://www.cmi.no/publications/file/4935-the-egyptian-military-in-politics-and-the-economy.pdf (accessed June 15, 2017).

Akcesme, Gokgan. "Poverty and Economic Inequality as the Leading Causes of the 2011 Egypt Revolution." *International Journal of Political Science and Development* 3, no. 9 (September 2015): 363–75. doi:10.14662/IJPSD2014.043.

Al-Ahram Gate. "April 6: Prosecuted inside and outside of Court." *Al-Ahram Gate, Cairo*, April 7, 2014. https://search-proquest-com.zdroje.vse.cz/docview/1513615310/citation/EB9D134953734672PQ/2?accountid=17203 (accessed June 15, 2017).

Al-Arian, Abdullah. "Egypt's Hollow Parliament," January 12, 2012. http://www.aljazeera.com/indepth/opinion/2016/01/egypt-hollow-parliament-160112071640089.html (accessed June 15, 2017).

Albaraa, Abdullah. "The Real Reason behind Thaw in EU-Egypt Tensions." *Al-Monitor*, March 9, 2017. http://www.al-monitor.com/pulse/originals/2017/03/egypt-relations-europe-improve-meetings.html (accessed June 15, 2017).

Aly, Abdel Monem Said, and Sobhy Essaila. "Egypt's 2015 Parliamentary Elections: A Prelude to Stability?" *Middle East Brief*, no. 98 (April 2016).

Aly, Abdel Monem Said, and Hussein Ibish. "Egypt-GCC Partnership: Bedrock of Regional Security Despite Fissures." *Arab Gulf States Institute in Washington*, December 12, 2016. http://www.agsiw.org/egypt-gcc-partnership-bedrock-regional-security-despite-fissures/ (accessed June 15, 2017).

Anani, Khalil al-. "Extremism Under Sisi." *Foreign Affairs*, January 8, 2017. https://www.foreignaffairs.com/articles/middle-east/2017-01-08/extremism-under-sisi (accessed June 15, 2017).

Barak, Michael. "The Al-Azhar Institute – A Key Player in Shaping the Religious and Political Discourse in Egypt." *International Institute for Counter-Terrorism*, March 28, 2016. https://www.ict.org.il/Article/1647/The-Al-Azhar-Institute (accessed June 15, 2017).

Benaim, Daniel. "What Does Trump Really Want From Sisi?" *Foreign Policy*, April 3, 2017. https://foreignpolicy.com/2017/04/03/what-does-trump-really-want-from-sisi/ (accessed June 15, 2017).

Brown, Nathan, and Yasser El-Shimy. "Did Sisi Save Egypt?" *Foreign Affairs*, January 25, 2016. https://www.foreignaffairs.com/articles/egypt/2016-01-25/did-sisi-save-egypt (accessed June 15, 2017).

Brownlee, Jason. "Violence Against Copts in Egypt." *Carnegie Endowment for International Peace*, November 14, 2013. http://carnegieendowment.org/2013/11/14/violence-against-copts-in-egypt-pub-53606 (accessed June 15, 2017).

Chebib, Nadine Kassem, and Rabia Minatullah Sohail. "The Reasons Social Media Contributed To The 2011 Egyptian Revolution." *International Journal of Business Research and Management (IJBRM)* 2, no. 3 (2011): 139–162.

CPJ. "Egyptian Human Rights Group Reports 64 Websites Blocked." *Committee to Protect Journalists*, June 13, 2017. https://cpj.org/2017/06/egyptian-human-rights-group-reports-64-websites-bl.php (accessed June 15, 2017).

Cunningham, Erin. "In Egypt Election, Low Turnout Undercuts Sisi's Goal of Sweeping Mandate (Posted 2014-05-29 03:12:57): Polling Stations across Egypt Were Deserted Even after Balloting in the Presidential Election Was Extended." *The Washington Post; Washington, D.C.* May 29, 2014, sec. FOREIGN. http://search.proquest.com/docview/1529712353/abstract/74E379FA92E94A11PQ/9 (accessed June 15, 2017).

Dunne, Michele, and Amr Hamzawy. "Egypt's Secular Political Parties: A Struggle for Identity and Independence." *Carnegie Endowment for International Peace – Papers*, March 31, 2017. https://search-proquest-com.zdroje.vse.cz/docview/1885880801/fulltext/A2E463CB55FE42A0PQ/1?accountid=17203 (accessed June 15, 2017).

EIU Democracy Index. "EIU Democracy Index 2016," 2017. https://infographics.economist.com/2017/DemocracyIndex/ (accessed May 9, 2017).

EL Medni, Bakry M. "Civil Society and Democratic Transformation in Contemporary Egypt: Premise and Promises." *International Journal of Humanities and Social Science* 12, no. 3 (June 2013): 14–26. http://www.ijhssnet.com/journal/index/1890 (accessed June 15, 2017).

El-Behary, Hend. "Egypt Annual Inflation Rates Hits the Highest Records since 30 Years, CAPMAS." *Egypt Independent*, April 10, 2017. http://www.egyptindependent.com/egypt-annual-inflation-rates-hits-highest-records-30-years-capmas/ (accessed June 15, 2017).

El-Fekki, Amira. "'I Don't Hope for Restoration, Rather Admission of Legal Violation in Presidential Decision': Hisham Geneina – ProQuest." *Daily News Egypt*, October 25, 2016. https://search-proquest-com.zdroje.vse.cz/docview/1832039390/1B575B1465EC4F25PQ/3?accountid=17203 (accessed June 15, 2017).

Elmasry, Mohamad. "Al Jazeera, Doha, Qatar, Mohamad Elmasry Column." *TCA Regional News; Chicago*. March 1, 2015. https://search-proquest-com.zdroje.vse.cz/docview/1658941948/abstract/8C556BEE89124C3CPQ/1 (accessed June 15, 2017).

Eshhad. "Eshhad Quarterly Report: Apr – June 2016." *The Tahrir Institute for Middle East Policy*, December 15, 2016. https://eshhad.timep.org/reports/eshhad-quarterly-report-apr-june-2016/ (accessed June 15, 2017).

Esposito, John L., Tamara Sonn, and John Obert Voll. *Islam and Democracy after the Arab Spring*. New York: Oxford University Press, 2016.

Freedom House. "Egypt | Country Report | Freedom in the World | 2001." *Freedom House*, 2001. https://freedomhouse.org/report/freedom-world/2001/egypt (accessed June 15, 2017).

–. "Egypt | Country Report | Freedom in the World | 2011." *Freedom House*, 2011. https://freedomhouse.org/report/freedom-world/2011/egypt (accessed June 15, 2017).

–. "Egypt | Country Report | Freedom in the World | 2013," 2013. https://freedomhouse.org/report/freedom-world/2013/egypt (accessed June 15, 2017).

–. "Egypt | Country Report | Freedom of the Press | 2017," 2017. https://freedomhouse.org/report/freedom-press/2017/egypt (accessed June 15, 2017).

Gallup. "Egypt: The Arithmetic of Revolution." *Gallup.com*, 2012. http://www.gallup.com/poll/157043/egypt-arithmetic-revolution.aspx (accessed June 15, 2017).

Glaeser, Edward, Giacomo Ponzetto, and Andrei Shleifer. "Why Does Democracy Need Education?" Working Paper. National Bureau of Economic Research, April 2006. doi:10.3386/w12128 (accessed June 15, 2017).

Halpern, Micah. "Egypt Has Figured Out How to Defeat ISIS: Defend Christians." *The New York Observer; New York, N-Y-*, March 31, 2017. https://search-proquest-com.zdroje.vse.cz/docview/1882491095/6AA57E4201724CD4PQ/3?accountid=17203 (accessed June 15, 2017).

Hamama, Mohamed. "Sisi Says Military Economy Is 1.5% of Egypt's GDP, but How Accurate Is This?" *Mada Masr*, November 2, 2016. http://www.madamasr.com/en/2016/11/02/feature/economy/sisi-says-military-economy-is-1-5-of-egypts-gdp-but-how-accurate-is-this/ (accessed June 15, 2017).

Hamas Covenant 1998. "Hamas Covenant 1988." *The Avalon Project*, 2008. http://avalon.law.yale.edu/20th_century/hamas.asp (accessed June 15, 2017).

Hammond, Joseph. "Egyptians Fight To Retool State Media." Lanham, United States: Federal Information & News Dispatch, Inc., March 4, 2011. https://search-proquest-com.zdroje.vse.cz/docview/855080030/abstract/668CF86493A140BEPQ/8 (accessed June 15, 2017).

Hamzawy, Amr. "How Sisi Is Using the Law as a Tool to Restore Tyranny." *TCA Regional News*, May 4, 2017. https://search-proquest-com.zdroje.vse.cz/docview/1894945523/B34969D170934939PQ/2?accountid=17203 (accessed June 15, 2017).

Hamzawy, Michele Dunne, Amr. "From Too Much Egyptian Opposition to Too Little—and Legal Worries Besides." *Carnegie Endowment for International Peace*, December 13, 2010. http://carnegieendowment.org/2010/12/13/from-too-much-egyptian-opposition-to-too-little-and-legal-worries-besides-pub-42128 (accessed June 15, 2017).

Hauslohner, Abigail. "An Insurgency Is Taking Root in Egypt's Restive Sinai Peninsula Following the July Coup." *The Washington Post*. July 30, 2013. https://search-proquest-com.zdroje.vse.cz/docview/1415480686/abstract/C44932604D3A447APQ/1 (accessed June 15, 2017).

Herrold, Catherine E. "NGO Policy in Pre- and Post-Mubarak Egypt: Effects on NGOs' Roles in Democracy Promotion." *Nonprofit Policy Forum; Berlin* 7, no. 2 (2016): 189–212. doi:http://dx.doi.org.zdroje.vse.cz/10.1515/npf-2014–0034.

HRW. "Egypt: Unprecedented Expansion of Military Courts." *Human Rights Watch*, November 17, 2014. https://www.hrw.org/news/2014/11/17/egypt-unprecedented-expansion-military-courts (accessed June 15, 2017).

Ibish, Hussein. "Egypt and Saudi Arabia: No Divorce Pending in a 'Dysfunctional Marriage.'" *Arab Gulf States Institute in Washington*, January 19, 2017. http://www.agsiw.org/egypt-saudi-arabia-no-divorce-pending-dysfunctional-marriage/ (accessed June 15, 2017).

Ibrahim, Hassan. "6 April: The Facts." *Daily News Egypt; Cairo*. December 12, 2012. http://search.proquest.com.zdroje.vse.cz/docview/1237272653/citation/7BF8901146E3495BPQ/4 (accessed June 15, 2017).

ICG. "Keeping Egypt's Politics on the Agenda." *International Crisis Group*, April 30, 2017. https://www.crisisgroup.org/middle-east-north-africa/north-africa/egypt/keeping-egypts-politics-agenda (accessed June 15, 2017).

Jones, Rory, and Tamer El-Ghobashy. "World News: Sinai Militants Forge Ties With Hamas, Officials Say." *The Wall Street Journal Asia; Hong Kong*. June 7, 2016. https://search-proquest-com.zdroje.vse.cz/docview/1794102983/abstract/6BB1C31CD8AD4087PQ/3 (accessed June 15, 2017).

Lappin, Robert. "Peace with Islam Now Possible." *Jewish Advocate* 206, no. 8 (February 20, 2015): 9. https://search-proquest-com.zdroje.vse.cz/docview/1658462580/54C8EFF69D1947F8PQ/2?accountid=17203 (accessed June 15, 2017).

Laub, Zachary. "Egypt's Muslim Brotherhood." *Council on Foreign Relations*, January 15, 2014. https://www.cfr.org/backgrounder/egypts-muslim-brotherhood?cid=ppc-google-grant-egypt_,uslim_brotherhood_backgrounder&gclid=Cj0KEQjwg47KBRDk7LSu4LTD8eEBEiQAO4O6rzbbS7kejqLqmSTfJjHyjQlTyZMWSXRrT1-gUEgdo0waAl988P8HAQ (accessed June 15, 2017).

Linn, Emily Crane. "The Army And Its President." *Foreign Policy*, January 28, 2016. https://foreignpolicy.com/2016/01/28/the-army-and-its-president-egypt-sisi/ (accessed June 15, 2017).

Linn, Emily Crane, and Nicholas Linn. "Sisi's Islam." *Foreign Policy*, June 2, 2015. https://foreignpolicy.com/2015/06/02/sisis-islam-egypt-muslim-brotherhood-arab-spring/ (accessed June 15, 2017).

Lynch, Marc, Deen Freelon, and Sean Aday. "How Social Media Undermines Transitions to Democracy." *PeaceTech Lab*, 2016. http://www.peacetechlab.org/blogs-bullets-iv/ (accessed June 15, 2017).

Maher, Stephen. "The Political Economy of the Egyptian Uprising – ProQuest." *Monthly Reviewer* 63, no. 6 (November 2011): 32–45.

Martini, Jeffrey, and Stephen M. Worman. "Voting Patterns in Post-Mubarak Egypt." *RAND Corporation*, 2013. https://www.rand.org/pubs/research_reports/RR223.html (accessed June 15, 2017).

McInerney, Stephen. "SCAF's Assault on Egypt's Civil Society." *Foreign Policy*, September 28, 2011. https://foreignpolicy.com/2011/09/28/scafs-assault-on-egypts-civil-society/ (accessed June 15, 2017).

McRobie, Heather. "Egypt: A Tale of Two Constitutions – ProQuest." *OpenDemocracy*, January 2014. https://search-proquest-com.zdroje.vse.cz/docview/1477833111/FC6C0D9E237247E5PQ/17?accountid=17203 (accessed June 15, 2017).

Metawe, Mohamed. "How and Why the West Reacted to the Arab Spring: An Arab Perspective – ProQuest." *Insight Turkey* 15, no. 3 (2013): 141–55.

Monitor, Sarah Gauch Special to The Christian Science. "Egyptian Human Rights Take a Hit with Tough New Law; Activists Are Watching the Implementation of 2002 Law on Nongovernmental Groups.: [ALL Edition]." *The Christian Science Monitor; Boston, Mass.* June 20, 2003, sec. WORLD.

Morajea, Hassan, and Erin Cunningham. "Militants Fill Void in Libya 'S Civil War – ProQuest." *The Washington Post*, June 7, 2015. https://search-proquest-com.zdroje.vse.cz/docview/1686257481/abstract/100915A244C34FDFPQ/1?accountid=17203 (accessed June 15, 2017).

Muhareb, Mahmoud. "Israel and the Egyptian Revolution." *Arab Center for Research and Policy Studies*, May 10, 2011. http://english.dohainstitute.org//home/getpage/5ea4b31b-155d-4a9f-8f4d-a5b428135cd5/35d3de00-35bf-4b6c-be54-323828feec50 (accessed June 15, 2017).

Mumtaz, Kashif. "The Fall of Mubarak: The Failure of Survival Strategies." *Strategic Studies; Islamabad* XXXI, no. 3 (September 30, 2011): 1–22. http://search.proquest.com.zdroje.vse.cz/docview/1231703271/abstract/A5A272BF435048A5PQ/7 (accessed June 15, 2017).

Noll, Jessica. "Egypt's Armed Forces Cement Economic Power." *SWP – Stiftung Wissenschaft Und Politik. German Institute for International and Security Affairs*, February 2017. https://www.swp-berlin.org/en/publication/egypts-armed-forces-cement-economic-power/ (accessed June 15, 2017).

Perra, Antonio. "Between Expectations and Reality: The Arab Spring in Egypt – ProQuest." *Hemispheres; Wroclaw* 29, no. 2 (2014): 55–78.

Rizk, Mariam, and Osman El Sharnoubi. "Egypt's Constitution 2013 vs. 2012: A Comparison -." *Ahram Online*, December 12, 2013. http://english.ahram.org.eg/NewsContent/1/0/88644/Egypt/0/Egypts-constitution--vs--A-comparison.aspx (accessed June 15, 2017).

RSF. "Egypt Falls Again in World Press Freedom Index, Now Ranked 159th | Reporters without Borders." *Reporters without Borders*, April 20, 2016. https://rsf.org/en/news/egypt-falls-again-world-press-freedom-index-now-ranked-159th (accessed June 15, 2017).

–. "Egypt: One of the World's Biggest Prisons for Journalists | Reporters without Borders." *Reporters without Borders*, 2017. https://rsf.org/en/egypt.

Sanchez, Raf, and Magdy Samaan. "Dozens Dead as Gunmen Attack Bus of Coptic Christians in Egypt." *The Telegraph*, May 26, 2017. http://www.telegraph.co.uk/news/2017/05/26/dozens-dead-gunmen-attack-bus-coptic-christians-egypt/ (accessed June 15, 2017).

Schanzer, Jonathan, and Merve Tahiroglu. "Ankara's Failure." *Foreign Affairs*, January 25, 2016. https://www.foreignaffairs.com/articles/turkey/2016-01-25/ankaras-failure (accessed June 15, 2017).

Sewilam, Hani, Orla McCormack, Marlene Mader, and Mohamed Abdel Raouf. "Introducing Education for Sustainable Development into Egyptian Schools." *Environment, Development and Sustainability* 17, no. 2 (April 1, 2015): 221–38. doi:10.1007/s10668-014-9597-7 (accessed June 15, 2017).

Sharp, Jeremy M. "Egypt: Background and U.S. Relations." *Congressional Research Service*, March 24, 2017. https://fas.org/sgp/crs/mideast/RL33003.pdf.

Tahhan, Zena. "Egypt-Israel Relations 'at Highest Level' in History." *TCA Regional News; Chicago*. November 20, 2016. https://search-proquest-com.zdroje.vse.cz/docview/1841807471/abstract/B63BD98FC2CF4B4DPQ/12 (accessed June 15, 2017).

The Carter Center. *Final Report of the Carter Center Mission to Witness the 2011–2012 Parliamentary Elections in Egypt. Carter Center; Atlanta*, 2012. https://www.cartercenter.org/resources/pdfs/news/peace_publications/election_reports/egypt-2011-2012-final-rpt.pdf (accessed June 15, 2017).

–. *Presidential Election in Egypt: Final Report*. Carter Center, 2012.

The Economist. "State of Denial; Egypt's Economy." *The Economist* 420, no. 9001 (August 6, 2016). https://search-proquest-com.zdroje.vse.cz/docview/1810532501/abstract/6700FB90340C48A5PQ/19?accountid=17203 (accessed June 15, 2017).

–. "Worse than Mubarak; Repression in Egypt." *The Economist; London*, May 2, 2015. https://www.economist.com/news/middle-east-and-africa/21650160-abdel-fattah-al-sisi-has-restored-order-egypt-great-cost-worse (accessed June 15, 2017).

The World Bank. "GDP Growth (Annual %) | Data," 2017. http://data.worldbank.org/indicator/NY.GDP.MKTP.KD.ZG?locations=EG (accessed June 15, 2017).

–"Unemployment, Youth Total (% of Total Labor Force Ages 15–24) (Modeled ILO Estimate) | Data." *Data World Bank*, 2017. http://data.worldbank.org/indicator/SL.UEM.1524.ZS?locations=EG (accessed June 15, 2017).

Trading economics. "Egypt Unemployment Rate | 1993–2017 | Data | Chart | Calendar | Forecast," 2017. tradingeconomics.com/egypt/unemployment-rate.

Trager, Eric. *Arab Fall: How the Muslim Brotherhood Won and Lost Egypt in 891 Days*. Georgetown University Press, Washington D.C., USA, 2016.

–. "Egypt Two Years After Morsi." *The Washington Institute for Near East Policy*, May 20, 2015. http://www.washingtoninstitute.org/policy-analysis/view/egypt-two-years-after-morsi (accessed June 15, 2017).

–. "Stuck With Sisi." *Foreign Affairs*, January 24, 2017. https://www.foreignaffairs.com/articles/egypt/2017-01-24/stuck-sisi (accessed June 15, 2017).

–. "The Unbreakable Muslim Brotherhood: Grim Prospects for a Liberal Egypt." *Foreign Affairs* 90, no. 5 (October 2011): 114–122,124–126.

Transparency International. "Research – CPI – Overview." *Transparency International*, 2016. https://www.transparency.org/research/cpi/overview.

–. "Transparency International – Egypt." *Transparency International*, 2017. https://www.transparency.org/country/EGY.

UNCTADstat. "UNCTADstat – Table View – Gross Domestic Product: Total and per Capita, Current and Constant (2005) Prices, Annual, 1970–2015," 2017. http://unctadstat.unctad.org/wds/TableViewer/tableView.aspx (accessed June 15, 2017).

UNESCO. "Country Profile: Egypt." *UNESCO*, November 4, 2014. http://en.unesco.org/countries/egypt (accessed June 15, 2017).

Walsh, Declan. "Egypt Roared as Mubarak Fell. It's Mute as He's Freed." *New York Times (Online); New York*, March 24, 2017. https://search-proquest-com.zdroje.vse.cz/docview/1880378909/abstract/DA6309BA097747D7PQ/1 (accessed June 15, 2017).

Weber, Peter C. "Modernity, Civil Society, and Sectarianism: The Egyptian Muslim Brotherhood and the Takfir Groups." *Voluntas; Baltimore* 24, no. 2 (June 2013): 509–27. doi:http://dx.doi.org.zdroje.vse.cz/10.1007/s11266–012-9299–4 (accessed June 15, 2017).

Wenig, Erica. "Egypt's Security and the Libyan Civil War." *The Washington Institute for Near East Policy*, 2016. http://www.washingtoninstitute.org/policy-analysis/view/egypts-security-and-the-libyan-civil-war (accessed June 15, 2017).

World Economic Forum. "Global Gender Gap Report 2016. Egypt." *Global Gender Gap Report 2016*, 2016. http://wef.ch/1OvkDKy (accessed June 15, 2017).

Aneta Hlavsová

Iraq

This chapter covers Iraqi democratization efforts since the US-led invasion of 2003; nonetheless, given the devastated state of the country's economy and society at that time, it is of absolute necessity to illustrate which foreign policy and political decisions led to such a gruesome situation. Additionally, even though Iraq experienced the Arab Spring, it is not a "textbook" case such as, for instance, Egypt, and therefore, the chapter closely follows certain indicators since the 1990s in order to fully analyse the roots of the current disintegration of the country.

The chapter mainly focuses on the internal factors which mostly damaged Iraq's democratization process. In fact, the country's history is a list of one catastrophe succeeding another – from Saddam Hussein's militarization of the economy in 1980s and his subsequent decision to invade Kuwait, the ruthless coalitional Operation Desert Storm and the corresponding UN sanctions regime which decimated Iraqi infrastructure and caused a severe humanitarian crisis; to the miscalculated political decisions of the post-2003 governments which increased sectarianism, corruption, and allowed for the so-called Islamic State (IS) to spread.

1. Internal institutional factors

1.1 Economic factors

The economic factors directly related to Iraq's democratization efforts are threefold: the state's overall levels of GDP will be analysed as the main internal economic factor; the world's oil price development as the external one; and lastly, the international community's sanctions against Iraq will be reviewed because they had an unprecedented and absolutely devastating effect on the country's well-being.

1.1.1 Internal economic factors

The World Bank provides data on Iraq's overall levels of GDP since 1960, including GDP per capita as a more specific indicator of the population's actual standard of living; similarly, information about the country's inflation rates is available for the 1970s onwards. It is necessary, however, to note that between 1990 and 2003 there are no data available – this period corresponds to the implementation of UN sanctions in response to Iraq's occupation of Kuwait in 1990 until the invasion of the US-led coalition forces in 2003 which forced Hussein out of power.

Upon its formal independence in 1932,[1] Iraq emerged as a poor Middle-Eastern country; however, the country's vast reserves of oil were soon able to generate significant profits from exports. The nationalization of Iraqi oil companies in 1972 marked a turning point in the country's GDP development – nominally, Iraq went from being worth 4 billion USD in 1972[2] to almost 38 billion in 1979[3] when Saddam Hussein officially[4] became the country's leader. This effectively translates into an increase of 388 USD per capita in 1972[5] to 2,852 USD in 1979.[6] Data tracking revenues from oil sales provide similar insight into the 1970s Iraqi economy – oil revenues rose from 1 billion USD in 1970 to 26 billion USD in 1980.[7] Hence, taking these indicators into account it can be presumed that on average, the well-being of the Iraqi population considerably improved during the 1970s as the government could allot more money to crucial sectors of the country's economy, such as infrastructure, social services, and the military.

Nonetheless, the 1980–1988 Iraq–Iran war prompted by Saddam's alleged fears of Iran's theocratic revolution's spill-over structurally damaged the Iraqi economy. Aside from the extreme human cost, there were several factors due to which the country's economy was in ruins by the end of the 1980s. Firstly, in spite of the Cold War atmosphere, most states of the international community chose to support Saddam in his aggression – including the United States as well as the Soviet Union; secondly, the Gulf states, similarly, decided to provide support to Iraq, this time in the form of substantial loans which enabled the war to be prolonged; and thirdly, the war caused structural changes to the country's industries through its colossal militarization of the economy (in 1988 at the war's end, 21% of Iraq's labour force was in the armed forces[8] as opposed to 3% in 1975). With the war's close, Iraq had accumulated a debt of 80 billion USD,[9] mostly owed to the Gulf states, which was soon to influence Iraq's foreign policy decisions.

---

1 Baxter and Akbarzadeh, *US Foreign Policy in the Middle East: The Roots of Anti-Americanism.*

2 World Bank, "GDP (Current US$)."

3 Ibid.

4 Vasselin, Hamelin, and Charmelot, *Saddam: America's Best Enemy.*

5 World Bank, "GDP per Capita (Current US$)."

6 Ibid.

7 Alnasrawi, "Iraq: Economic Sanctions and Consequences, 1990–2000."

8 Ibid.

9 Baxter and Akbarzadeh, *US Foreign Policy in the Middle East: The Roots of Anti-Americanism.*

Concerning Iraqi GDP levels, there is no data covering the UN sanctions period between 1991 and 2003 provided by the World Bank (while the actual human and economic losses caused by the sanctions will be discussed in detail below). However, some sources claim that the humanitarian catastrophe was mirrored in GDP per capita which "in the 1990s was lower than that of 1950."[10] Furthermore, from 2003 when the US coalition forces entered Iraq and attempted to democratize the state by removing the ruling Baath party from power, Iraq's GDP steadily rose for a decade (from 36 billion USD in 2004[11] to 234 billion USD in 2013[12] with 1,391 and 6,879 USD per capita[13] respectively). Unfortunately, the emergence of the so-called IS swiftly reversed this trend and the country's GDP and GDP per capita figures began sharply decreasing in 2014.

1.1.2 External economic factors

The price of oil on the world markets necessarily (and significantly) influenced the well-being of Iraq's economy, given the country's heavy dependence on its oil exports. Before Iraq attacked Iran in 1980, the price of oil was skyrocketing at almost 116 USD[14] per barrel (in prices adjusted for inflation) while at the end of the conflict the price level plummeted to around 27 USD. Consequently, this was bound to immediately affect the country's revenues – in 1990, the oil sector generated 61%[15] of Iraq's GDP. Still, during the course of the Iraq–Iran war, in 1986, the oil prices experienced a collapse which prompted the OPEC (Organization of the Petroleum Exporting Countries) exporting countries to agree on a cartel price which would sustain their revenues and therefore the social and economic development of their countries.[16] However, some countries still made the decision to break this agreement and therefore made a short-term profit based on market inefficiencies – Kuwait happened to be one of them.[17]

Similarly, it is noteworthy that by January 1990, Iraq's dependency on oil exports translated into a 1 billion USD loss in government revenue per year with

10 Alnasrawi, "Iraq: Economic Sanctions and Consequences, 1990–2000."
11 World Bank, "GDP (Current US$)."
12 Ibid.
13 World Bank, "GDP per Capita (Current US$)."
14 "Crude Oil Prices - 70 Year Historical Chart."
15 Shehabaldin and Laughlin Jr, "Economic Sanctions against Iraq: Human and Economic Costs."
16 Alnasrawi, "Iraq: Economic Sanctions and Consequences, 1990–2000."
17 Ibid.

a drop in price of 1 USD per barrel.[18] In the case of post-war Iraq, such high dependency on oil exports, combined with the militarization of the economy and substantial indebtedness to third states must have played a role in Saddam Hussein's decision to invade Kuwait.

The one-dimensionality of Iraq's economy remains a structural problem up to the present. Ever since the US occupation of Iraq, the world price of oil has been steadily rising (in fact, it began to increase in the aftermath of the 9/11 attacks in 2001) with a brief drop in prices between 2008 and 2009. Nonetheless, no other country in the world was more affected by the IS insurgency more than Iraq as the price of crude oil began to drop in the summer of 2014.[19] According to the IMF, in 2014, "oil exports represented almost 100 percent of total exports; oil sector GDP was more than 50 percent of the total (with much of the non-oil activity indirectly driven by oil revenues); and oil exports constituted over 93 percent of government revenues."[20] Given the IS threat affecting the world oil markets and Iraq's extreme dependency on its oil revenues, the medium-term forecasts for the country's economic recovery remain modest.

Aside from the world oil prices, there were other external factors which gravely affected Iraq's development, that is, the UN sanctions regime of the 1990s and early 2000s (which resulted from Saddam's decision to invade Kuwait) and the protracted ensuing humanitarian crisis catalysed by the Operation Desert Storm.

With hindsight, Iraq's invasion of Kuwait was not necessarily a madman's move – Saddam Hussein was receiving the support of the international community following his aggression towards Iran and the United States gave absolutely no warning signs concerning Kuwait. Quite the opposite: in July 1990, "the US ambassador April Glaspie delivered to Saddam Hussein in Bagdad the most publicized 'green light' signal of them all: '*... our opinion is that you should have the opportunity to rebuild your country... we have no opinion on Arab-Arab conflicts like your border disagreement with Kuwait.*'"[21] Still, the invasion was immediately met with a response from the international community – the United Nations Security Council passed several resolutions on the matter. The foremost was Resolution 660[22] of August 2, 1990, the day of the invasion, condemning Iraq's actions and calling for

18 Ibid.
19 "Crude Oil Prices – 70 Year Historical Chart."
20 "IRAQ: 2015 ARTICLE IV CONSULTATION AND REQUEST FOR PURCHASE UNDER THE RAPID FINANCING INSTRUMENT—PRESS RELEASE; STAFF REPORT; AND STATEMENT BY THE EXECUTIVE DIRECTOR FOR IRAQ."
21 Simons, *The Scourging of Iraq: Sanctions, Law, and Natural Justice.*
22 "UN SC Res. 660."

a withdrawal from Kuwait's territory. Given Iraq's non-compliance, four days later, the Security Council passed Resolution 661[23] implementing all-encompassing economic sanctions against Saddam's regime.

Additionally, because of Iraq's continued violations of the preceding resolutions, the Security Council authorized a military action providing the "all means necessary" clause in Resolution 678[24] on November 29, 1990. The ensuing US-led Operation Desert Storm, combined with the inexplicable consequences of the sanctions regime, completely destroyed the Iraqi economy and infrastructure and inflicted immense suffering on the country's population.

Operation Desert Storm has been considered a military success as it did indeed result in Iraq's withdrawal from the occupied Kuwaiti territories. Nonetheless, the US-led coalition committed many breaches of "international law and morality, including the UN Charter, the Hague and Geneva Conventions, the Nuremberg Charter, and the laws of armed conflict."[25] Within the military campaign, the United States used napalm and depleted uranium projectiles (which further hindered future environmental conditions and had an adverse impact on the Iraqi population's health); targets of the coalition included – among the more obvious military targets – water treatment facilities, infant milk formula factories, universities and colleges, hospitals and clinics and many others; testimonies of US-dug mass graves exist.[26] And additionally, "the assets that were not bombed were rendered dysfunctional because of the destruction of power generating facilities."[27]

In other words, the military operation completely wiped out Iraq's infrastructure systems, severely damaged its oil producing sector (as basically the only source of income for the country), and bombed a wide array of purely civilian targets. Still, some political commentators view the operation as a clear success – having as a sole regret the failure to remove Saddam Hussein from power right away which was "the most basic object of strategy."[28] This is despite the fact that "the impact of the war and of the draconian economic sanctions on Iraqi civilians in general and on Iraqi children in particular was well known to Washington and the rest of the international community *[already]* in 1991."[29]

23 "UN SC Res. 661."
24 "UN SC Res. 678."
25 Simons, *The Scourging of Iraq: Sanctions, Law, and Natural Justice.*
26 Ibid.
27 Alnasrawi, "Iraq: Economic Sanctions and Consequences, 1990–2000."
28 Mahnken, "The Gulf War in Retrospect."
29 Simons, *The Scourging of Iraq: Sanctions, Law, and Natural Justice.*

In terms of the humanitarian catastrophe, the sanctions implemented by the UN Resolution 661 were aimed at the complete economic isolation of the Iraqi regime – they included a "ban on all trade, an oil embargo, a freezing of Iraqi financial assets abroad, an arms embargo, suspension of international flights, and banned financial transactions"[30] and were all readily executed by naval and air blockades. The embargo was quite simple to monitor as "Iraq ha[d] no friendly neighbours and only one small sea outlet,"[31] which was easily controlled by the naval blockade.

Given the country's high dependence on the import of foodstuffs (between 70 and 80%), the "blockade had an immediate impact on food availability in Iraq."[32] In fact, at that time, Iraq also had to import 100% of capital goods and about 50% of consumption goods.[33] The acute lack of food and medical supplies, in combination with the two wars' destructive impact on the country's infrastructure, economy, and society, immediately pushed Iraq to the verge of a humanitarian crisis.

The international community, however, was well-aware of the imminent dangers posed to the Iraqi people. A UN report from March 1991 by the UN Secretary General Javier Pérez de Cuéllar specifically calls for action based on a detailed review of the situation on-the-ground: "*... there needs to be a major mobilization and movement of resources to deal with aspects of this deep crisis in the fields of agriculture and food, water, sanitation and health... It is unmistakable that the Iraqi people may soon face a further imminent catastrophe, which could include epidemic and famine, if massive life-supporting needs are not rapidly met.*"[34]

The hypocrisy in the international community's approach towards the inhuman suffering of Iraqis can be further highlighted by the UN Security Council Resolution 666[35] which was meant to, at least theoretically, prevent a catastrophe by granting exemptions to foodstuffs in humanitarian circumstances. However, due to the fact that Iraq's assets were frozen and the country was not allowed

30 Alnasrawi, "Iraq: Economic Sanctions and Consequences, 1990–2000."

31 Shehabaldin and Laughlin Jr, "Economic Sanctions against Iraq: Human and Economic Costs."

32 Alnasrawi, "Iraq: Economic Sanctions and Consequences, 1990–2000."

33 Shehabaldin and Laughlin Jr, "Economic Sanctions against Iraq: Human and Economic Costs."

34 de Cuellar, "Report to the Secretary-General on Humanitarian Needs in Kuwait and Iraq in the Immediate Post-Crisis Environment by a Mission to the Area Led by Mr. Martti Ahtisaari, Under-Secretary-General for Administration and Management, Dated 20 March 1991."

35 "UN SC Res. 666," 666.

to sell any of its oil to generate revenue, the regime could literally not afford to purchase any of the foodstuffs (or medical supplies).[36,37] Within the UN sanctions regime, "the U.S. position was simply to block everything possible, regardless of the humanitarian impact, as much as possible, as long as possible."[38] Similarly, the 1995/1996 oil-for-food program was widely criticized as it "failed to reverse the deterioration in the social and economic conditions of the country" and even tightened the regime's grip over its population.[39]

Overall, with the devastation caused by the sanctions well-documented by various agencies, "the brunt of these intensive sanctions was borne by the civilian population of the country."[40] In fact, estimates of the sanctions' victims "range up to 1.5 million people, including more than 500 000 children."[41] Not only should the international community be aware that the sanctions were "unprecedented in [their] comprehensiveness, severity and length, and in the enormous human and economic cost,"[42] their actual goal of removing Saddam Hussein from power was not attained. "It was assumed that sanctions would increase economic hardships and motivate the Iraqis to protest Saddam's policy and, if necessary, overthrow the regime"[43] which was finally achieved only in 2003 with a new US military campaign against the country.

1.2 Civil society and media

Overall, in terms of Iraqi society, the country has fairly specific demographics. Ethnically, the majority of Iraqis are Arab (75–80%); there is a Kurdish minority (between 15 and 20%) as well as other ethnics, such as the Yazidis, Turkmen or Assyrians.[44] However, the religious, or sectarian, distinctions are less clear – it is assumed that Iraq has a slight Shia majority (between 50 and 60%)[45] as opposed to

36 Alnasrawi, "Iraq: Economic Sanctions and Consequences, 1990–2000."
37 Simons, *The Scourging of Iraq: Sanctions, Law, and Natural Justice.*
38 Gordon, "Joy Gordon on Iraq Sanctions."
39 Alnasrawi, "Iraq: Economic Sanctions and Consequences, 1990–2000."
40 Baxter and Akbarzadeh, *US Foreign Policy in the Middle East: The Roots of Anti-Americanism.*
41 Alnasrawi, "Iraq: Economic Sanctions and Consequences, 1990–2000."
42 Ibid.
43 Shehabaldin and Laughlin Jr, "Economic Sanctions against Iraq: Human and Economic Costs."
44 "The World Factbook — Iraq."
45 Lipka, "The Sunni-Shia Divide."

about 40% of Sunni[46] population; only a fraction of Iraqis claim to be Christians or followers of other religions.

Still, the internal turmoil which engulfed the country in 2003 and rose to new mortifying levels since 2014 caused many people to relocate and therefore flee the terror. Currently, it is near-impossible to delineate Iraq's ethnic and religious structure; there is evidence that the country's Christian minority shrank by about 50% post-2003 invasion[47] as well as the "refugees arriving in Iraq due to the conflict in Syria or leaving Iraq due to its own turmoil may have affected the composition of Iraq's population."[48] Discretion concerning Iraq's current demographics is therefore necessary.

1.2.1 Civil society

The state of civil society in Iraq is currently dim, to say the least. For decades, civil society as such was near non-existent under the dictatorship and since the 2003 overthrow of the regime, many factors still limit and undermine the process of its evolution. Additionally, in the case of Iraq, it is necessary to link today's existence of what resembles a civil society to the country's repeated decimation of its society in history.

In 1980, commencing the Iraq–Iran war, "Saddam Hussein launched what he hoped would be an easy victory over a disorganized enemy," tragically underestimating the Iranians.[49] The war could have had an early end if it was not for the involvement of third states – including the financial support of the Gulf states, military intelligence and satellite imagery provided by the United States,[50] and "armaments and raw materials for gas and chemical weapons" supplied by European states.[51] A combination of these factors allowed Saddam to continue his war effort which, by its end, resulted in about 500,000 dead Iraqis[52] (excluding those injured or displaced). The 1980s, marked by military mobilization and the corresponding militarization of the country's economy, therefore constituted uneasy times for the Iraqis.

46 "The World Factbook — Iraq."
47 Ibid.
48 Lipka, "The Sunni-Shia Divide."
49 Black, "Iran and Iraq Remember War That Cost More than a Million Lives."
50 Vasselin, Hamelin, and Charmelot, *Saddam: America's Best Enemy*.
51 Black, "Iran and Iraq Remember War That Cost More than a Million Lives."
52 Ibid.

Subsequently, the 1990s brought a new and intensified form of human suffering. The on-the-ground consequences of the UN sanctions regime have been already illustrated; nonetheless, the acute food and health crises also had a sociopolitical dimension. Firstly, the international community's wishful thinking that the sanctions-hit population would rise and oust Saddam Hussein from power crucially underestimated the Baath party's potency in controlling the people. The regime's "authoritarian étatisation of civil society; that is, the repression of political opposition or difference, coupled with an incorporation of all institutions and associations into the state" effectively resulted in a virtually non-existent civil society.[53] Furthermore, this absence of opposition left the population with no alternative sources of information other than the regime-controlled television, radio or newspapers,[54] strengthening the party's domination over Iraqis.

It is estimated that about three million Iraqis managed to escape the regime's terror, while "those that remained [in the country] were reduced to voices of the rulers, often persecuted and humiliated by party and security thugs put in charge of universities and cultural institutions."[55] The Baath party's grip on the country's society was immense – for instance, university applicants were obliged to be party members, and once enrolled, they were required to "report other students' activities every week."[56] The Iraqi government could not have been overthrown – the population was either afraid to voice any opposition to the regime or, at the same time, decimated by the lack of food, medical supplies, and basic sanitation.

The generations raised by the Baath government and under the sanctions regime were predicted to "suffer from increasing rates of illiteracy, technological gaps, decline in productivity, and most importantly, *declining moral values which may lead to disbelief, hate, and surrender.*"[57] Combined with Saddam's open support for tribalism[58] and the US insensitive de-Baathification campaign[59] after the 2003 invasion, the society was undermined and fractured enough for the IS to find fertile ground and conquer significant parts of the country.

53 Zubaida, "The Rise and Fall of Civil Society in Iraq."
54 Shehabaldin and Laughlin Jr, "Economic Sanctions against Iraq: Human and Economic Costs."
55 Zubaida, "The Rise and Fall of Civil Society in Iraq."
56 Shehabaldin and Laughlin Jr, "Economic Sanctions against Iraq: Human and Economic Costs."
57 Ibid.
58 Zubaida, "The Rise and Fall of Civil Society in Iraq."
59 Gerges, *ISIS: A History.*

In 2003, when the international community still could have been (cautiously) optimistic about Iraq's possibilities of democratization, there were "no credible independent institutions or associations within the country… that could serve as agents of governance and transformation."[60] The simple overthrow of Saddam Hussein and his Baathist regime could not lead to proper democratization – not with the deep structural decimation of the country's economy and its population. In fact, according to the Human Development Index (as measured by the UN) Iraq fell from 1990's 76th place globally to 126th in 2000, meaning that the degradation of Iraqi society and economy during the 1990s was well-shown; however, in 2013, a decade after the initial US invasion, Iraq further deteriorated and ranked 131st out of 186 countries.[61]

Even though the removal of an authoritarian regime technically allowed for civil society to emerge, its progress has been sluggish, halted by security challenges and terrorist threats, and damaged by the country's economic underperformance. In 2010, in the aftermath of the violence caused by the 2003 occupation, Iraq's Presidency Council passed a law[62] regulating the conduct of non-governmental organizations (NGOs) in the country, which was supposed to help and structure the activities of Iraqi civil society – 1770 organizations immediately met the requirements set by the law.[63] The new rule was celebrated as it was supposed to install a formal relationship between the country's civil society and the official government (thereby fully and explicitly legalizing the civil society organizations' (CSOs) existence); nonetheless, the implementation of the law has been extremely slow.[64] Additionally, "in 2015 the government began requiring new NGOs to obtain approval from the de-Baathification commission in order to officially register" – still, by the year's end, almost 2600 organizations were registered with the government.[65]

According to Ali Taher, professor of political sociology at Baghdad University, Iraq's CSOs can be classified into four groups: (1) "charitable organizations, which receive funds from religious institutions or political parties" which in reality translates into political parties' own public relations campaigns; (2) anti-establishment leftist organizations which are the ones usually responsible for street protests and social media campaigns; (3) elitist "forums, conferences, seminars, and media

---

60 Zubaida, "The Rise and Fall of Civil Society in Iraq."

61 United Nations Development Program, "Iraq Human Development Report 2014."

62 "Law of Non-Governmental Organizations."

63 Taher, "Iraqi Civil Society Struggles to Stay Relevant, Effective."

64 "Iraq Civil Society Organizations – Iraq Research."

65 Freedom House, "Iraq | Country Report | Freedom in the World | 2016."

outlets" mostly functioning on US aid which do not "represent genuine groups of Iraqi society"; and lastly, (4) organizations representing "those that do the impossible amid a climate of violence and mistrust to achieve their stated objectives", usually fighting for the rights of Iraqi minorities such as women, Yazidis, or Christians.[66]

According to the Iraqi Research Foundation for Analysis and Development, the estimates of active, operational, and functional CSOs in Iraq range from about 800 to 1,800, while the numbers of "unregistered CSOs have ranged from 6000 to 12000 total organizations."[67] It appears near-impossible to pinpoint the exact number of Iraq's CSOs. Similarly, the organizations' funding remains an important element in their development – as local fundraising has almost no potency to generate funds, what remains is either political affiliation or out-of-country donors. Both sources of finance can be troublesome in today's Iraq. CSOs funded by the country's internal government (either central or local), by definition, pursue the interests of the particular political factions; the same could be applicable for the foreign funding. Still, as the country's civil society "industry" is in its beginnings and its building it up will take decades, the role of Western support and funds remains vital. In terms of the international community's official involvement, UN Security Council Resolution 1500[68] established a political mission to Iraq: The United Nations Assistance Mission for Iraq (UNAMI), which is tasked also "with working with government partners and civil society to coordinate the humanitarian and development efforts of the UN agencies, funds and programmes."[69]

In spite of the undeniable widespread efforts of the Iraqi society to push for democratization, the country's civil society faces tremendous obstacles to its development. Apart from violence and security concerns which frequently halt efforts of the CSOs,[70] observers, such as the United Nations, call attention to the state's internal shortcomings – the country's literacy and employment rates flag up an enormous challenge especially concerning the Iraqi youth. In 2011, within Iraqi provinces, male youth unemployment (ages 15–29) was over 15% with 33.3% unemployment rate between young women; in Kurdistan, the figures were 10.1% and 37.6% respectively.[71] High youth unemployment is a dangerous economic factor, especially combined with high youth illiteracy rates (as predicted in the

66 Taher, "Iraqi Civil Society Struggles to Stay Relevant, Effective."
67 "Iraq Civil Society Organizations – Iraq Research."
68 "UN SC Res. 1500."
69 United Nations Iraq, "United Nations Iraq – UN Assistance Mission for Iraq."
70 Freedom House, "Iraq | Country Report | Freedom in the World | 2016."
71 United Nations Development Program, "Iraq Human Development Report 2014."

1990s) – in 2012, there was a 13.9% total youth illiteracy rate in Iraqi governorates (10.3% males and 18.5% females); Kurdistan scores a bit better with 8% total youth illiteracy rate (4.6% males and 11.6% females).[72] Additionally, the country's road to economic and political recovery seems to be obstructed by "the concepts, values, and behaviours of the rentier state, which are deeply rooted in the minds of society and government."[73]

It is of acute importance for the state to engage its youth in the country's rebuilding and provide them with opportunities to learn and work – a disengaged young generation is a structural and deep concern halting Iraq's attempts at modernization and democratization. Still, it is necessary to acknowledge that since the 1980s and 1990s when the civil society was brutally suppressed, Iraq's society has already started to take shape and make valid demands.

1.2.2 Media

Iraq's media are closely interconnected with the country's fractured civil society – when civil society was non-existent under the dictatorship, all media were controlled by the government. The post-invasion constitution guarantees freedom of expression; nonetheless, in reality, there are only a "few truly independent media outlets in Iraq."[74] Most are affiliated with either political parties or religious groups.[75] In 2014, in an effort to enhance the uncertain position of journalists in Iraq, the al-Abadi administration "issued an order that withdrew all pending government cases against journalists and media outlets."[76] Nonetheless, since the amnesty, new court cases have been filed. The biggest institutional obstacle the Iraqi journalists face might be the lack of law-making regulations as there are no laws which would grant the public (or journalists) access to government information[77] – in a future post-conflict Iraq, an increase of transparency, such as access to information, must be a top priority if the country wishes to improve its democratization process.

Nonetheless, the constitutional or legislative obstructions Iraqi journalists currently face are of lower priority compared to the physical danger posed by IS. Reporters Without Borders designated the so-called IS as the most dangerous

---

72 Ibid.
73 Ibid.
74 Freedom House, "Iraq | Country Report | Freedom in the World | 2016."
75 "Iraq Profile – Media."
76 "Iraq – Freedom of the Press 2016."
77 Ibid.

threat to journalists;[78] no other state government or sub-state actor in the world exterminates independent journalism more diligently than IS.[79] Additionally, IS does not allow a free flow of information and systematically targets those who attempt to share other information than the official IS propaganda which is shared through the established "media-points."[80] Unfortunately, journalists in the IS-held territories are regularly kidnapped and tortured; several times they were used by IS in their propagandist videos. For instance, the cases of American journalist James Foley and British war correspondent John Cantlie who were kidnapped in November 2012 absolutely horrified the international community.[81]

1.3 Extremism and religion

Political and religious extremism is almost inherent to Iraq's history and politics. The Baath party's secularism, which favoured tribalism and employed religious symbolism when it served Saddam Hussein's purpose, coupled with the erroneous US-installed policies post-2003, corrupt government, and sectarianism, produced a fractured and divided society which then, in turn, favoured the spread of IS and allowed it to assert enormous control in parts of Iraq and Syria.

It is impossible not to connect the current situation in Iraq with the country's Baath party ideology and its implementation as well as with the subsequent de-Baathification campaign of government and its institutions. The Baath party was established in 1947 and (even though it eventually split into an Iraqi and Syrian factions), "its major focus was Arab nationalism, emphasizing the unifying factors of shared history, culture and language… informed by socialism, anti-imperialism and militarism."[82] In Iraq, the Baathists seized power in 1968 and in fact, quickly installed "ruling cliques based on tribal and communal solidarities" and the party's propaganda became a means for "penetration and control of all public institutions and functions."[83] Saddam Hussein then asserted his leadership position in 1979[84]

---

78 "Worldwide Round-Up of Journalists Who Are Detained, Held Hostage or Missing 2016."

79 The second leading threat to journalists are the Houthis in Yemen, for more information, please refer to the Yemen chapter.

80 Freedom House, "Iraq | Country Report | Freedom in the World | 2016."

81 James Foley was beheaded by the IS in August 2014 in a video titled "A Message to America"; John Cantlie remains hostage.

82 Baxter and Akbarzadeh, *US Foreign Policy in the Middle East: The Roots of Anti-Americanism.*

83 Zubaida, "The Rise and Fall of Civil Society in Iraq."

84 Vasselin, Hamelin, and Charmelot, *Saddam: America's Best Enemy.*

and coupled with the extensive network of the regime's police and secret forces and surveillance systems,[85] the party terrorized the Iraqi people and virtually eliminated all dissent in the state.

It is interesting to note that in spite of the Baathists' "clear secular-nationalist orientation, Saddam did seek Islamic legitimacy when it was politically expedient."[86] It became politically viable to employ religious symbolism in the 1990s when the party was rallying against the United States and coalition involvement in Kuwait and Iraq; additionally, the ever-present anti-Iranian rhetoric had an adverse effect on the country's own (majority) Shia population as it projected a "sectarian dimension of hostility."[87] And while "a wave of new religious observance of prayer and rituals"[88] was witnessed under the autocratic Baathist regime, Gerges points out that despite the increased adherence to religion, radicalism never flourished under the dictatorship and it took "America's dismantling of the state apparatus to open the floodgate for Zarqawi and his cohorts."[89]

The Islamic State of Iraq first proclaimed its existence on October 13, 2006,[90] that is, 8 years prior to its mortifying conquest of parts of Iraq and Syria in the summer of 2014. The same year, due to the US misunderstanding of the on-the-ground political, social, and religious situation in Iraq, Barack Obama was informed by his intelligence officers that IS constituted only a minor threat. He recalled this in a *New Yorker* interview, describing "the constellation of jihadist groups in Iraq and Syria as terrorism's 'jayvee team.'"[91]

The international community at times continues to misunderstand IS – not only due to the lack of information concerning its internal mechanisms. It is of importance not to confuse or equate IS and al-Qaeda. The organizations differ on several fronts; most importantly, they do not agree on the prioritization of their enemies – while al-Qaeda prioritizes the struggle against the distant enemy, that is, the West and particularly the United States, IS highlights above all the fight against the close enemy, that is, the Shia, the Kurds, and also the Sunnis

---

85 Shehabaldin and Laughlin Jr, "Economic Sanctions against Iraq: Human and Economic Costs."

86 Baxter and Akbarzadeh, *US Foreign Policy in the Middle East: The Roots of Anti-Americanism.*

87 Zubaida, "The Rise and Fall of Civil Society in Iraq."

88 Ibid.

89 Gerges, *ISIS: A History.*

90 Ibid.

91 Goldberg, "The Obama Doctrine."

who do not support their cause.[92] Similarly, IS proved to be more ruthless and violent than its ideological predecessor, as shown by the frequent IS-produced videos of beheadings – "social-media posts from the [IS-held] region suggest that individual executions happen more or less continually, and mass executions every few weeks."[93] The thirst for violence of the common IS members can also be illustrated by the organization's recruitment strategy of systemic rape "to lure men from deeply conservative Muslim societies" into their ranks.[94]

Given their extremely purist and radical ideology, there is a debate about to what degree it may ultimately be to the organization's detriment, because "other Islamist groups, such as the Muslim Brotherhood and Hamas, have succumbed to the blandishments of democracy and the potential for an invitation to the community of nations, complete with a UN seat" – such steps are unthinkable through IS ideology.[95]

It is of importance to highlight that experts describe IS a "youth movement"[96] given its appeal mostly to younger generations of men – the same Iraqi young men who might not have access to education or cannot find work in their proximity. This is to stress that Iraq's rebuilding must be carried out with special attention paid to the country's youth.[97]

2. Internal institutional factors

2.1 Security and defence structures

The capacity of Iraq's armed forces and the country's security situation are both interlinked with the 2003 US-led invasion. In an effort to rid the country of all elements of the former dictatorship, the Coalition Provisional Authority's second order was to dissolve tens of organizations which were originally vital for the functioning and security of the country – including the Iraqi Army, Air Force, Navy, and the Iraqi Republican Guard. This signified a sudden loss of income for hundreds of thousands of Iraqis: estimates range between 300,000[98] and 400,000.[99] According to Gerges, army dissolution, "coupled with the de-Baathification

92 Gerges, *ISIS: A History*.
93 Wood, "What ISIS Really Wants."
94 Gerges, *ISIS: A History*.
95 Wood, "What ISIS Really Wants."
96 Gerges, *ISIS: A History*.
97 For more information about the IS, please refer to the chapter on Syria.
98 Gerges, *ISIS: A History*.
99 Freedom House, "Iraq | Country Report | Freedom in the World | 2016."

campaign, which dismissed people based on rank and affiliation, not behaviour, and which was mainly seen as a punitive and discriminatory policy against Sunnis by Iraq's newly installed Shia rulers, left widespread feelings of injustice and bitterness within the Sunni community."[100] Iraq was heading towards a civil war and high unemployment, "security vacuum, widespread looting, and acute electricity and water shortages"[101] acted as catalysts accelerating the crisis.

The chaos which marked the post-2003 developments was fuelled by the growing sectarianism of the country which both the coalition planners and the terrorists attempted to employ. The new Shia-favouring governance system aggravated the Sunnis who were then left vulnerable to IS (at the time still being al-Qaeda Iraq) infiltration at the most local levels while the United States "tried to build a wedge between the Sunni and Shia communities" as they were both resisting the occupation forces.[102] Even though both the Shia and the Sunni resistance shared a similar goal of ending the US-led occupation of Iraq, "the Shia fight was framed as a fight against decades of inequalities that they believed the transitional government had failed to overturn, [while] the Sunni fight was framed as one against foreign invaders, based on a widespread perception that the occupiers had handed Iraq to Shia-dominated Iran on a silver platter."[103]

The 2003 US-led invasion and the subsequent internal struggle had an enormous civilian death toll – during the peak of resistance between 2006 and 2007, the death toll was the highest. Over 29,000 people died in 2006 and more than 26,000 more in 2007.[104,105] However, these statistics do not involve the people wounded or those who died of war-related causes; let alone internally displaced people. In fact, it was estimated that between 2003 and 2011, roughly 500,000 Iraqis died because of the war – "coalition forces were blamed for 35 percent of the killings, followed by militias at 32 percent."[106]

Subsequently, IS made its claims over significant parts of Iraq (and Syria) and the death toll spiked again – claiming over 20,000 civilian lives in 2014. The figure keeps slowly decreasing each year; nonetheless, with IS currently being on the

---

100 Gerges, *ISIS: A History*.
101 Freedom House, "Iraq | Country Report | Freedom in the World | 2016."
102 Gerges, *ISIS: A History*.
103 Ibid.
104 "2016: Another Year of Relentless Violence in Iraq."
105 "Civilian Deaths in Iraq War 2003–2016 | Statistic."
106 Vergano, "Half-Million Iraqis Died in the War, New Study Says."

defensive against the Iraqi army, it may resort to even more violence and thus increase the civilian death toll again.[107]

Certain groups have been especially targeted by IS, such as women or the Yazidis, and they "were subject to forced conversion, beheading, crucifixion, enslavement, massive theft of property, and rape."[108] The causes of the unbridled violence carried out by IS members are threefold – it is partly because of its founder's legacy (al-Zarqawi), partly because of "its Iraqization through the instrumentalization of Baathist tools of repression as well as the country's bitter legacy of violence"; and finally, because of the organization's "ruralisation."[109] The organization's internalization of Baathist "know-how" effectively transformed a "mafia-like network into a skilled and professionalized army."[110] As a result of the many factors, a minimum of three million Iraqis have become internally displaced.[111]

2.2 Political factors

Iraq's internal politics have been for decades strongly influenced by its leading personalities – unfortunately, both Saddam's personality cult and post-2003 officials' political manoeuvring were mostly to the detriment of the Iraqi people.

Saddam's legacy is ever-present in Iraq. He came to be known as the party's "hit man," a ruthless torturer, and the way he assumed power in 1979 left no space for optimism as he publicly, in a meeting, named 19 "conspirators" who were subsequently escorted out of the room, never to be seen again.[112] Saddam dealt brutally with any signs of dissent, implementing a network of secret police,[113] skilfully exploited support of both the Soviet Union and the United States (possibly collaborating with the CIA),[114] and his miscalculated foreign policy decisions brought enormous suffering to the Iraqi people.

---

107 Even though Iraq's Prime minister declared victory over IS in December 2017, IS still poses a threat to the country's stability as they continue to launch sporadic attacks and most importantly, it is unlikely that their ideological legacy halts to lure men into their ranks.

108 Freedom House, "Iraq | Country Report | Freedom in the World | 2016."

109 Gerges, *ISIS: A History*.

110 Ibid.

111 "Report on the Protection of Civilians in the Armed Conflict in Iraq: 1 May – 31 October 2015."

112 Vasselin, Hamelin, and Charmelot, *Saddam: America's Best Enemy*.

113 Shehabaldin and Laughlin Jr, "Economic Sanctions against Iraq: Human and Economic Costs."

114 Vasselin, Hamelin, and Charmelot, *Saddam: America's Best Enemy*.

The US-led coalition then implemented an insensitive de-Baathification campaign which, combined with Western arrogance and insufficient analysis of Iraqi society, resulted in increased and violent sectarianism. Zakaria describes an anecdote illustrating the US self-confidence prior to the invasion when the Americans "lectured the [UN] inspectors – who had spent weeks combing through Iraq – on the evidence of weapons of mass destruction," disregarding the UN's actual findings.[115] This approach, coupled with several unthought-through decisions of the newly installed government, led to increased anti-US sentiment in Iraq.

The Arab Spring did not bypass Iraq either – even though people in Iraq were manifesting against an "on-paper" democratic government unlike in other Middle Eastern or North African countries where people were demonstrating against decades of dictatorships. Before the protests degenerated into a sectarian struggle, in 2011, "thousands of Iraqis came together, in a rare display of cross-sectarian harmony around the country."[116] They were asking for social and economic reforms, and an end to corruption and the foreign presence. The wave of protests was then gradually transformed into a sectarian struggle between the Sunnis and the Shia community which controlled the government. And even though the Al-Maliki government was ravaged by corruption and fuelled the cross-sectarian violence in Iraq, he managed to be re-elected in the 2010 general elections. It is worth noting that the "elections were able to go forward in an atmosphere remarkably free of violence, political conflicts were peacefully resolved within the rules of the democratic game, both the electoral process and its results met with general acceptance."[117]

Nonetheless, after his re-election, "Maliki's grip on state institutions soon expanded, encompassing the military, police, the courts, and the central bank;"[118] and the government's growing authoritarianism further exacerbated the society's grievances. Still, the government remained in power until IS overran the Iraqi Army in Mosul in 2014 which "finally put an end to Al-Maliki's government and exposed the serious weaknesses of the rump state created by the US and its allies."[119]

The election of al-Abadi initially sparked optimism as he campaigned to rid Iraq of sectarianism which considerably worsened under the preceding administration.[120] It is worth noting that al-Abadi was assuming power over Iraq when

115 Zakaria, *The Post-American World and the Rise of the Rest.*
116 Ahmed, "Iraq after the Arab Spring."
117 Dawisha, "Iraq."
118 Gerges, *ISIS: A History.*
119 Ahmed, "Iraq after the Arab Spring."
120 Freedom House, "Iraq | Country Report | Freedom in the World | 2016."

the country almost ceased to exist: about a third of its territory was occupied by IS, "including Mosul, the country's second-largest city; the Kurds had moved to take oil-rich Kirkuk and threatened to secede; and the Shia were bracing for further [IS] advances."[121]

2.3 Rule of law – judiciary system

Related to the IS security threat which materialized in 2014, al-Abadi did not fully deliver on his promises and the people began protesting against the new government, demanding an end to corruption and improved living conditions (such as water quality or electricity availability) and judiciary.[122] Iraq's rule of law remains "heavily influenced by political, tribal and religious forces, as well as by bribery,"[123] similar to most other aspects of Iraqi politics.

The al-Abadi government, however, did take specific steps in its fight against widespread corruption; for instance, 50,000 "ghost soldiers" were identified and removed from the government's payroll.[124] Still, according to Corruption Perceptions Index 2016, Iraq ranks 166th out of 176 countries evaluated.[125]

Overall, the al-Abadi administration's tenure has been most focused on corruption-control and the fight against IS (which aligned Iraq more with Russia as al-Abadi welcomed Russia's involvement and installed an intelligence-sharing platform between Iraq, Russia, Iran, and Syria).[126] And despite some progress and attempts at reforms, the Iraqi government remains "hampered by ongoing security crises, corruption, ethno-sectarian power sharing, and the state's limited administrative capacity."[127]

3. External factors

In fact, this chapter has already discussed in detail most of the external factors which could influence a country's democratization development process. In the case of Iraq, neighbouring countries played a specific, albeit marginal role – under Saddam's regime, it was the Iranian revolution which prompted his aggression towards Iran; concerning Kuwait, the country's vast oil reserves, its behaviour

121 Almaliky, "Mending Iraq."
122 Khoder, "Iraq."
123 Freedom House, "Iraq | Country Report | Freedom in the World | 2016."
124 Evans, "Iraq Says It Found 50,000 'Ghost Soldiers' on Payroll."
125 Transparency International, "Corruption Perceptions Index 2016."
126 al-Abadi, Prime Minister Abadi.
127 Freedom House, "Iraq | Country Report | Freedom in the World | 2016."

within OPEC and Iraq's enormous indebtedness paved the way to the 1990 invasion. Recently, the Syrian civil war most influences Iraq as the violence, including the spread of IS, fluidly spills over from one country to another.

International shocks have played a significant role in Iraq's development. As thoroughly demonstrated, the UN sanctions regime of the 1990s and early 2000s decimated the already war-affected Iraqi population – without reaching the political goal of removing Saddam Hussein from power. Similarly, given Iraq's dependence on oil revenues (currently around 43% of GDP),[128] the country is sensitive to oil price developments and shocks on the world market.

Systemic wars certainly affect the country's well-being. In fact, since 1979 when Saddam seized power, the country has only gone through a few years without violence – Iraq went from the Iraq–Iran war, the invasion of Kuwait, the subsequent Operation Desert Storm, and the UN sanctions regime and its consequences, to the 2003 invasion and occupation which triggered anti-American resistance and increased sectarianism which, in turn, cleared a path for IS and unprecedented levels of violence and brutality.

In terms of establishment of new states, Iraqi Kurds enjoyed favourable developments following the 2003 invasion. Kurds, who represent about 20% of the country's population, lived through extreme oppression under the dictatorship – in particular, Saddam targeted Kurds through the Anfal campaign of the late 1980s and employed chemical weapons in achieving his objective.[129] Nonetheless, the new 2005 Iraqi constitution finally "recognizes an autonomous Kurdistan region in the north of the country," the first time in history Kurds have been granted their own state, though not fully independent.[130] Still, the Kurdish struggle for independence is ever-present as the Iraqi Kurds went to cast their votes in a September 2017 referendum for the state's full-pledged independence. While more than 90% of Kurds voted *yes* for a separate state,[131] the Iraqi government rejected the legality of the referendum. More importantly, as the neighbouring states such as Turkey or Syria have significant Kurdish minorities, the referendum and its results disconcerted foreign leaders who worry the same fate would be pursued by "their" Kurds as well.

In fact, Kurds proved to be reliable allies in the coalition's fight first of all against Saddam and currently against IS – the Kurdistan Regional Government,

---

128 Kennedy, "Iraq On The Brink Of Chaos As Oil Revenues Fall."

129 "Profile: Who Are the Peshmerga?"

130 "Iraqi Kurdistan Profile."

131 Cockburn, "Kurdish Referendum: UN Offers to Help Resolve Iraqi Kurds' Independence Crisis."

the Peshmerga, its main fighting force, and the US share intelligence.[132] Related to Kurdish cooperation with the CIA, "the role of the Peshmerga was key in the eventual toppling of Saddam Hussein"[133] as well as being the principal fighting force against IS.

4. Conclusion

This chapter has evaluated Iraqi democratization efforts since 2003 when the US-led coalition forces overthrew Saddam's Baathist regime. Nonetheless, as most of the country's current structural economic and sociopolitical challenges stem from Iraq's history, it was necessary to illustrate some of the events which preceded the invasion.

It can be summarized that Iraq's economy was affected by the 1980s militarization of the regime and then the Operation Desert Storm eradicated the country's infrastructure. The Baathist regime brutally oppressed any forms of dissent and the UN sanctions regime which lasted from 1990 until 2003 decimated the country's population through acute lack of foodstuffs and medical supplies. The generations brought up during 1980s and 1990s have lower literacy rates, suffer from technological gaps, and some have become morally skewed.

The 2003 euphoria from the ousting of the Baathist regime was swiftly replaced by growing sectarianism, corrupt governments, and people's aggravation with non-improving basic living conditions and opportunities to work – especially influencing the younger generations. Iraq's civil society, which should be the country's main democratization driver, remains fractured and frequently positioned along political or sectarian lines. Additionally, the extreme security threat posed by IS suggests further limits to the country's democratization progress – when the country's most vital institutions need to focus their energy and funds on re-assuming the power monopoly, the democratization agenda may not be a top priority.

5. References

"2016: Another Year of Relentless Violence in Iraq." *Iraq Body Count*. March 13, 2017. https://www.iraqbodycount.org/analysis/numbers/2016/.

Abadi, Haider al-. Prime Minister Abadi: Iraq welcomes Russia in Islamic State fight. September 30, 2015. http://www.pbs.org/newshour/bb/prime-minister-abadi-iraq-welcomes-russia-islamic-state-fight/.

132 "Kurdish Peshmerga."

133 "Profile: Who Are the Peshmerga?"

Ahmed, Nasim. "Iraq after the Arab Spring." *Middle East Monitor.* January 19, 2016. https://www.middleeastmonitor.com/20160119-iraq-after-the-arab-spring/.

Almaliky, Muhamed H. "Mending Iraq." *Foreign Affairs.* January 16, 2015. https://www.foreignaffairs.com/articles/middle-east/2015-01-16/mending-iraq.

Alnasrawi, Abbas. "Iraq: Economic Sanctions and Consequences, 1990–2000." *Third World Quarterly* 22, no. 2 (2001): 205–18.

Baxter, Kylie, and Shahram Akbarzadeh. *US Foreign Policy in the Middle East: The Roots of Anti-Americanism.* London and New York: Routledge, 2008.

Black, Ian. "Iran and Iraq Remember War That Cost More than a Million Lives." *The Guardian*, September 23, 2010, sec. World news. https://www.theguardian.com/world/2010/sep/23/iran-iraq-war-anniversary.

"Civilian Deaths in Iraq War 2003–2016 | Statistic." *Statista.* March 19, 2017. https://www.statista.com/statistics/269729/documented-civilian-deaths-in-iraq-war-since-2003/.

Cockburn, Harry. "Kurdish Referendum: UN Offers to Help Resolve Iraqi Kurds' Independence Crisis." *The Independent.* September 28, 2017. http://www.independent.co.uk/news/world/middle-east/un-help-resolve-baghdad-iraq-kurdistan-kurdish-referendum-crisis-syria-a7972911.html.

"Crude Oil Prices – 70 Year Historical Chart." *Macrotrends.* March 10, 2017. http://www.macrotrends.net/1369/crude-oil-price-history-chart.

Cuellar, Javier Perez de. "Report to the Secretary-General on Humanitarian Needs in Kuwait and Iraq in the Immediate Post-Crisis Environment by a Mission to the Area Led by Mr. Martti Ahtisaari, Under-Secretary-General for Administration and Management, Dated 20 March 1991." United Nations. March 20, 1991. http://www.un.org/Depts/oip/background/reports/s22366.pdf.

Dawisha, Adeed. "Iraq: A Vote Against Sectarianism." *Journal of Democracy* 21, no. 3 (2010): 26–40. doi:10.1353/jod.0.0181.

Evans, Dominic. "Iraq Says It Found 50,000 'Ghost Soldiers' on Payroll." *Reuters.* December 1, 2014. http://www.reuters.com/article/us-mideast-crisis-iraq-soldiers-idUSKCN0JF2RZ20141201.

Freedom House. "Iraq | Country Report | Freedom in the World | 2016," 2016. https://freedomhouse.org/report/freedom-world/2016/iraq.

Gerges, Fawaz. *ISIS: A History.* Vol. 2016. Princeton and Oxford: Princeton University Press, n.d.

Goldberg, Jeffrey. "The Obama Doctrine." *The Atlantic.* April 2016. http://www.theatlantic.com/magazine/archive/2016/04/the-obama-doctrine/471525/.

Gordon, Joy. "Joy Gordon on Iraq Sanctions." Interview. *Public Ethics Radio*. Canberra, Australia, August 5, 2010. http://www.cappe.edu.au/media/docs/PER_Transcript_Gordon.pdf.

"Iraq – Freedom of the Press 2016." *Freedom House*, 2016. https://freedomhouse.org/report/freedom-press/2016/iraq.

"IRAQ: 2015 ARTICLE IV CONSULTATION AND REQUEST FOR PURCHASE UNDER THE RAPID FINANCING INSTRUMENT—PRESS RELEASE; STAFF REPORT; AND STATEMENT BY THE EXECUTIVE DIRECTOR FOR IRAQ." The International Monetary Fund, August 2015. https://www.imf.org/external/pubs/ft/scr/2015/cr15235.pdf.

"Iraq Civil Society Organizations – Iraq Research." *Iraqi Research Foundation for Analysis and Development*, 2014. http://www.irfad.org/iraq-civil-society/.

"Iraq Profile – Media." *BBC News*, May 2, 2016, sec. Middle East. http://www.bbc.com/news/world-middle-east-14546541.

"Iraqi Kurdistan Profile." *BBC News*, February 5, 2016, sec. Middle East. http://www.bbc.com/news/world-middle-east-28147263.

Kennedy, Charles. "Iraq On The Brink Of Chaos As Oil Revenues Fall." *OilPrice.com*. February 19, 2016. http://oilprice.com/Energy/Energy-General/Iraq-On-The-Brink-Of-Chaos-As-Oil-Revenues-Fall.html.

Khoder, Salam. "Iraq: The End of Sectarian Politics?" *Al Jazeera*. May 2, 2016. http://www.aljazeera.com/news/2016/05/iraq-sectarian-politics-160502093754018.html.

"Kurdish Peshmerga." *The Kurdish Project*. March 20, 2017. http://thekurdishproject.org/history-and-culture/kurdish-nationalism/kurdish-peshmerga/.

"Law of Non-Governmental Organizations." *Iraqi Local Governance Law Library*. March 1, 2010. http://www.iraq-lg-law.org/en/content/law-non-governmental-organizations.

Lipka, Michael. "The Sunni-Shia Divide: Where They Live, What They Believe and How They View Each Other." *Pew Research Center*. June 18, 2014. http://www.pewresearch.org/fact-tank/2014/06/18/the-sunni-shia-divide-where-they-live-what-they-believe-and-how-they-view-each-other/.

Mahnken, Tom. "The Gulf War in Retrospect." *Foreign Policy*. January 20, 2011. https://foreignpolicy.com/2011/01/20/the-gulf-war-in-retrospect/.

"Profile: Who Are the Peshmerga?" *BBC News*. August 12, 2014, sec. Middle East. http://www.bbc.com/news/world-middle-east-28738975.

"Report on the Protection of Civilians in the Armed Conflict in Iraq: 1 May – 31 October 2015." United Nations Assistance Mission for Iraq UNAMI. January 19, 2016. http://www.ohchr.org/Documents/Countries/IQ/UNAMIReport1May31October2015.pdf.

Shehabaldin, Ahmed, and William M. Laughlin Jr. "Economic Sanctions against Iraq: Human and Economic Costs." *The International Journal of Human Rights* 3, no. 4 (1999): 1–18.

Simons, Geoff. *The Scourging of Iraq: Sanctions, Law, and Natural Justice*. 2. Vol. 1998. London: Macmillan Press, n.d.

Taher, Ali. "Iraqi Civil Society Struggles to Stay Relevant, Effective." *Al-Monitor.* September 23, 2013. http://www.al-monitor.com/pulse/originals/2013/09/civil-society-organizations-iraq-donations-effectiveness.html.

"The World Factbook — Iraq." Central Intelligence Agency, June 21, 2017. https://www.cia.gov/library/publications/the-world-factbook/geos/iz.html.

Transparency International. "Corruption Perceptions Index 2016," 2016. https://www.transparency.org/country/IRQ.

"UN SC Res. 660." United Nations Security Council, August 2, 1990. https://documents-dds-ny.un.org/doc/RESOLUTION/GEN/NR0/575/10/IMG/NR057510.pdf?OpenElement.

"UN SC Res. 661." United Nations Security Council, August 6, 1990. https://documents-dds-ny.un.org/doc/RESOLUTION/GEN/NR0/575/10/IMG/NR057510.pdf?OpenElement.

"UN SC Res. 666." United Nations Security Council, September 13, 1990. https://documents-dds-ny.un.org/doc/RESOLUTION/GEN/NR0/575/16/IMG/NR057516.pdf?OpenElement.

"UN SC Res. 678." United Nations Security Council, November 29, 1990. https://documents-dds-ny.un.org/doc/RESOLUTION/GEN/NR0/575/28/IMG/NR057528.pdf?OpenElement.

"UN SC Res. 1500." United Nations Security Council, August 14, 2003. http://www.un.org/press/en/2003/sc7843.doc.htm

United Nations Development Program. "Iraq Human Development Report 2014." *UNDP in Iraq*. March 16, 2017. http://www.iq.undp.org/content/iraq/en/home/operations/projects/democratic_governance/Iraq-NHDR-2014.html.

United Nations Iraq. "United Nations Iraq – UN Assistance Mission for Iraq." March 17, 2017. http://www.uniraq.com/index.php?option=com_k2&view=item&layout=item&id=943&Itemid=637&lang=en.

Vasselin, Pascal, Arnaud Hamelin, and Jacques Charmelot. *Saddam: America's Best Enemy*. Documentary, 2005. https://www.youtube.com/.

Vergano, Dan. "Half-Million Iraqis Died in the War, New Study Says." *National Geographic News*. October 16, 2013. http://news.nationalgeographic.com/news/2013/10/131015-iraq-war-deaths-survey-2013/.

Wood, Graeme. "What ISIS Really Wants." *The Atlantic*. March 2015. https://www.theatlantic.com/magazine/archive/2015/03/what-isis-really-wants/384980/.

World Bank. "GDP (Current US$)." March 7, 2017. http://data.worldbank.org/indicator/NY.GDP.MKTP.CD?end=2015&locations=IQ&start=1960.

–. "GDP per Capita (Current US$)." March 13, 2017. http://data.worldbank.org/indicator/NY.GDP.PCAP.CD?end=2015&locations=IQ&start=1960.

"Worldwide Round-Up of Journalists Who Are Detained, Held Hostage or Missing 2016." Reporters Without Borders. December 9, 2016. https://rsf.org/sites/default/files/rsf_2016-en_0.pdf

Zakaria, Fareed. *The Post-American World and the Rise of the Rest*. 2nd ed. London and New York: Penguin Books, 2011.

Zubaida, Sami. "The Rise and Fall of Civil Society in Iraq." *openDemocracy*. February 5, 2003. http://www.opendemocracy.net/conflict-iraqwarquestions/article_953.jsp.

Yvona Novotná and Jana Samadová

Lebanon

Lebanon, which was called the "Switzerland of the Middle East" in the 1960s, is an exceptional country. Lebanon is an Arab state, but it is not a typical Islamic state. It is characterized by a multicultural, multi-confessional society where individual religious communities live in coexistence. There are 18 officially recognized confessional groups with different religious, political, and cultural views in Lebanon.

Lebanon witnessed several crucial moments through its history. It was under the reign of the Ottoman Empire before being ruled by yet another foreign power since the French got a mandate over the country. Lebanon became an independent state and was designated as a formal democracy on November 22, 1943 with a multi-confessional society of pluralist character. Lebanon always had a strong commitment to Europe, especially to countries such as France, Italy, and the United Kingdom. Later it turned to the United States. From these sources Lebanon took and developed a model of republicanism, parliamentarism, and democracy with a mosaic of political cultures. Lebanon has never established a cantonal system on its territory, such as Switzerland, and the Lebanese territorial units are still religiously heterogeneous.

Then, a civil war took place in Lebanon as the tension grew between the Palestinian refugees fleeing their country and the government, as well as between Lebanon and Syria on one hand, and Israel on the other. The war lasted almost 15 years and damaged the country and Lebanon is still suffering from the consequences. Since then, Lebanon is struggling to overcome the religious polarization of the population and essential things, such as insufficient water and electricity problems. Furthermore, Lebanon faced another war in 2006 with Israel, with Hezbollah the leading Lebanese actor in that conflict.

This chapter deals with the process of democratization in Lebanon, focusing on the period after the so-called Arab Spring. The Arab Spring touched Lebanon and its system indirectly, but nevertheless, influenced it in many fields; especially through the war in Syria. However, for a better understanding of the current Lebanese political system and the country's political culture, it is necessary to mention the historical context from which emerged the Lebanese confessional democracy. This chapter analyses important historical factors and milestones that laid the foundation for the emergence and subsequent development of the democratization process in Lebanon.

1. Internal non-institutional factors

Democratization elements in Lebanon emerged during the historical period, especially under the reign of the Ottoman Empire in the 19th century. There were major changes in the ethnic and religious structure of the population, along with the development of trade, craft production, monetary relations, the first factories, and workshops with a capitalist basis. At the same time, European powers, such as France, Great Britain, and Tsarist Russia, began to penetrate Lebanon and interfere into its internal affairs. Each of these European countries supported individual confessions in Lebanon. After the outbreak of the Maronite-Druze rebellion in 1860 and under the pressure of European states, Lebanon was divided into two governorships – Maronite and Druze.[1] Two principles began to emerge in Lebanon with the creation of these two governorships – a territorial principle and the principle of religious affiliation.[2]

An important democratization element in the development of the Lebanese state was the Organic Statute of 1861, which laid the foundations for the confessional democracy after the Druze-Maronite conflict in 1860. This document abolished the existence of the two governorships, guaranteed autonomy to the Lebanese population, and set up an autonomous area headed by a non-Lebanese Christian governor. It was named Mountain (Small) Lebanon and was completely independent from the Ottoman Empire. This status of autonomy lasted until the outbreak of the First World War.[3]

After the First World War, the Ottoman Empire collapsed in 1920, and an independent modern Lebanon emerged at the initiative of France: Mountain Lebanon expanded into the so-called Great Lebanon, whose borders are valid up to the present. France then obtained a mandate over Lebanon according to the Sykes-Picot agreement of 1916.[4] The established Lebanese state was founded primarily on the initiative of the Lebanese Maronites, supported by France, as a challenge to Arab nationalists who intended to integrate Lebanon into Syrian territory.[5] They considered it to be an end to the effort of autonomy of Christians throughout the Levant.[6] But the extension of the borders from Small to Great Lebanon violated the principle of religious self-determination. For example, Christians, who

1 G. Corm, *Le Liban Contemporain, Histoire et Société*, 59.
2 A. N. Messarra, *Théorie Générale Du Systeme Politique Libanais*, 67–69.
3 G. Corm, *Le Liban Contemporain, Histoire et Société*, 62–65.
4 Dib, *Tarikh Souriya al-Mouaaser*, 37.
5 S. H. Longrigg, *Syria and Lebanon under the French Mandate*, 71.
6 G. Corm, *Le Liban Contemporain, Histoire et Société*, 70.

accounted for 80% of Lebanon's population in 1910, were only 55% of the total Lebanese population after 1918.[7] The French mandate created legal, institutional, and political entities out of the individual confessional groups in Lebanon.[8] The Second World War contributed to greater awareness of political identity.[9] The national struggle for Lebanon's independence prompted all Lebanese religious groups to cooperate. The French mandate over Lebanon lasted until the declaration of independence in 1943.[10]

The very act of Lebanon's creation can be considered as exceptional in terms of democratization principles. It was based on an inter-communal, verbal agreement from two major Lebanese politicians, namely Lebanon's president Beshara al-Khoury (a Maronite, elected on September 21, 1943) and the Lebanese Prime Minister Riyadh al-Solh (a Sunni Muslim, in office since September 1943). Lebanese Christians abandoned the idea of creating a Lebanon which would be under the protection of the Western powers, and thus completely dissociated from the surrounding Arab world. On the other hand, Lebanon's Muslims ceased to demand the division of Lebanon's territory into the neighbouring Syria or the complete extinction of Lebanon, which would become part of any Pan-Arab Union.[11] Thus, Independence Day was proclaimed on November 22, 1943 by the so-called National Pact (also the National Act), that is, by an oral agreement that divided, on the basis of confessionalism (see section 2.3) the political power between the two most powerful communities, namely the Maronites and the Sunnis.[12]

The National Pact certainly contributed to the stability of post-war Lebanon and became an important factor for the nation's dynamic economic development, which began in the early 1950s.[13] Lebanese Christians have constantly strived for maximum rapprochement with the West, including intensive development of relations with European countries at all levels and in all areas while Lebanese Muslims are considered to be under the prolonged influence of Arab states, in order to create a united Islamic world or Pan-Arab empire. The National Pact was therefore a compromise between these two currents. Lebanese Christians were supposed to give up their demand for Western protection, to reduce the influence

7 G. Figuié, *Le Point Sur Le Liban*, 23.
8 G. Corm, *Le Liban Contemporain, Histoire et Société*, 71–84.
9 A. N. Messarra, *Théorie Générale Du Systeme Politique Libanais*, 22.
10 S. H. Longrigg, *Syria and Lebanon under the French Mandate*, 93.
11 E. Rabbath, *La Formation Historique Du Liban Politique et Constitutionel*, 140.
12 See A. N. Messarra, *Théorie Générale Du Systeme Politique Libanais*. And A. N. Messarra, *Le Pact Libanais*.
13 A. N. Messarra, *Théorie Générale Du Systeme Politique Libanais*, 77.

of France, and Lebanese Muslims were supposed to give up any demand to create, for example, a union with Syria or other neighbouring country. It is also necessary to mention the complicated post-war situation in the region, where the influence of the European powers, that is France and Great Britain, has been limited, and the Jewish state has been formed and consolidated.

In the process of democratizing Lebanon, nothing major happened in the period that followed, until the civil war in 1975 that ended with the Taif agreements. The Taif agreements[14] (see section 2.2) have made significant progress, bringing about many important changes concerning constitutional and political reforms, the functioning of the Lebanese state, its political system and, in particular, the resumption of the coexistence of the Lebanese population after almost 15 years of the civil war.[15] The presence of Palestinians that quit their country from war to settle on Lebanese territory in refugee camps, played an important role in the events that led to the war. Furthermore, PLO's activity expanded into Lebanon and received the support of the Syrian regime, which will become later a pretext for a military intervention. Additionally, the Lebanese scene split between those in favour of the Palestinian opposition in Lebanon and those against it.[16] As for the civil war itself, it can be divided into several periods: the Syrian intervention (1976 – see section 3), the war between militias (1980), the Israeli invasion (1982), and the intra-Christian wars (1988).[17]

1.1 Economic factors

Lebanon was one of the most advanced states in the region after Second World War. Lebanon's geographical location and its long-standing tradition as a mediator between the West and the Arab world have laid the foundations for Lebanon's economic and service development, especially in banking, finance, and tourism. The international trade developed intensively, and Beirut became one of the most important Mediterranean ports. The great development of the Lebanese economy, in which 70% of GDP is provided by the service sector, occurred in the 1950s and

14 S. Khalaf, *Civil and Uncivil Violence in Lebanon*, 290–91.

15 These peace agreements were signed in the Saudi-Arabian town of Taif on 22 October 1989 by 58 Lebanese members of the Parliament at the suggestion of Saudi Arabia, Algeria, and Morocco. Interestingly, the signing agreements took place in Saudi Arabia, that is in a state in which, unlike Lebanon, there is no democratic system and political and religious freedom is totally missing.

16 Hassan Krayem, 'The Lebanese Civil War and the Taif Agreement'.

17 Haugbolle Sune, 'The Historiography and the Memory of the Lebanese Civil War'.

lasted until the outbreak of the civil war in Lebanon in April 1975.[18] In connection with the development of the oil industry after the Second World War and the outbreak of Islamic revolutions, regime changes and military coups in neighbouring countries, Arab states have largely transferred their financial resources to Lebanese banks which became the intermediaries of their financial operations. Rich Arab societies have transferred their financial capital and the so-called petrodollars to Lebanon for fear of sudden political changes in their countries. Unlike the neighbouring states which employed a direct economy without the goal of engaging in international trade, Lebanon decided to apply a liberal economy open to the world's markets.[19]

Economic development followed again after the end of the civil war in 1990. The war has destroyed the productive facilities and infrastructures; indirectly damaged the potential of renewing capital assets and developing human resources. Furthermore, the war caused the human capital flight and the country's loss of its elite.[20] During the reign of Prime Minister Rafic Hariri in the 1990s, a plan called the "Horizon 2000 for Reconstruction and Development" was established to restore the Lebanese economy.[21] The national currency stabilized, with the private sector already accounting for 90% of GDP in 1996.[22] Lebanon regained its prominent position in regional economic relations. However, Horizon 2000 was primarily financed by foreign donors and institutions, along with national budget surplus and internal borrowing.[23] Thus, the country's debt grew rapidly[24]: the government debt reached 169.03% of the country's GDP in 2003 as opposed to year 2000 when it was 146.10%.[25] There was a major impact on the Lebanese economy also from the conflict in 2006 when Israel attacked Lebanese Hezbollah. During the so-called Second Lebanon War, the Israeli army bombed Beirut harbour, Beirut International Airport, attacked power stations, bridges, roads, and destroyed almost all of Lebanon's infrastructure.[26]

18 J. Bertrand and N. Picaudou, *L'industrie Libanaise et Marchés Arabes Du Golfe*, 159.
19 Ibid., 163.
20 Maroun Kisirwani, 'The Rehabilitation and Reconstruction of Lebanon'.
21 'Economy of Lebanon'.
22 'Le Commerce Du Levant'.
23 Maroun Kisirwani, 'The Rehabilitation and Reconstruction of Lebanon'.
24 G. Corm, *Le Liban Contemporain, Histoire et Société*, 236.
25 'Lebanon Government Debt to GDP 2000–2017'.
26 G. Corm, *Le Liban Contemporain, Histoire et Société*, 250.

The GDP of the country in 2000 represented 17.26 billion US dollars[27] (5,334 US dollars per capita[28]). It remained in the same marge until 2007 when it grew to 24.577 billion US dollars[29] (6,014 US dollars per capita[30]). It grew further to 40.079 billion US dollars in 2011[31] (8,734 US dollars per capita[32]). Finally, in 2016 the GDP was 47.537 billion US dollars[33] (7,914 US dollars per capita[34]).

As for the problem of unemployment, Lebanon suffers from a high rate of unemployment, that reached 25% in 2016 from which 36% are formed by the youth.[35] Nevertheless, several sources present different numbers due to poor governance and the lack of official statistics. Noting that the last official census in Lebanon was conducted in 1932, even the population statistics are inexact.[36] However, the fact that there are way more demands of jobs than there are offers remains present in the Lebanese reality. It is resulting in massive emigration of the Lebanese, especially of the youth, and in illegal activities.[37]

Furthermore, the impact of the actual Syrian conflict on the Lebanese economy is large. At the end of the Syrian occupation of Lebanon in 2005, Lebanon's GDP grew by 8% each year.[38] After the Syrian conflict, Lebanese GDP hit a sharp decline in annual growth from 8% in 2010 to 0.9% in 2011.[39] In the following years, GDP growth did not take place, with only 1.3% growth in GDP in the 2015, and 1.8% in 2016.[40] The biggest reason for slowing economic growth is the ongoing conflict in Syria and the associated influx of more than 1 million[41] registered Syrian refugees, which subsequently increased internal tensions in Lebanon and slowed the economic growth.[42] Poor economic growth reduces tax revenues, while the largest government spending targets debt services, government salaries,

27 'GDP (Current US$)'.
28 'GDP per Capita (Current US$)'.
29 'GDP (Current US$)'.
30 'GDP per Capita (Current US$)'.
31 'GDP (Current US$)'.
32 'GDP per Capita (Current US$)'.
33 'GDP (Current US$)'.
34 'GDP per Capita (Current US$)'.
35 'Nisbat Al-Batala Fi Loubnan Wasalat Ila 25% Wa 47% Menhom Toulab Jamiaat'.
36 'The Lebanese Demographic Reality'.
37 'Crippling the Youth'.
38 'Lebanon – Data'.
39 Ibid.
40 Ibid.
41 Refugees (UNHCR), 'UNHCR Syria Regional Refugee Response'.
42 Amal Mudallali, 'The Syrian Refugee Crisis Is Pushing Lebanon to the Brink'.

and transfers to power engineering and electricity. These things restrict other government spending, limiting the government's ability to invest in necessary infrastructure improvements such as water, electricity, and transport. The subsequent economic crisis has hit many economic sectors. Significantly, the sectors of construction, logistics, health, education, and tourism have been affected.[43]

The Syrian conflict in 2011 also has a major impact on Lebanon's international trade. Lebanon's most important trading partners include neighbouring Syria, where Lebanon exports around 15% of all its exports, and Turkey, which accounts for almost 12% of Lebanese exports. Lebanese exports are mainly agricultural products: 95% of agricultural products are exported to the neighbouring Middle Eastern countries. The share of the agricultural sector in the total GDP is 4.7%, and in the agriculture sector, about 10% of the Lebanese population work.[44] Furthermore, the Lebanese job market was already saturated and with the influx of refugees, the situation got more complicated as the Lebanese and the Syrians are competing for jobs and resources. By 2015, the unemployment rate is estimated to have doubled to almost 20% and economic losses up to 7.5 billion US dollars have been registered.[45]

1.2 Civil society and media

1.2.1 Civil society

Civil Society Organisations are a widespread practice in the Lebanese reality but they face many difficulties and obstacles in fulfilling their goals. The Lebanese environment is unstable in terms of politics and security while the socioeconomic conditions of the population are in bad shape, which negatively affects the work of CSOs.[46] CSOs are registered at the Ministry of Interior and their number has reached 8,000.[47] Their activity is visible within the Lebanese society as they organize demonstrations, prepare position papers, and lobby on certain issues. However, the war in Syria has put security issues in the spotlight and diminished the advocacy role of CSOs. They primarily advocate for women's rights, human rights, the environment, and against domestic violence, human trafficking, refugees, and corruption.[48]

---

43 Ibid.

44 'IDAL – Investment Development Authority of Lebanon'.

45 'ILO Response to Syrian Refugee Crisis in Lebanon'.

46 'Mapping Civil Society Organizations in Lebanon'.

47 David Schenker, 'Lebanon's [Un]Civil Society'.

48 Ibid.

Under the reign of the Ottoman Empire and the French mandate, CSOs were given a legal framework. Thus, a law organising the work of the new organisations, that had essentially a religious purpose, was established in 1909. The functioning law that provides the legal environment for the Lebanese CSOs is the 1909 Ottoman Law on Associations. It is rather liberal with the only obligation to notify the government immediately after the establishment of a new organization and the only barrier to activities is the prohibition of secret and undeclared associations.[49] During the civil war (from 1975 to 1990), the civil society tried to replace the government, which was damaged by the war. However, the role of CSOs was executed by armed militias which sometimes negated the purpose of the existence of the civil society. After the war, the civil society regained its position complementing the government.[50]

The Lebanese civil society has made a considerable contribution to the humanitarian crisis of the refugees in Lebanon. Many factors stand in the way of the CSOs' work. First, Lebanon is not a member state to the 1951 Convention Relating to the Status of Refugees and the 1967 Protocol of the same name,[51] that protects and implements the facilitation of refugee travels, the principle of unity of the family, the welfare services and the international cooperation in the field of asylum and resettlement.[52] Second, the Lebanese government does not want to grant asylum status to the refugees and hence consider them as Internally Displaced Peoples. Third, the responsibility of taking care of the refugees falls on communal institutions and CSOs as policies on the national level are not implemented in that matter. Thus, CSOs provide food, shelters, medical assistance, and other services to refugees, especially Syrians, coming to the country.[53] Furthermore, activists in this field are not only Lebanese, but they are joined by middle-class Syrian refugees that are committed to helping Syrians at Syria and Lebanon. Those Syrians are establishing their own civil society in exile which is not an easy task: their organisations cannot get officially registered in Lebanon and have bank accounts along with the discrimination they face.[54]

---

49 'Civic Freedom Monitor: Lebanon'.

50 Geoffroy d'Aspremont, 'The Development of Civil Society in Lebanon from the Ottoman Empire to the XXIst Century'.

51 Carmen Geha, 'The Syrian Refugee Crisis and Lebanon's Endemic Deadlocks'.

52 'Convention and Protocol Relating to the Status of Refugees: 1951 Convention Relating to the Status of Refugees and 1967 Protocol Relating to the Status of Refugees'.

53 Carmen Geha, 'The Syrian Refugee Crisis and Lebanon's Endemic Deadlocks'.

54 Frances Topham Smallwood, 'Refugee Activists' Invovlvement in Relief Effort in Lebanon'.

Currently, one prominent CSO is the "You Stink" movement, which was established in response to the Garbage Crisis of 2015. The nomination aimed to reflect the crisis of uncollected garbage and long-term structural problems: it coincided with the presidential vacuum while the contract of the company responsible for collecting trash in Beirut and other cities expired and the responsible politicians were unwilling to negotiate new contracts because of the individual interests they have in such companies and the high level of corruption.[55] Moreover, the movement did not radically change the course of actions as the government tried to undermine them by suggesting that the organizers join political parties, which was immediately rejected. However, those events signified a remarkable progress within civil society, since it was unprecedented for the Lebanese people to demonstrate without any political banners and for general socioeconomic concerns. [56]

1.2.2 Media

The media's status in Lebanon is one of the best in the Arab World. However, it still struggles by global standards to be independent and free. In fact, according to the Freedom of Press report of 2017, the Lebanese Press Freedom Status is "partly free" with a score of 56 out of 100 (0 being the most and 100 the least free).[57] The report from 2016 shows that the biggest challenge for the Lebanese media is the legal environment. Despite the fact that the Constitution provides for the freedom of press, expression and assembly (Article 13), the laws implementing the limits of those freedoms "are chaotic, contradictory, and ambiguously worded"[58]. There are many restrictions to media practices such as loopholes which allow for the prosecution of journalists in the penal code, the Publications Law, the 1994 Audio-visual Media Law, and the military justice code.[59] In terms of politics, a censorship bureau exists and has the power to censor all foreign media prior to their diffusion in Lebanon with the pretext of defending national security and the wellbeing of the country.[60] In addition, religious authorities exert a certain influence by consulting different reviews and bans on publications.[61]

---

55 Zogby, 'You Stink'.
56 Sami Nader, 'Why Lebanon's "You Stink" Movement Lost Momentum'.
57 'Lebanon – Country Report 2017'.
58 'Lebanon – Country Report 2016'.
59 'Lebanon's Media Landscape'.
60 'Lebanon – Country Report 2016'.
61 Ibid.

The Lebanese media landscape is very rich and diverse. There are up to 1,500 privately owned newspapers in several languages (Arabic, French, and English)[62] and these outlets are often associated with ethnic, religious, or political groups[63]: for example, al-Mustakbal Tv (Future Tv) is owned by the pro-Saudi Sunni Hariri family (the prime minister is the son of the deceased Rafic al-Hariri, Saad), al-Manar Tv is affiliated with Hezbollah, NBN Tv was founded by Nabih Berri (the speaker of the parliament) and LBC channel was founded as a platform for the Christian Lebanese Forces party.[64] Moreover, there are many television stations, digital cable companies, and radio stations. All those media sources have a strong online presence through their own websites and social media.[65] The social media in Lebanon became an important part of the political and social life, since they are used to express political, religious, and communal views.[66]

Finally, the media's reactions to the refugee crisis in Lebanon are diverse. On one hand, the media is reacting negatively by dealing with the refugees as a block not as individual issues. For example, when the Lebanese army clashed with some Syrian militants in Arsal (near the Syrian border – see section 2.2), some media tended to label all Syrian refugees as terrorists, spreading hate-speech and stereotyping. On the other hand, some media are trying to point out the humanitarian crisis of the refugees and incite the empathy of the Lebanese people. Overall, the media's position is rather negative and xenophobic.[67]

1.3 Extremism and religion

The whole Lebanese experience is built on a religious basis. This part will present the religious composition of the country and some examples of extremism, such as the Salafist movements and Hezbollah.

In the unique case of Lebanon, the Constitution recognizes 18 confessions of faith, from which 15 are managed by the Laws of the Directorate General of Personal Status, since matters of personal status like marriage, divorce, child custody, and inheritance differ from one denomination to another.[68] Furthermore, according to Article 9, the Constitution grants the freedom of conscience.

---

62 Ibid.
63 Nabil Dajani, 'The Myth of Media Freedom in Lebanon'.
64 Lorenzo Trombetta, 'Lebanon'.
65 'Lebanon's Media Landscape'.
66 'Survey'.
67 Magda Abu-Fadil, 'Media Put Humanity in the Picture as Refugee Crisis Takes Hold'.
68 'Lebanon – 2012 Report on International Religious Freedom'.

Lebanese society is 54% Muslim, 40.5% Christian, and 5.5% Druze (they consider themselves as an autonomous group but their faith is similar to Islam).[69]

The Muslim community is constituted of the Sunnis, Shias, Ismailis, and Alawites. As for the Christians, they are divided between those with an affiliation to the Roman Catholic Church and those associated with the Eastern Orthodox Church. The Catholics encompass the Maronite, the Greek Catholic, the Armenian Catholic, the Syriac Catholic, and the Chaldean Churches. On the other hand, the Orthodox confessions include the Greek Orthodox, the Armenian Orthodox, the Syriac Orthodox, the Jacobite, the Nestorian, the Evangelist, and the Coptic Churches. Lastly, a small community of Jews lives in Lebanon.[70]

As for the Salafists, their presence on the Lebanese scene increased after the Syrian uprising in 2011. "Salafism today can be separated into three main categories: quietists, activists, and Salafi jihadists. The quietists focus on Islamic education [...] propagation, while the activists, unsatisfied with Arab rulers, want to exert power and influence on their governments. As for Salafi jihadists -- epitomized by Usama bin Laden -- they believe the way to return to the golden age of Islam and Islamic society is through holy war, or jihad".[71] For example, Ahmad al-Assir is a Salafi radical cleric who was present on the Lebanese scene primarily in 2013. He emerged in the city of Sidon preaching against Hezbollah, the Syrian regime and Iran.[72] He and his men were behind an attack on the Lebanese army that turned the city to a battleground in June 2013 and an attack on the Iranian embassy in Beirut in November 2013.[73]

Finally, Hezbollah is the continuing movement of resistance that emerged in the 1982 against the Israeli invasion of South Lebanon. It received the support of the Iranian Islamic Revolutionary Guards, which makes Iran today the main sponsor of the movement in terms of finances, weapons, human resources, and propaganda.[74] It turned later to a Shia Islamist organisation whose main enemies are the United States and Israel, as it carried out several attacks against them, such as the 1983 attack on the Marine barracks or the suicide attack on the Israeli embassy in Buenos Aires in 1992.[75] It fought the Israeli invasion of South Lebanon

69 'The World Factbook – Lebanon'.

70 'Lebanon – 2012 Report on International Religious Freedom'.

71 Robert Rabil, 'Salafism in Lebanon'.

72 Shaheen, 'Fugitive Lebanese Cleric Ahmad Al-Assir Fails to Avoid Arrest with "70s Makeover"'.

73 Mona Alami, 'Radical Sheikh Still Wields Influence from Lebanese Prison'.

74 'Hezbollah'.

75 Ibid.

that lasted from 1982 to 2000. Hezbollah was credited for freeing Lebanon but refused to disarm and maintained a military presence in the South, under the pretext of protecting the Southern borders with Israel.[76] Furthermore, the tension between Hezbollah and Israel grew into another war in 2006, when Hezbollah launched a military operation against Israel. Then, Israel reacted with a major military offensive that paralysed Lebanon for 34 days.[77] Today, Hezbollah plays a major role in Lebanese politics as a political party: before the civil war of 1975 it was a militia group which emerged as a political party in the post-war era[78] with its leader Hassan Nasrallah; and is a member of the March 8 Alliance (see section 2.2). Furthermore, Hezbollah is directly engaged in the war in Syria (see chapter about Syria) which put more tension into national politics and complicated the situation in the country.[79] The movement is listed as a terrorist organization in many counties and organizations of the world: the United States,[80] the Arab League,[81] the EU,[82] Australia,[83] and many others.

2. Internal institutional factors

2.1 Security and defence structures

Lebanon has never had a large, powerful army. The Lebanese Army was founded by General Fuad Shihab on August 1, 1945, and had a special role from the very beginning. Its main goal has always been to keep order in the country, trying to prevent any conflicts with other Arab states.[84] Throughout its history, the Lebanese army had only participated in one regional conflict, namely the first Arab-Israeli war in 1948 as part of the United Arab Military. The Lebanese army did not even have the power to enter the Palestinian armed camps in Lebanon, due to the

76 'Profile'.
77 'Hezbollah: Lebanese Militant Group & Political Party'.
78 Ibid.
79 'Profile'.
80 'Foreign Terrorist Organizations'.
81 'Profile'.
82 Justyna Pawlak and Adrian Croft, 'EU Adds Hezbollah's Military Wing to Terrorism List'.
83 Safi, 'Hezbollah's "External Security" Branch Remains Listed by Australia as Terrorist Group'.
84 Yvona Šabacká, 'The Role of the International Organizations in the Middle East with the Focus on the United Nations'.

so-called Cairo international agreements of November 1969 that gave Palestinians in Lebanon under Yasser Arafat's command considerable autonomy on Israel.[85]

After the end of the civil war in Lebanon in 1989, all armed militias had to be disarmed, except for the Hezbollah movement. Syria as the occupying power left this movement armed, and continued to support it in its resolute struggle against the Israeli occupation of Lebanon. In 2015, military spending stood at 4.76% of GDP.[86] In 2015 Saudi Arabia and the United States increased financial and material assistance to the Lebanese Armed Forces (LAF, including ground forces, the Lebanese Navy and the Lebanese Air Force), for the following period by 30–40%.[87] The US military assistance in the last eight years has reached the value of one billion dollars,[88] thanks to which the Lebanese army has greatly strengthened. The foreign aid (provided by the United States, Saudi Arabia, France, and China) for the LAF is mainly focused on strengthening its ability to face rebel and terrorist groups and ensuring full control of Lebanese borders. LAF elite units under the training of US instructors focus on fighting in city districts and counterinsurgency. The LAF are thus relatively well prepared for a possible spillover of the Syrian conflict into Lebanon (see section 3).

2.2 Political factors

The Taif agreements of 1989 signify the first written agreement that has been concluded between Lebanese political parties, militias, political party leaders, and confessional groups. The agreements deal with Lebanon as an Arab country, a country with Arab identity and affiliation, the founder of the League of Arab States, and a member of the UN, whose Charter is fully respected by Lebanon. The system of the state is based on the principle of the division of power, the people are the source of power and sovereignty, and exercise their rights through constitutional institutions.[89] The economic system is based on the principle of a market economy that respects private ownership. The main objective of the state, and hence its stability, is the development in the area of economy, culture, social affairs in all regions of Lebanon. Although the demographic ratio of the population changed in the second half of the twentieth century to the benefit of Muslims, the

85 G. Figuié, *Le Point Sur Le Liban*, 150.
86 'Military Expenditures'.
87 Amal Mudallali, 'The Syrian Refugee Crisis Is Pushing Lebanon to the Brink'.
88 Ibid.
89 G. Corm, *Le Liban Contemporain, Histoire et Société*, 232.

Taif Accords guarantee the Christian population of Lebanon half the power in the state. The National Pact is still valid after the conclusion of the Taif agreements.[90]

The Lebanese regime has been going through a political crisis for some time now. The assassination of then Lebanese Prime Minister Rafic Hariri was committed on February 14, 2005 and was attributed to Syria, then Hezbollah, but a particular attacker has not yet been investigated. This assassination became the trigger for the so-called Cedar Revolution; massive demonstrations and manifestations began in Lebanon invoking the withdrawal of the Syrian army from Lebanon and the end of the 29-years Syrian occupation. Syrian troops, including blue-collar workers and intelligentsia, had to leave Lebanon on April 30, 2005.

In 2005, the Lebanese government was divided into two coalitions – the March 8 Alliance and the March 14 Alliance. These two coalitions stand in opposition and are made up of different political parties. Block 8 March is led by the Hezbollah Shia movement, while other members are the Amal Shia movement, the Druze Progressive Socialist Party, and the Maronite Free Patriotic Movement (headed by Michel Aoun). The March 14 Movement is formed by the Sunni Party of the Future (Mustaqbal – led by Saad Hariri), the Christian Lebanese Forces and the Christian Kataeb. The March 8 Alliance, supported by Syria and Iran, was in favour of the Syrian presence in Lebanon while March 14, supported by Saudi Arabia and Western powers, protested it.[91]

The Lebanese electoral system is a very complicated process, as each religious community is represented in the parliament according to its demographic importance, noting that the 128 seats are equally distributed between Muslims and Christians.[92] This mosaic spreads further to the functioning of the public sector and government. For example, according to the National Pact, the President of the Republic ought to be a Maronite, the Speaker of the Parliament a Shiite and the Prime Minister a Sunni.[93]

The whole political system has caused many crises to the concept of democratization. The latest crisis was the presidential vacuum that endured for more than two years. The parliament elects the President and was unable to agree on a candidate, due to the political division of the country that deepened further with the civil war in Syria.[94] On May 25, 2014, the term of office of President Michel Suleiman (Maronite, Former Chief of Staff of the Lebanese Army, President

90 Ibid., 141.

91 'The World Factbook – Lebanon'.

92 'The Lebanese Electoral System'.

93 Charles Rizk, *Le Régime Politique Libanais*, 30.

94 'Lebanon', 31 October 2016.

2008–2014) ended and the new President, Michel Aoun, was elected on October 31, 2016 (elected on the 46th attempt).[95] In addition, the parliament was incapable of coming up with a new electoral law and therefore prolonged its own mandate: new elections were supposed to take place in June 2013 but the parliament extended its mandate until June 2017.[96] Hence, this postponement is violating Article 25 of the International Covenant on Civil and Political Rights[97], which Lebanon ratified in 1972.[98] According to the Economist Intelligence Unit's Democracy Index, Lebanon scores 4.86 out of 10 (0 being an authoritarian regime and 10 a full democracy). Overall, since 2006, when Lebanon scored 5.82, the situation has been deteriorating but still qualifies as a "hybrid regime".[99] This is caused by the challenging security context that set back the institutional reform process, the ineffective functioning of the government and the repeated postponement of elections.[100]

The conflict in Syria undoubtedly has an impact on the current political crisis in Lebanon. The 8 March Movement, including Hezbollah are on the side of Bashar al-Assad and support his regime. On the contrary, the March 14 Movement opposes the Assad regime and supports the Syrian opposition.[101] This is how the tension between these two Lebanese political coalitions is increasing, and the polarization of the Lebanese political system is deepening.[102] This also reflected in the presidential vacuum and the discord of the parties over presidential candidates. At the same time, the security of the Lebanese state is at risk. There have been several armed clashes in Lebanon since the outbreak of the conflict in Syria, especially in the border village of Arsal between the Lebanese army and Syrian jihadis.[103] During 2012, there were a number of riots and violence in Lebanon that killed more than two dozen Lebanese people. This was seen as a spillover of the

95 'The World Factbook – Lebanon'.
96 Hassan Abbas, 'Iza Aradtom Dimoukratiya La Tahtarem Houkouk Al-Insan, Youmkinokom Estensakh Al-Tajrouba Al-Loubnaniya'.
97 Article 25 of the International Covenant on Civil and Political Rights states that "every citizen has the right to vote and to be elected in regular elections to be held on the basis of universal and equal voting rights, by secret ballot ensuring freedom of vote".
98 'Lebanon', 4 November 2014.
99 'EIU Democracy Index 2016'.
100 'Democracy Index 2016: A Year of Political Stagnation in MENA'.
101 Khatib, 'Regional Spillover'.
102 'Lebanon on a Knife-Edge'.
103 'Arsal in the Crosshairs'.

Arab Spring into Lebanon, since people were demonstrating against Lebanon's sectarian political system using the same slogans used in Tunisia and Egypt.[104]

2.3 Rule of law – judicial system

Religious diversity, already presented, influences the rule of law in the country along with the repartition of assembly seats on a confessional basis. This represents characteristics of confessionalism. "Confessionalism is a system of government that proportionally allocates political power among a country's communities—whether religious or ethnic—according to their percentage of the population".[105] Furthermore, confessionalism is also part of a broader concept: a type of consociationalism which is the functioning of a state despite internal division along ethnic, religious, or linguistic lines without a dominating majority.[106]

The judicial branch is an independent institution whose independence is granted by the Lebanese Constitution (Article 20). There are several types of courts in the system: ordinary (criminal and civil courts) and exceptional courts.[107] As for personal status matters, they are left to each denomination. For example, Sharia Courts and Ecclesiastical Courts exist within the Personal Status Courts division.[108] Lebanon is democratic in its constitutional basis but the practice of the law contradicts it: religious and sectarian considerations surmount the prevalence of law. The practice of political life in the country allows the powerful and the wealthy to abuse their power, at the expense of vulnerable social groups.[109] Furthermore, the rule of law draws its legitimacy from its enforcement by religious instances rather than from its compliance with human rights and justice.[110]

3. External factors

Lebanon's internal as well as foreign policy are mainly influenced by external factors or international actors, whether global or regional. Syria, a significant regional actor, has long been influencing the internal political development of Lebanon, including its foreign-political relations. In fact, the Syrian occupation of Lebanon began in 1976, during the civil war in Lebanon, and lasted until May 2005. During

---

104 'Thousands Protest against Lebanon's Sectarian System'.
105 Imad Harb, 'Lebanon's Confessionalism'.
106 'Understanding Lebanese Confessionalism'.
107 'Lebanon Legal System'.
108 Firas El Samad and Lara Eid, 'The Lebanese Legal System and Research in Brief'.
109 Matthias Koetter, 'Lebanon – Understandings of the Rule of Law'.
110 Vida Hamd, 'Overview of the Rule of Law in Lebanon'.

the Syrian occupation, no democratic changes could have taken place in Lebanon, since Syria had all the state-owned Lebanese apparatus under its control and the Lebanese presidential candidate had to be approved by Syria.

Syria supported PLO in its struggles against Israel. As well as supporting the removal of the PLO from Lebanon in 1982, Syria supported the Lebanese Hezbollah movement.[111] It used this movement as an instrument of its foreign policy towards Israel, for example in the question of the Golan Heights.[112] Hezbollah, now a Lebanese political party, is supporting the Bashar Assad regime in the fight against the Islamic State and the Syrian opposition (see chapter about Syria). The impact of the conflict in Syria on Lebanon means the stagnation of the democratization process in the country (see section 2.2).[113]

One of the main factors influencing the internal political developments in Lebanon are the Syrian refugees. In 2016, 1,011,366 Syrian refugees were registered in Lebanon.[114] With illegal migration, the figure has reached almost 1.5 million Syrian refugees since the beginning of the conflict in 2011.[115] Lebanon, which has about 4.5 million inhabitants, has the largest refugee density relative to the domestic population. The influx of refugees has a negative impact on the country, in particular its infrastructure, the public finances of Lebanon, the provision of services and the environment. It is expected that the crisis will significantly increase the incidence of poverty among Lebanese residents and increase income inequality. It is estimated that, as a result of the Syrian crisis, some 200,000 other Lebanese will find themselves below the poverty line, adding up to 1 million poor.[116]

Up to December 31, 2016, the largest number of refugees is in the Beqaa Valley (361,104), Beirut capital (280,170), northern Lebanon (252,369), and southern Lebanon (at least 117,273).[117] Thousands of refugees live in poor conditions, since Lebanon's state is not able to provide sufficient assistance.[118] It can be said that the presence of Syrian refugees is a major burden on the Lebanese economy and has only minor benefits, for example by improving the situation for property

111 Marius Deeb, *Syria's Terrorist War on Lebanon and the Peace Process*, 182.

112 There is a territorial dispute over the Golan Heights mainly between Syria and Israel. It has a political and strategic significance as Damascus is exposed from the Golan Heights and they form a natural buffer for Israel. Source: 'Golan Heights Profile'.

113 'Democracy Index 2016: A Year of Political Stagnation in MENA'.

114 'The World Factbook – Lebanon'.

115 'Lebanon Overview'.

116 Ibid.

117 Refugees (UNHCR), 'UNHCR Syria Regional Refugee Response'.

118 Amal Mudallali, 'The Syrian Refugee Crisis Is Pushing Lebanon to the Brink'.

owners: among the refugees there are many wealthy Syrians searching for accommodation who can rent expensive apartments, and not only in Beirut.[119] Another benefit may be the fact that the financial assistance provided to the refugees by the international community is being spent directly in Lebanon for Lebanese goods.

At the beginning of the Syrian conflict in 2011, the Lebanese borders were open and Syrian refugees could enter Lebanese territory where they were looking for security. However, Lebanon is gradually closing its borders with the rapid rise in numbers of Syrian refugees.[120] Lebanon introduced new criteria, issued by the General Directorate of General Security, under the Lebanese Ministry of the Interior, for the admission of Syrians seeking renewal of residence permits from the beginning of 2015, as well as new conditions for Syrians coming to Lebanon. However, very little information was made about these new changes. The situation among Syrian refugees in Lebanon is unsatisfactory, since 70% of Syrian refugees in Lebanon live below the poverty line[121] and UN financial assistance is their only source of income. Noting that wealthy Syrians that left their country in the early stages of the conflict, are leading a normal life in Lebanon, buying or renting houses and sending their kids to school. However, the acquisition of the funds, helping the poor majority of the refugees, is threatened. If this extraordinary financial assistance were to be refused, the United Nations High Commissoner for Refugees would be forced to stop all its projects for Syrian refugees in Lebanon and Jordan.[122]

The role of Iran in Lebanon comes through Syria and Hezbollah (see section 1.3 and chapter about Syria). As for Israel, its relationship with Lebanon is conflictive with closed borders in the South of Lebanon and no diplomatic relations between the countries (see section 1.1 and 1.3).

4. Conclusion

The process of democratization in Lebanon began in the 19th century, when the so-called confessional democracy was born in Lebanon. Under the reign of the Ottoman Empire, Lebanon gained certain autonomy within a specific position, forming the first Lebanese institutions. After the First World War, the modern

119 Ibid.

120 Ibid.

121 Refugees, 'UNHCR and Partners Warn in Syria Report of Growing Poverty, Refugee Needs'.

122 Leo Dobbs, 'Funding Shortage Leaves Syrian Refugees in Danger of Missing Vital Support'.

Lebanon emerged: in 1920, at the initiative of France, which acquired a mandate over Lebanon, Lebanon expanded into the so-called Great Lebanon, whose borders are still valid today. The National Pact, within the declaration of independence of 1943, is between the three most numerous religious communities that have thus divided power in the state. Furthermore, the major democratization changes occurred after the end of the 15-year Lebanese civil war at the turn of 1989 and 1990 under the so-called Taif Peace Accords, concluded between political Lebanese parties and their leaders, religious leaders or militias with the aim of re-establishing the functioning of the state, the political system, and especially the coexistence between political and confessional groups in Lebanon. During the 1990s until 2005, there were virtually no democratization changes in Lebanon, and the democratization elements could not be further developed because of the Israeli and Syrian occupation of Lebanon.

The Arab Spring, which broke out in Tunisia in December 2010 and further expanded in the Middle East and North Africa (MENA) region, did not take place in Lebanon, but touched Lebanon indirectly. The Arab Spring, particularly in terms of the conflict in Syria which started in 2011, has major implications for the Lebanese state and thus for the evolving democratization process. The impact of the Syrian conflict on Lebanon is extensive, especially concerning the issue of Syrian refugees, which have a major effect on the Lebanese economy. As a result, Lebanon's international trade and investment are influenced, and Lebanon also has financial, social, political, and security problems. The Syrian conflict also affected the political situation in Lebanon, where from 2014 until 2016 the Lebanese Parliament failed to elect a president, and the Lebanese Parliament extended its mandate in 2014 until the year 2017, which is considered unconstitutional and illegitimate by the UN. The Syrian conflict further supports Lebanon's political and, in turn, religious confessional polarization. The Hezbollah movement, now a political party, is one of the main supporters of the Syrian regime and president Bashar al-Assad, while the opposition is formed by Lebanese Sunnis. The security situation in Lebanon is especially threatened by the Syrian conflict.

5. References

Abbas, Hassan. 'Iza Aradtom Dimoukratiya La Tahtarem Houkouk Al-Insan, Youmkinokom Estensakh Al-Tajrouba Al-Loubnaniya'. *Rasif 22*, 13 April 15AD. http://raseef22.com/politics/2015/04/13/democracy-lebanese-style/.

Abu-Fadil, Magda. 'Media Put Humanity in the Picture as Refugee Crisis Takes Hold'. Ethical Journalism Network, 6 July 2017. http://ethicaljournalismnetwork.org/resources/publications/moving-stories/lebanon.

Alami, Mona. 'Radical Sheikh Still Wields Influence from Lebanese Prison'. Al-Monitor, 3 February 2017. http://www.al-monitor.com/pulse/originals/2017/02/sheikh-assir-lebanon-influence-prison.html.

'Arsal in the Crosshairs: The Predicament of a Small Lebanese Border Town'. *Crisis Group*, 23 February 2016. https://www.crisisgroup.org/middle-east-north-africa/eastern-mediterranean/lebanon/arsal-crosshairs-predicament-small-lebanese-border-town.

Bertrand, J., and N. Picaudou. *L'industrie Libanaise et Marchés Arabes Du Golfe*. Beirut, Lebanon: Cermoc, 1979.

'Civic Freedom Monitor: Lebanon'. *The International Center for Not-for-Profit Law*, 15 January 2017. http://www.icnl.org/research/monitor/lebanon.html.

'Convention and Protocol Relating to the Status of Refugees: 1951 Convention Relating to the Status of Refugees and 1967 Protocol Relating to the Status of Refugees', n.d.

Corm, G. *Le Liban Contemporain, Histoire et Société*. Paris: La Decouverte, 2003.

'Crippling the Youth: Unemployment in Lebanon at an All-Time High'. *Newsroom Nomad*, 19 August 2016. https://newsroomnomad.com/crippling-youth-unemployment-lebanon-time-high/.

d'Aspremont, Geoffroy. 'The Development of Civil Society in Lebanon from the Ottoman Empire to the XXIst Century: A Driver of Political Changes?' *Institut MEDEA*, 23 December 2011. http://www.medea.be/2011/12/the-development-of-the-civil-society-in-lebanon-from-the-ottoman-empire-to-the-xxist-century-a-driver-of-political-changes/.

Dajani, Nabil. 'The Myth of Media Freedom in Lebanon'. Arab Media & Society, 12 May 2013. http://www.arabmediasociety.com/?article=833.

Deeb, Marius. *Syria's Terrorist War on Lebanon and the Peace Process*. New York, USA: Palgrave, 2003.

'Democracy Index 2016: A Year of Political Stagnation in MENA'. *The Economist*, 27 January 2017. http://country.eiu.com/article.aspx?articleid=755057259&Country=Lebanon&topic=Politics&subtopic=Forecast&subsubtopic=Democracy+index.

Dib, Kamal. *Tarikh Souriya al-Mouaaser*. Beirut, Lebanon: Dar al-Nahar, 2012.

Dobbs, Leo. 'Funding Shortage Leaves Syrian Refugees in Danger of Missing Vital Support'. UNHCR, 25 June 2015. http://www.unhcr.org/news/latest/2015/6/558acbbc6/funding-shortage-leaves-syrian-refugees-danger-missing-vital-support.html.

'Economy of Lebanon'. *Fanack Chronicle*, 29 September 2009. https://chronicle.fanack.com/lebanon/economy/.

'EIU Democracy Index 2016'. *The Economist,* 5 July 2017. https://infographics.economist.com/2017/DemocracyIndex/.

El Samad, Firas, and Lara Eid. 'The Lebanese Legal System and Research in Brief'. *GlobaLex*, February 2016. http://www.nyulawglobal.org/globalex/Lebanon1.html.

Figuié, G. *Le Point Sur Le Liban*. Beirut, Lebanon: Anthologie, 1998.

'Foreign Terrorist Organizations'. *U.S. Department of State,* 25 June 2017. http://www.state.gov/j/ct/rls/other/des/123085.htm.

Frances Topham Smallwood. 'Refugee Activists' Involvement in Relief Effort in Lebanon'. Forced Migration Review. University of Oxford, Refugee Studies Centre, September 2014.

'GDP (Current US$)'. *The World Bank,* 5 July 2017. http://data.worldbank.org/indicator/NY.GDP.MKTP.CD?locations=LB.

'GDP per Capita (Current US$)'. *The World Bank,* 5 July 2017. http://data.worldbank.org/indicator/NY.GDP.PCAP.CD?locations=LB.

Geha, Carmen. 'The Syrian Refugee Crisis and Lebanon's Endemic Deadlocks: Trading Reform for Resilience'. *Middle East Institute*, 17 March 2016. http://www.mei.edu/content/map/syrian-refugee-crisis-and-lebanon%E2%80%99s-endemic-deadlocks-trading-reform-resilience.

'Golan Heights Profile'. *BBC News*, 27 November 2015, sec. Middle East. http://www.bbc.com/news/world-middle-east-14724842.

Hamd, Vida. '*Overview of the Rule of Law in Lebanon*', *in Matthias Koetter / Gunnar Folke Schuppert, Understandings of the Rule of Law in various legal orders of the World, Rule of Law Working Paper Series Nr. 21, Berlin.*

Harb, Imad. 'Lebanon's Confessionalism: Problems and Prospects'. *United States Institute of Peace*, 30 March 2006. https://www.usip.org/publications/2006/03/lebanons-confessionalism-problems-and-prospects.

'Hezbollah'. *Counter Extremism Project,* 25 June 2017. https://www.counterextremism.com/threat/hezbollah.

'Hezbollah: Lebanese Militant Group & Political Party'. *Encyclopedia Britannica,* 5 July 2017. https://www.britannica.com/topic/Hezbollah.

'IDAL – Investment Development Authority of Lebanon', 28 June 2017. http://investinlebanon.gov.lb/.

'ILO Response to Syrian Refugee Crisis in Lebanon'. *International Labour Organization,* 5 July 2017. http://www.ilo.org/beirut/areasofwork/syrian-refugee-crisis/lebanon/lang--en/index.htm.

James, Zogby. 'You Stink'. Huffington Post, 29 August 2015. http://www.huffingtonpost.com/james-zogby/you-stink_b_8056484.html.

Khalaf, S. *Civil and Uncivil Violence in Lebanon*. New York, USA: Columbia University Press, 2002.

Kisirwani, Maroun. 'The Rehabilitation and Reconstruction of Lebanon'. American University of Beirut, 1997. http://ddc.aub.edu.lb/projects/pspa/kisirwani.html.

Koetter, Matthias. 'Lebanon – Understandings of the Rule of Law'. Wikis Der Freien Universität Berlin, 31 August 2012. http://wikis.fu-berlin.de/display/SB projectrol/Lebanon.

Krayem, Hassan. 'The Lebanese Civil War and the Taif Agreement'. *American University of Beirut*, 3 July 2017. http://ddc.aub.edu.lb/projects/pspa/conflict-resolution.html.

'Le Commerce Du Levant', no. 5437 (23 January 1997): 15.

'Lebanon – 2012 Report on International Religious Freedom'. *U.S. Department of State*, 20 May 2013. http://www.state.gov/j/drl/rls/irf/2012/nea/208400.htm.

'Lebanon – Country Report 2016'. *Freedom House*, 25 June 2017. https://freedom house.org/report/freedom-press/2016/lebanon.

'Lebanon – Country Report 2017'. *Freedom House*, 25 June 2017. https://freedom house.org/report/freedom-press/2017/lebanon.

'Lebanon – Data'. *The World Bank*, 3 July 2017. http://data.worldbank.org/country/lebanon.

'Lebanon – Right to Vote For Parliament Under Threat'. *Human Rights Watch*, 4 November 2014. https://www.hrw.org/news/2014/11/04/lebanon-right-vote-parliament-under-threat.

'Lebanon Government Debt to GDP 2000–2017'. *Trading Economics*, 5 July 2017. tradingeconomics.com/lebanon/government-debt-to-gdp.

'Lebanon Legal System'. *Mattar Law Firm*, 24 June 2017. http://mattarlaw.com/lawyers-articles/lebanon-legal/.

'Lebanon: Michel Aoun Elected President, Ending Two-Year Stalemate'. *BBC News*, 31 October 2016, sec. Middle East. http://www.bbc.com/news/world-middle-east-37821597.

'Lebanon on a Knife-Edge: Anti-Syrian Tensions Rising'. *RT International*, 20 October 2012. https://www.rt.com/news/lebanon-attack-bomb-syria-847/.

'Lebanon Overview'. *The World Bank*, 1 April 2017. http://www.worldbank.org/en/country/lebanon/overview.

'Lebanon's Media Landscape: An Overview'. *Fanack Chronicle*, 23 March 2017. https://chronicle.fanack.com/lebanon/society-media-culture/lebanon-media/.

Lina, Khatib. 'Regional Spillover: Lebanon and the Syrian Conflict'. *Carnegie Middle East Center*, 9 June 2014. http://carnegie-mec.org/2014/06/09/regional-spillover-lebanon-and-syrian-conflict-pub-55829.

Longrigg, S. H. *Syria and Lebanon under the French Mandate*. Oxford: Oxford University Press, 1957.

'Mapping Civil Society Organizations in Lebanon'. The European Union – Civil Society Facility South, 2015.

Messarra, A. N. *Le Pact Libanais*. Beirut, Lebanon: Librairie Orientale, 1997.

–. *Théorie Générale Du Systeme Politique Libanais*. Paris: Cariscript, 1994.

'Military Expenditures'. The World Factbook – Central Intelligence Agency, 28 June 2017. https://www.cia.gov/library/publications/the-world-factbook/rankorder/2034rank.html#le.

Mudallali, Amal. 'The Syrian Refugee Crisis Is Pushing Lebanon to the Brink'. *Wilson Center*, 22 February 2013. https://www.wilsoncenter.org/publication/the-syrian-refugee-crisis-pushing-lebanon-to-the-brink.

Nader, Sami. 'Why Lebanon's "You Stink" Movement Lost Momentum'. Al-Monitor, 23 October 2015. http://www.al-monitor.com/pulse/originals/2015/10/lebanon-civil-movement-protests-violence.html.

'Nisbat Al-Batala Fi Loubnan Wasalat Ila 25% Wa 47% Menhom Toulab Jamiaat'. GreenArea.me, 20 April 2016. http://greenarea.me/ar/129783/%d9%86%d8%b3%d8%a8%d8%a9-%d8%a7%d9%84%d8%a8%d8%b7%d8%a7%d9%84%d8%a9-%d9%81%d9%8a-%d9%84%d8%a8%d9%86%d8%a7%d9%86-%d9%88%d8%b5%d9%84%d8%aa-%d8%a7%d9%84%d9%89-25-%d9%8847-%d9%85%d9%86%d9%87%d9%85-%d8%b7/.

Pawlak, Justyna, and Adrian Croft. 'EU Adds Hezbollah's Military Wing to Terrorism List'. *Reuters*. 22 July 2013. http://www.reuters.com/article/us-eu-hezbollah-idUSBRE96K0DA20130722.

'Profile: Lebanon's Hezbollah Movement'. BBC News, 15 March 2016, sec. Middle East. http://www.bbc.com/news/world-middle-east-10814698.

Rabbath, E. *La Formation Historique Du Liban Politique et Constitutionel*. Université Libanaise, 1973.

Rabil, Robert. 'Salafism in Lebanon'. The Washington Institute, 20 February 2015. http://www.washingtoninstitute.org/policy-analysis/view/salafism-in-lebanon.

Refugees (UNHCR), United Nations High Commissioner for. 'UNHCR Syria Regional Refugee Response'. UNHCR Syria Regional Refugee Response, 6 June 2017. http://data.unhcr.org/syrianrefugees/regional.php.

Refugees, United Nations High Commissioner for. 'UNHCR and Partners Warn in Syria Report of Growing Poverty, Refugee Needs'. UNHCR, 5 July 2016. http://www.unhcr.org/news/press/2016/7/577b717a4/unhcr-partners-warn-syria-report-growing-poverty-refugee-needs.html.

Rizk, Charles. *Le Régime Politique Libanais*. Paris: Librairie générale de droit et de jurisprudence., 1966.

Šabacká, Yvona. 'The Role of the International Organizations in the Middle East with the Focus on the United Nations'. *The UN and Conflict Resolution*, 2007.

Safi, Michael. 'Hezbollah's "External Security" Branch Remains Listed by Australia as Terrorist Group'. The Guardian, 22 June 2015, sec. Australia news. https://www.theguardian.com/australia-news/2015/jun/22/hezbollahs-external-security-group-remains-listed-by-australia-as-terrorist.

Schenker, David. 'Lebanon's [Un]Civil Society'. *The Washington Institute*, March 2016. http://www.washingtoninstitute.org/policy-analysis/view/lebanons-uncivil-society.

Shaheen, Kareem. 'Fugitive Lebanese Cleric Ahmad Al-Assir Fails to Avoid Arrest with "70s Makeover"'. The Guardian. 17 August 2015, sec. World news. https://www.theguardian.com/world/2015/aug/17/fugitive-lebanese-cleric-ahmad-al-assir-arrest-70s-makeover-beirut.

Sune, Haugbolle. 'The Historiography and the Memory of the Lebanese Civil War'. *Sciences Po Violence de Masse et Résistance – Réseau de Recherche*, 25 October 2011. http://www.sciencespo.fr/mass-violence-war-massacre-resistance/fr/document/historiography-and-memory-lebanese-civil-war.

'Survey: Social Media Increasingly Popular in Lebanon'. Naharnet, 13 December 2012. http://www.naharnet.com/stories/en/64402.

'The Lebanese Demographic Reality'. Lebanese Information Center, 14 January 2013.

'The Lebanese Electoral System'. The International Foundation for Electoral Systems Lebanon, March 2009.

'The World Factbook – Lebanon'. Central Intelligence Agency, 23 June 2017. https://www.cia.gov/library/publications/the-world-factbook/geos/le.html.

'Thousands Protest against Lebanon's Sectarian System'. Reuters, 6 March 2011. http://www.reuters.com/article/us-lebanon-protest-idUSTRE7251SR20110306.

Trombetta, Lorenzo. 'Lebanon'. European Journalism Centre (EJC), 3 July 2017. http://ejc.net/media_landscapes/lebanon.

'Understanding Lebanese Confessionalism'. CJPME, May 2007. http://www.cjpme.org/fs_026.

Kristýna Stejskalová

Libya

Libya is a country that was probably never meant to unite. Three main regions – Cyrenaica, Tripolitania and Fezzan – that created the Great Socialist People's Libyan Arab Jamahiriya in 1977 have so many differences that one would hardly believe that it is possible to unify them. Muammar Gaddafi believed and proved it, but failed to give the country a strong system anchored in institutions that would allow this unification to work even under a different regime. That is the main reason why the regime change in Libya in 2011 did not end with democracy but with a civil war taking place in Libya ever since 2011.

The regime change in Libya started in 2011, at the time when Arab Spring was developing in different countries in the Middle East and North Africa (MENA) region. Nevertheless, Libya is not an example of a country that changed its regime due to Arab Spring influence. Regime change in Libya was imposed from abroad, therefore it is qualified as Foreign Imposed Regime Change (FIRC),[1] and due to its speed and the various interests of western countries that participated, Libya did not have enough time to realise Gaddafi was gone after 42 years of rule. Libya is an example of a country where democracy was imposed too fast, with low and underestimated preparations.

Regime change in Libya is sometimes associated with the Arab Spring, as it happened at the same time and had a slightly similar beginning. Protests in Libya began in February 2011 in Benghazi and turned into a fight between forces loyal to Gaddafi and protesters trying to oust his government. These protests then switched into a rebellion that spread across the country and led to the establishment of an interim governing body, named the National Transitional Council (NTC).[2] Gaddafi's military responded by conducting airstrikes against Libyan rebels. This situation led to a request for a no-fly zone that was sent to the UN by Libyan officials[3] as well as by international organizations.[4] The no-fly zone was established by UN resolution 1973 authorising Member States to take all

1 Reiter, *Foreign-Imposed Regime Change.*
2 Barker and wires, "Time Running out for Cornered Gaddafi."
3 "Global Arab Network | Libyan Ambassador to UN Urges International Community to Stop Genocide | Libya Politics | Politics."
4 "Arab States Seek Libya No-Fly Zone – Al Jazeera English."

necessary measures to protect civilians under threat of attack in the Libyan Arab Jamahiriya.[5] This no-fly zone then transformed into military intervention chasing Gaddafi, led by France and Great Britain, with the aim of changing Gaddafi's regime. Gaddafi was killed in October 2011 and it did not prevent the protests turning into civil war.

The NTC was formed in February 2011 to play the role of a government until democratic elections take place and governed the country for ten months. Then it held elections to the National General Congress (NGC) in July 2012.[6] The NGC was the legislative authority and its main task was to transition Libya to a permanent democratic constitution and after the election replaced the NTC, with the deadline being set for two years. When this deadline passed the NGC had to hold an election for a newly established House of Representatives, which took over power in August 2014.[7] Nevertheless, there was a minority of NGC representatives that were not re-elected and who cast doubt upon the election. Later, they declared themselves the new self-proclaimed General National Congress (GNC). This new GNC is supported by Islamist groups, dominated by the Libya Revolutionaries Operations Room (LROR) and the Libya Shield Force.[8] The GNC is neither recognised by the Libyan House of Representatives nor by foreign governments.

Since 2014, these two governments claim they are legitimate and refuse to give up power or cooperate with each other. This situation became the core of the current Libyan civil war and is the highest concern affecting the future of Libya. There were several initiatives to mediate the talks between the two governments, still with no visible progress. The latest attempts to mediate the talks were initiated by the United Nations, who established a third unity in Libya with the aim to include both fighting parties into a new government.[9] Until June 2017 this effort did not bring any significant improvement of the situation.

Libya is a unique example of a democratization effort which is publicly admitted as a failure of western countries, led by France and Great Britain, with the USA leading from behind. Barack Obama claimed that Libya was his worst mistake during his presidential era. He said that together with European partners they

5 "S/RES/1973 (2011) | United Nations Security Council Subsidiary Organs."

6 "Q&A."

7 "Congress Votes to Replace Itself with New House of Representatives."

8 Rosenthal, *The Jihadist Plot*.

9 "Libya's Unity Government Leaders in Tripoli Power Bid."

underestimated the need to come in full force, and that there had to be a much more aggressive effort to rebuild societies that did not have any civic traditions.[10]

This study focuses on the change in factors before 2011 and after the FIRC, explaining the failure of the democratization process. A detailed study of the factors influencing the progress of the regime change might allow a search for focus points for the establishment of democracy in this country that is currently in chaos and despair.

1. Internal non-institutional factors

Before studying any factors that might have an impact on regime change in Libya in 2011, it is crucial to understand how Gaddafi gained his power and what political and economic concept he imposed on the country. Muammar Gaddafi, who was then Captain of the Military, became the ruler of the country through a military coup in 1969 when he overthrew King Idris I. He immediately imposed a regime change and began a series of political and social reforms in the country. His main goal is described in his revolution motto: "Libya from the Libyans and for the Libyans." This signalised that the time when tribes were interfering into politics was over and that a voice was now given to popular participation.[11] Even though Gaddafi was considered a dictator, it is clear that it was him who gave the diverse population a feeling of citizenship and belonging as one nation. His thoughts of how the Libyan nation should be reformed can be found in his fundamental guidance book called *The Green Book*.[12] The system he prepared for the country was sustainable only under one condition: that he was the ruler. As *The Green Book* is based on his philosophy and how he perceived the Libyan nation as united, he always had the last word in all the country functioning processes in order to make sure Libya was aiming in the right direction. Therefore, his concept of functioning as a "one-man show" could not endure after he was overthrown.

1.1 Economic factors

Libya is an example of a democratization process where the economic process was tightly connected to the political situation. To understand the current crisis in Libya, it is necessary to reveal the principles on which the Libyan economy was based and how it functioned during Gaddafi's regime and after his fall. Therefore,

10 Tierney, "The Libya Intervention: Obama's 'Worst Mistake' as America's Worst Habit"
11 Lellou, "Libya: From All-Seeing Eye to the Evil Eye of Chaos."
12 Gaddafi, *Gaddafi's "The Green Book."*

the economic point of view will play a significant part in the explanation of the Libyan democratization milestones.

Economic development in Libya began in 1959 when American prospectors announced the discovery of petroleum deposits in eastern Libya. The following decade witnessed significant increases in both production and revenues. Nevertheless, the price of oil posted by the foreign companies was consistent and therefore Libya had to orientate its policy towards volume instead of price, fearing a confrontation with oil companies that might slow the development of the industry.[13] From the beginning, revenues from petroleum exports increased rapidly, growing more than fifteen-fold from $40 million in 1962 to $625 million in 1967. Within eight years of its first shipment, Libya became the fourth largest exporter of crude oil in the world. During this process Libya changed from a stagnant to an exploding economy, the state switched from capital-deficit to capital-surplus and the country became an aid extender instead of an aid recipient. By 1969 Libyan oil exports exceeded 3 million barrels per day. Despite such a rate of expansion that did not appear anywhere else in the industry's history, revenues received per barrel of oil remained one of the lowest in the world due to the low posted price.[14]

When Gaddafi took over power in 1969, he focused his first efforts on economic reforms aimed directly at oil companies. He opened negotiations with the oil companies working in Libya that concluded by either Gaddafi gaining a majority control in them through modified participation agreements or by complete nationalization.[15] Since then, petroleum has become the most effective political weapon in Libya.

Another stepping stone in the Libyan economy is the era after 1992 when the UN exposed sanctions on Libya due to little Libyan cooperation with investigations into two major terrorist attacks.[16] Sanctions led to increased isolation and mounting discontent in Libya and forced Gaddafi's regime to cooperate in the investigation. Finally, the UN abolished the sanctions, while the USA maintained them.[17]

The suspension of the UN sanctions happened at a time when the global demand for petroleum products strengthened and oil prices increased. As a result, Libya's hydrocarbon-based revenues increased sharply from 1999–2003, contributing around 50% of GDP, 97% of exports, and 75% of government revenues.

13 John, "The Changing Libyan Economy: Causes and Consequences."
14 Bakar Mahmud and Russell, "An Analysis of Libya's Revenue per Barrel from Crude Oil Upstream Activities, 1961–93."
15 Nathan Alexander, "Libya: The Continuous Revolution."
16 Deeb, "Qadhafi's Changed Policy: Causes and Consequences."
17 John, "The Changing Libyan Economy: Causes and Consequences."

Due to the high dependency on the oil and gas sector, the economy remained largely state-controlled. The International Monetary Fund (IMF) estimated in March 2005 that 75% of employment remained in the public sector, with private investment being low at 2% of GDP. The Libyan economy also faced a serious employment problem, caused by a high rate of population growth and a low rate of job creation.[18]

After the suspension of the UN sanctions, Gaddafi launched a wave of new initiatives in Africa and Europe with the aim of ending Libya's economic and political isolation. Despite the commitment to a course of economic liberalization, real progress in the non-petroleum sectors of the Libyan economy remained the subject of uncertainty.[19] In contrast, the process of liberalization in the oil and gas sector was more efficient. Libya had been for a long time an attractive investment destination for Europe, given its closeness to major European markets, relatively low extraction costs, and high-quality crude oil. This was especially significant when the UN sanctions were suspended, and the US embargo continued to block American companies from returning to Libya. When the National Oil Corporation offered more than 140 new oil blocks in 1999–2000, several European operators took advantage of expanded acreage in Libya.[20]

Libya's oil wealth, being spread over a small population of around 6 million people, allowed for a relatively high living standard compared to its neighbouring countries. Despite one of the highest unemployment rates in the region (20.7 % in 2009, 19.5 % in 2011)[21], there was a continuous lack of labour force, with over a million migrant workers present in the market. These migrant workers formed the bulk of the refugees who left Libya after the beginning of the hostilities.[22]

The regime change in Libya in 2011 caused a significant decrease of the Libyan economic potential and was reflected in many areas. According to the World Bank, The Libyan economy is near collapse as political stalemate and civil conflict prevent it from fully exploiting its crucial natural resource– oil. With oil production being on the level of just a fifth of its potential, revenues have sunk significantly, pushing fiscal and current account deficits to record highs. The Dinar rapidly lost its value and inflation rates changed according to the political situation, peaking

18 International Monetary Fund, "Socialist People's Libyan Arab Jamahiriya : Staff Report for the 2004 Article IV Consultation."

19 John, "The Changing Libyan Economy: Causes and Consequences."

20 Ronald, "Libya's Oil & Gas Industry: Blending Old and New."

21 "Libya Unemployment Rate | 2005–2017 | Data | Chart | Calendar | Forecast."

22 Garland, *2011 Libyan Civil War.*

in 2012 and again in 2016 at around 30%.[23] In addition to near-term challenges of macroeconomic and social/political stability, medium-term challenges include the need to rebuild the infrastructure and establish economic diversification for job creation and inclusive growth.[24]

Political and security instability in Libya have continued to affect the economy. Economic growth declined by 8.1% in 2016. The projected real GDP growth rate is estimated at -4.9% and -3.0% in 2017 and 2018, due to the projected rise in oil prices and the anticipated recovery of the crude oil production. A considerable decrease in oil production and a high degree of volatility in oil prices have affected both the current account and budget revenue. To control expenditure amidst reduced oil revenues, the Central Bank of Libya continues to provide funds only for wages and essential subsidies, while unemployment remains high, reaching 19.2% in 2016. Plans to implement industrial and entrepreneurship strategies have failed due to the ongoing unstable political situation. Limited institutional coordination within the Libyan public sector and a decrease in oil revenues negatively affect government revenue collection, obstruct budget revenues and fiscal management, and delays efforts and projects to diversify the economy from the oil sector towards more general industrialisation.[25]

The economic outlook in 2017 and 2018 largely depends on political unity and the extent of improvements in security. If progress is achieved, the economy will recover slowly, especially in the crude oil industry. Prospects also depend on the outcome of efforts to diversify the economy. Necessary reform programmes, enhanced ability to mobilise external resources, and diversification of the economy could release growth potential and produce important economic changes for Libya.[26] Nevertheless, all this is conditional to the stabilization of the political situation. If Libya does not have a unified government, it is not possible to run needed reforms or create the budget for the following years.

Building its economic growth solely on oil resources gave Gaddafi strong political power and allowed rocketing economic growth. On the other hand, it limited the economic potential of the country only to crude oil. An economic model which is highly dependent on political power becomes difficult to maintain during regime change, as the case of Libya confirmed. To ensure economic stability for the future, once the political situation stabilizes in Libya, the economic system needs to get institutional anchoring independent on political power and therefore

23 "Libya Inflation Rate | 2004–2017 | Data | Chart | Calendar | Forecast."

24 "Libya's Economic Outlook – October 2016."

25 Eita, "Libya."

26 Ibid.

sustainable under different political leadership. The other room for improvement is the political culture itself, which not only allows institutional principles to be anchored, but also allows the creation of civil society.

1.2 Civil society and media

Civil society almost does not exist in Libya[27] due to three main factors: diverse population, tribalism, and Gaddafi's way of ruling the country. The Libyan population is generally based on a tribal structure and in many areas people still identify themselves as part of the tribe. The most traditional tribes are Warfallah, Magarha, Zintan, Obeidat, Zawiya, and Kdadfa – from which Muammar Gaddafi also came.[28] Tribal structure was always typical for Libya and under the reign of King Idris, from 1951 to 1969[29], it was institutionalised. At that time, most significance and most seats in the federal government was given to tribes in Cyrenaica, from which King Idris came, even though tribes in Tripolitania were demographically stronger.[30] Therefore, the origin of people plays another important factor in people's identification.

There are significant differences among people from different regions. Tripolitania is generally perceived as the most developed region. People who were born here identify themselves as Libyans and incline to perceive themselves as responsible for the development of Libya.[31] Most important decisions have been made in Tripolitania since the revolution in 1969, when Gaddafi transported the centre of the country from Benghazi in Cyrenaica to Tripoli in Tripolitania. Cyrenaica is still perceived as region with a strong tribal structure. For Gaddafi, it was always the most problematic region in terms of opposition, caused mainly by Cyrenaica's loss of position as the most important region once Gaddafi seized power. Fezzan is a region with an extreme climate. Most of the region consists of desert and rough rocks, and due to the southwest location of Fezzan, its population is closer to sub-Saharan Africa than to the Middle East. Due to difficult life conditions, people from the Fezzan region had to cohere and create a strong tribal structure. These three regions have existed as separate units for more than three thousand years, and they differ by climate, by population structure, and by the Arabic language,

27 Boose, "Democratization and Civil Society: Libya, Tunisia and the Arab Spring."
28 Lellou, "Libya: From All-Seeing Eye to the Evil Eye of Chaos."
29 "Idris I | King of Libya."
30 Haimzadeh, *Au Coeur de La Libye de Kadhafi.*
31 Lellou, "Libya: From All-Seeing Eye to the Evil Eye of Chaos."

which has its own strong dialect in different areas. Therefore, it is fundamentally very difficult to unite people in Libya.

Gaddafi also prohibited political parties, and only a few civil-society organizations were legalized. After his defeat, political and administrative structures were destroyed and that created a short-term vacuum that enabled civil society to evolve. After Gaddafi's fall hundreds of non-governmental organisations were quickly organized (4,000 by the end of 2014). The formation of political parties started at the end of 2011, as parliamentary elections were scheduled for 2012.[32] In February 2011, Gaddafi's son, Saif al-Islam, appeared in a TV broadcast and warned people that Libya is made up of tribes, clans, and loyalties and that now there was going to be a civil war.[33] Today, civil society in Libya consists only of fragmented militias competing for power, and weak organisations focusing on democratization.[34]

The difficulties with the establishment of a functioning civil society are also connected to the role of the media. Under Gaddafi's regime, the government owned most of the national media, such as the TV network *Great Jamahiriyah TV* and *Great Jamahiriyah Radio,* both of which had national coverage and significant importance.[35] Regarding printed media, there was one weekly newspaper owned by government, *Al Jamahiria,* and others were owned by private companies, but had pro-government rhetoric.[36] Gaddafi's son, Saif al-Islam, who was then widely considered a reformer, set up another two private newspapers, which groused about problems in governance but did not attempt to challenge Gaddafi's rule.[37] Gaddafi also controlled all civilian communications and due to restrictions on the import of satellite telephones, the population was forced to use state-controlled networks. There were two main telephone operators, both state-owned.[38]

Within months of the regime change in February 2011, the Libyans founded an independent media to fill the market gap and get as much independent information as possible. There was a hope of establishing real freedom of speech. Nevertheless, with the new government taking over the country after Gaddafi, the situation did not significantly improve. The Libyan congress (GNC) passed a

32 Mattes, "Libya since 2011: Political Transformation and Violence."

33 "Libya Protests."

34 Boose, "Democratization and Civil Society: Libya, Tunisia and the Arab Spring."

35 Press, *Libya Media, Internet & Telecommunications Complete Profile: This All-Inclusive Profile Includes All Three of Our Communications Reports.*

36 Ibid.

37 Thorne, "In Libya, Media Freedom Isn't Bulletproof."

38 Ripley, "War of Words – Social Media as a Weapon in Libya's Conflict."

law allowing authorities to censor TV stations if they criticized the 2011 regime change, undermined security, or propagated discord amongst Libyans. Originally, this law was aimed at two pro-Gaddafi TV stations, but due to its vague wording it allowed for a potentially much wider application that threatened freedom of speech and allowed the media only to present opinions from one party's point of view.[39]

A special role in the process of regime change in Libya was given to the social media. These allowed domestic and international audiences to watch the arising conflict almost live. Military intervention in Libya gave social media a new international prominence, because it was the very first time in history when social media provided real-time coverage of a major conventional conflict involving NATO, the USA, and other armed forces.[40] In the first days of the Libyan uprising, Twitter feeds, YouTube sites, Facebook pages, and Internet blogs run by opposition groups or by Libyan exiles became the main sources of information and imagery of what was happening.[41] These were also the only sources able to react promptly to the situation, unlike government-owned media.[42]

After the fall of Benghazi in March 2011, Gaddafi closed down the mobile services, landline-based internet, and other telephone services to the east of the country, and all internet and mobile data services, including SMS, were closed down across the country. These moves aimed to prevent opposition groups getting their messages out and using the advantages of social networks to influence the local and international public. Opposition groups succeeded in restarting mobile telephone coverage across the east of the country in April 2011 after tapping into the national cellular network that allowed limited internet and SMS text connectivity to rebel units.[43]

Recovery of communication networks and the internet also introduced another role of the social media – assistance to military forces. People tweeted target information that NATO could use for its air strikes against Gaddafi's forces. Even though NATO claimed that air strikes were not conducted according to tweets from Libya, this tool played an important role for the exploration of the area.[44]

A few international journalists (mainly British and American journalists from the BBC, Sky, CNN, Fox, Reuters, Associated Press, and Chinese television),[45]

39 Thorne, "In Libya, Media Freedom Isn't Bulletproof."
40 Ripley, "War of Words – Social Media as a Weapon in Libya's Conflict."
41 Ibid.
42 Ibid.
43 Ibid.
44 Ibid.
45 Sherwood, "Libya Conflict."

operated in Libya at the beginning of the conflict in 2011. These journalists worked under the close supervision of the Libyan government and were not allowed to travel freely. Therefore, international news organizations frequently relied on phone reports from people who were currently on the ground then. This meant that the media could not independently verify accounts and so reported them as "claims" or "allegations" rather than "facts."[46] The restrictions on and the attempts to control the media by the Gaddafi-led regime continued until the government fled from Tripoli.

Gaddafi's opposition, on the other hand, took a completely different approach to international journalists. As soon as the opposition acquired the territorial base of Benghazi, foreign reporters could join them. These reporters were free to travel wherever they wanted and could talk to whomever they wished within opposition-controlled areas. This proximity and relative freedom of travel, combined with reporters' natural sympathies for what they saw as genuine popular rebellions against despotic regimes, undoubtedly aided the opposition and hurt Gaddafi's government in getting their respective messages out.[47]

1.3 Religion and extremism

Almost 97% of Libyans are Muslims and most of these belong to the Sunni branch of Islam and a small community of Christians, most of which creates the Christian Church of Egypt.[48] After the fall of Gaddafi's regime, when Libya turned into a civil war, many extremist groups from the ultra-conservative strains of Islam and armed militias arose. The Islamic State (IS) posed one of the biggest threats. Libya is strategically important for groups like IS, because it gives them a relatively calm environment to operate, in comparison to Iraq and Syria where it faces daily bombardment by US-led coalition airstrikes. IS in Libya also took advantage of oil resources that became core funding for the group's terror activities. Even though IS is only one of many fractions trying to take control over Libya, their activities are considered as most dangerous. Luckily, IS faces strong resistance from the citizens within Libya and it is more difficult for them to attract Libyans by their ideology than citizens in Iraq and Syria.[49] IS made their base in the city of Derna in eastern Libya in 2014[50] and was taken over by the Shura Council of Mujahideen in Derna,

46 "BBC – The Editors."
47 "Libya: Media on the Frontlines of Revolution – Al Jazeera English."
48 "The World Factbook — Central Intelligence Agency."
49 Besheer, "UN: Libya at Risk From Forces of Extremism."
50 "Derna."

one of the ultra-conservative Islamic militias, after the Libyan parliament failed to liberate the city in 2016.[51]

From February 2015, IS took over the strategically crucial coastal city of Sirte after clashes with militias there.[52] The Battle of Sirte happened from May until December 2016, when the Libyan Government of National Accord (GNA), backed up by the USA, retook the city.[53] Nevertheless, IS still poses the biggest threat to Libya as a country, since a civil war creates a convenient environment for terrorist groups and militias.

2. Internal institutional factors

Internal institutional factors are affected by the regime change in Libya the most, mainly due to the fact that they function according to the principles set by Gaddafi. After the regime change, institutions were not ready for the transition and therefore the political and security situation turned into chaos and despair.

2.1 Security and defence structures

The security situation in Libya worsened significantly after the regime change. During the reign of Muammar Gaddafi, the military structures were almost wholly subordinated to the political structures of Gaddafi's regime.[54] This system allowed Gaddafi to take control over the whole of Libya and make sure there were no uprisings or local conflicts. During the reign of Gaddafi, the National Army consisted of approximately 25,000 professional soldiers plus 25,000 conscripts.[55]

Gaddafi's National Army was defeated in 2011 by the uprising and NATO and it was disbanded. The new Libyan National Army was founded by the NTC in 2011. The loss of state control also caused emerging conflicts between cities and ethnic groups and tribes, which had been repressed for years, and generated armed struggles for power and resources.[56]

Militias are currently present in Libya on a large scale. They started as small groups of three or five men. Over time, these small units gained more supporters and merged based on existing social ties. They transformed into a form of

51 Times, "Al-Qaida-Linked-Militants-Attack-Is-Affiliate-in-Libya."

52 Besheer, "UN: Libya at Risk From Forces of Extremism."

53 "US AFRICOM Ends Military Operation against IS Radicals in Libya."

54 Vandewalle, "After Qaddafi: The Surprising Success of the New Libya."

55 Under the Gaddafi's regime, conscription was mandatory for the duration of 18 months ("The World Factbook — Central Intelligence Agency.")

56 Terrill, "The Libyan Revolution and Its Aftermath."

autonomous fighting groups, known as revolutionary brigades, which usually consist of 30 to 70 combatants.[57] These fighting groups might have both positive and negative impacts on security. In cities, where they have strong support from the local communities, they cooperate quite well with local security structures. This prevents conflicts and increases the security level. On the other hand, in cities where these fighting groups are not associated with local authorities but operate on their own, the probability of conflict rises, and they often get into fights with other armed militias trying to gain power in the area.

2.2 Political factors

Before the regime change in 2011, the political system in Libya was based on Gaddafi's idea of creating the Great Socialist People's Libyan Arab Jamahiriya on 2 March 1977 by adopting the Declaration of the Establishment of the People's Authority.[58] This concept of state was unique to Libya, but Gaddafi tried to propose it as a concept suitable for all Third World states – as a concept of his Third International Theory. This concept is a unique mixture of Islamic socialism, Arab nationalism, and African nationalism and is enriched by several principles of direct democracy.[59] Gaddafi's concept of government principles was unique and progressive in comparison with the majority of countries in the MENA region.

Gaddafi rejected the democratic form of government, because it is a system that allows a minority to take the lead over a majority. He also did not support the concept of parliament as representatives of the people, because representatives who were elected created in his opinion a separation between the people and the government of the country. As stated in *The Green Book*, "*A parliament is originally founded to represent the people, but this in itself is undemocratic as democracy means the authority of the people and not an authority acting on their behalf. The mere existence of a parliament means the absence of the people.*"[60] For Gaddafi, real democracy meant only direct democracy, therefore direct participation of the people in the decision-making process. Because this was one of the main principles of the government that Gaddafi spread amongst the Libyan population, it became rooted in people's perception of the government. This might be one of the reasons why today in Libya there are two parliaments which struggle to get recognition by people who may not believe in the principle of parliament itself.

57 McQuinn, "Assessing (In) Security after the Arab Spring: The Case of Libya."
58 "ICL – Libya – Declaration on the Establishment of the Authority of the People."
59 St. John, *Libya*.
60 Gaddafi, *Gaddafi's "The Green Book."*

The perception of democracy in Libya is still affected by Gaddafi's concept of an Islamic socialist republic, therefore the transition is difficult. According to the Democracy Index, Libya was ranked as an authoritarian regime during Gaddafi's rule and this ranking did not change even after the regime change in 2011, and today Libya is still marked as authoritarian regime.[61]

2.3 Rule of law

Gaddafi also applied his thoughts about democracy to the instrument of the rule of law. He refused the principle of committees and assemblies making the laws of society binding to the general public. The origin of natural law is rooted in either tradition or religion, and any constitution is justified based on these traditions, but is customised to the needs of the current government. Gaddafi supported religion as being the supreme supervising instrument covering all the needs of society and allowing people to coordinate their behaviour naturally. His concept of social supervision was driven by a core thought of society being self-supervised according to traditions and religion.[62]

3. External factors

Gaddafi's policy towards Libya's neighbours was often a matter of dispute within the international community. As he was trying to gain more power and influence in the region, western leaders became fearful of his expansion and therefore changed their policies towards him, culminating in the Foreign Imposed Regime Change in 2011. The cause of the regime change is highly affected by Gaddafi's behaviour on the international scene.

3.1 Neighbouring countries

Libya has six countries as neighbours – Egypt, Sudan, Chad, Niger, Algeria, and Tunisia. Libya has always maintained bilateral relations with these countries. Moreover, it has acted as an African leader initiating larger scale projects.[63] Gaddafi could maintain positive bilateral relationships with its neighbouring countries only as long as these countries did not cooperate with the West, particularly the USA.

Libya–Egypt relations were always more or less cooperative. Egypt did not specifically support Gaddafi during the regime change in 2011, as it had to face

61 "Democracy Index – Knoema.com."
62 Gaddafi, *Gaddafi's "The Green Book."*
63 "Groundwater in International Law."

its own revolution as well. The revolution in Egypt might have influenced Libya's opposition movements, supported by information spreading through the social media network. Egypt supported Libya militarily during the fight with IS in the city of Derna from 2014 until 2016.[64]

Gaddafi always tended to intervene in Sudan's internal politics and supported the Darfur rebel movements, and had even greater ambitions in the Darfur region. His financial and military support to the Darfur rebel movements became one of the triggers of the Sudan crisis. As a revolt, Sudan also participated in the regime change in Libya 2011, through effective collaboration with the NTC, and the international community standing against Gaddafi. The Sudanese government provided security and military assistance to the Libyan rebels against the Gaddafi's regime, and helped the NTC to gain political and military power in Libya.[65]

Gaddafi always tried to maintain his influence in Niger, mainly by the means of financial aid to the country. Therefore, Niger never intervened into Gaddafi's policies with other states or reacted to his way of ruling Libya. Although after regime change in 2011 Niger recognised the NTC as the legitimate governing authority,[66] the country tried to maintain good relationships with the former Libyan government as well. In September 2011, a convoy arrived in Niger carrying several members of the former Gaddafi government as well as stockpiles of gold bullion belonging to the Libyan treasury. After NTC's requests to stop the convoy and extradite these people back to Libya, Niger's government firstly denied any presence of the convoy in Niger, and later decided to give refugee status to the Libyans as they were not sought by the International Criminal Court. Shortly after that, Niger's government gave asylum to one of Gaddafi's sons, as-Saadi Gaddafi.[67] The NTC still requires the extradition of Gaddafi's generals and his son, but Niger's government refuses to extradite them due to humanitarian reasons, as in Libya they would face the death penalty.

There is a similar story with the Algeria–Libya relations, which were always friendly during the rule of Gaddafi. After the regime change in 2011, Algeria was accused by the NTC of supporting Gaddafi by allowing him to traffic military equipment through Algerian territory.[68] Relationships between Algeria and the NTC became tense, and that culminated in the closing of borders between these two countries. It was initially requested from the NTC's side due to Algeria's loyalty

64 "Derna."
65 Elhag, "The Sudanese Role in Libya 2011 | Reinventing Peace."
66 "Niger, Benin and Togo Recognise Libyan Rebels | Reuters."
67 "Gaddafi Generals Seek Asylum in Niger."
68 Al Baik, "Rebel Council Calls on UN to Hit Mercenary Bases."

to Gaddafi, but Algeria decided to keep the border closed arguing a worsening security situation in Libya that might have threatened Algeria as well.[69]

Libya–Tunisia relations were always unpredictable, with ups and downs during the history of both states. Their good or neutral relationship was always based on economic cooperation and trade exchange. For Tunisia, Libya was always the most important trade partner in Africa. In 2009, total trade reached €1.25 billion in value terms, while Libya absorbed about 6.9% of Tunisia's exports, mainly industrial products. Since the regime change in Libya in 2011, Tunisia's main concern is the security threat posed by terrorist groups training their fighters very close to the Tunisian border. These fighters also attract Tunisian citizens from terrorist groups such as Ansar al-Sharia. These Tunisian terrorist groups are then reinforced by jihadists who gained experience on the Middle East's battlefields and then return via Libya to their home. Another security risk is the smuggling of weapons and ammunition over the border. For this reason, a wall was also built on the Tunisian border with Libya.[70]

3.2 Foreign relations

With such a strong anti-western approach, it was obvious that many countries had issues with Gaddafi, especially when his influence on the African Continent grew. Gaddafi's most difficult relationship was with the USA. Disputes between the USA and Libya began when Gaddafi nationalised the oil industry in the country and therefore removed American oil companies.[71] The situation improved after 9/11, when Gaddafi started to cooperate with western intelligence services by sharing information about Al-Qaeda and another Islamic group that were threatening both the USA and Gaddafi. The first big step towards improvement of Libya–US relations was the decision of President George W. Bush to follow up diplomatic relations with Libya, and to nominate a new ambassador in 2007, the first since 1972. Nevertheless, he failed to push this idea through Congress, which blocked this confirmation as well as funding for the new embassy in Tripoli.[72]

Barack Obama was very restrained when it came to relations with Gaddafi. A famous picture from the meeting ahead of the G-8 summit shows Obama and

69 "Algeria's Military Chief Calls Alert over Libyan Frontier."

70 AfDB, *North Africa Quaterly Analytical – Impact of Libya's Conflict on the Tunisian Economy – A Preliminary Assessment – Issue 2.*

71 Asser, "The Muammar Gaddafi Story."

72 John, "LIBYA AND THE UNITED STATES: A FAUSTIAN PACT?"

Gaddafi shaking hands as a sign of the renewed US–Libya relationship.[73] When the air strikes led by NATO took place in Libya, Gaddafi wrote a three-page letter to Barack Obama, calling him "our son," asking him to stop the strikes and wishing him all the best of luck in the upcoming presidential elections.[74] Nevertheless, Barack Obama hailed the death of Muammar Gaddafi as a foreign policy success.[75]

Gaddafi also had complicated relations with the United Kingdom. Gaddafi became very close to former UK Prime Minister Tony Blair, whose handshake with Gaddafi in a tent on the outskirts of Tripoli in 2004 confirmed the "Deal in the Desert" that set the tone for Gaddafi's transformation from an international pariah into a favoured ally. This deal made Gaddafi agree to abandon his nuclear and chemical weapons programmes, and confirmed Libya's complicity in US rendition operations. British oil firms benefited from that deal by gaining lucrative contracts, while the Gaddafi family moved billions of dollars in assets to London and ensured access to influential circles, with Gaddafi's son Saif acquiring a PhD from the London School of Economics.[76] The United Kingdom's approach to Libya completely changed with the election of the Conservative Prime Minister David Cameron. He wanted to distinguish his foreign policy from his Labour predecessor, and together with then French president Nikolas Sarkozy he became one of the main leaders of the military intervention in Libya in 2011.[77]

Gaddafi supported, financially and/or militarily, several rebel groups and terrorist organisations. These were the Provisional Irish Republican Army (IRA) in Ireland,[78] Basque Fatherland and Liberty (ETA),[79] the Polisario Front in Western Sahara,[80] the Moro National Liberation Front in the Philippines,[81] and Umkhonto we Sizwe – Xhosa in South Africa.[82]

---

73 "Obama Shakes Hands With Libya's Qaddafi | Fox News."

74 "READ QADDAFI'S LETTER TO OBAMA: 'Our Dear Son, Excellency, Baraka Hussein Abu Oumama' – Business Insider."

75 MacAskill, "Obama Hails Death of Muammar Gaddafi as Foreign Policy Success."

76 "A Brief History of UK-Libya Relations."

77 Wintour and Watt, "David Cameron's Libyan War."

78 "The 38-Year Connection between Irish Republicans and Gaddafi – BBC News."

79 "Colonel Gaddafi."

80 Fiddian-Qasmiyeh, *South-South Educational Migration, Humanitarianism and Development*.

81 "Moro National Liberation Front | Mapping Militant Organizations."

82 Kirchick, "South Africa Stands With Qaddafi."

4. Conclusion

Libya does not fit into the concept of the Arab Spring, because foreign western countries imposed the regime change in 2011. As a result of the democratization process Libya became a stagnant state. Two opposite sides are struggling over power in the country, oil resources are in many areas occupied by rebel and terrorist groups, and the country is tormented by a civil war.

The failure of the regime transition in Libya was predictable. Given the 42 years of Gaddafi's rule that set the country into a unique concept of a Socialist Islamic Republic with democratic patterns, the Libyan population got used to a different concept of a political system than was applied after Gaddafi's regime was defeated. Moreover, given the structure of the Libyan population, defined by regional differences and tribal structures, it was highly predictable that the country would fall into civil war. To unite three different regions is possible only by strong rule in combination with the principle of recognition of local communities. Gaddafi was able to establish this system and maintain a united Libya while working on the country's development for more than four decades. Nevertheless, after he left it was obvious that his system was not sufficiently institutionally rooted and was highly dependent on him. The loss of state control enabled conflict constellations between cities, ethnic groups and tribes, which had been repressed for years, to surface with force, and generated armed struggles for power and resources.

The chaos taking place in Libya today threatens not just the Libyan population, but also the whole African continent, and moreover the European Security Area. Libya became an unguarded haven for terrorist groups, armed rebel militias, functioning as a trafficking route for arms smuggling and for migrants from Africa who want to get to the European continent. The future of Libya is unsure, even though the international community admitted responsibility for the failure of the Libyan state and tries to act as a mediator between the two fighting parties. One thing is clear – if Libya's desperate situation is not solved soon, it will threaten international security in many aspects.

Political instability with an unclear governmental structure is causing the main obstruction in the way of the Libyan transition to democracy. Solving this situation will be the first step for Libya to recover from its civil war. Nevertheless, due to the population structure and large number of influential groups fighting over power, the legitimacy of any new government will always be questioned by other parties, and political stability will be more or less always threatened in Libya.

References

"A Brief History of UK-Libya Relations." June 16, 2017. http://www.aljazeera.com/indepth/features/2015/12/history-uk-libya-relations-151210095534126.html.

AfDB, AfDB. *North Africa Quarterly Analytical – Impact of Libya's Conflict on the Tunisian Economy – A Preliminary Assessment – Issue 2.* African Development Bank, 2011. June 10, 2017: http://EconPapers.repec.org/RePEc:adb:adbcbr:323.

Al Baik, Duraid. "Rebel Council Calls on UN to Hit Mercenary Bases." *GulfNews*, March 2011. http://gulfnews.com/news/mena/libya/rebel-council-calls-on-un-to-hit-mercenary-bases-1.771287.

Alexander, Nathan. "Libya: The Continuous Revolution." *Middle Eastern Studies* 17, no. 2 (1981): 210–27.

"Algeria's Military Chief Calls Alert over Libyan Frontier." *Reuters*, March 14, 2016. http://www.reuters.com/article/us-algeria-security-idUSKCN0WG1EE.

"Arab States Seek Libya No-Fly Zone – Al Jazeera English." June 28, 2017. http://www.aljazeera.com/news/africa/2011/03/201131218852687848.html.

Asser, Martin. "The Muammar Gaddafi Story." *BBC News*, October 21, 2011, sec. Africa. http://www.bbc.com/news/world-africa-12688033.

Bakar Mahmud, Mustafa, and Alex Russell. "An Analysis of Libya's Revenue per Barrel from Crude Oil Upstream Activities, 1961–93." OPEC Review, September 1999. Vol. 23, No. 3 (213–249).

Barker, AM Middle East correspondent Anne, and wires. "Time Running out for Cornered Gaddafi." Text. *ABC News*, February 24, 2011. http://www.abc.net.au/news/2011-02-24/time-running-out-for-cornered-gaddafi/1955842.

"BBC – The Editors: The Difficulty of Reporting from inside Libya." June 10, 2017. http://www.bbc.co.uk/blogs/theeditors/2011/02/reporting_from_libya.html.

Besheer, Margaret. "UN: Libya at Risk From Forces of Extremism." Lanham: Federal Information & News Dispatch, Inc., December 11, 2015. 1748603929. ProQuest Central. https://search.proquest.com/docview/1748603929?accountid=17203.

Boose, Jason William. "Democratization and Civil Society: Libya, Tunisia and the Arab Spring." *International Journal of Social Science and Humanity* 2, no. 4 (July 2012): 310–n/a. doi:10.7763/IJSSH.2012.V2.116.

"Colonel Gaddafi." *History TV*, April 21, 2017. http://www.history.co.uk/biographies/colonel-gadaffi.

"Congress Votes to Replace Itself with New House of Representatives." *Libya Herald*. June 11, 2017. https://www.libyaherald.com/2014/03/30/congress-votes-to-replace-itself-with-new-house-of-representatives/.

Deeb, Mary-Jane. "Qadhafi's Changed Policy: Causes and Consequences." *Middle East Policy* 7, no. 2 (February 2000): 146–53.

"Democracy Index – Knoema.com." *Knoema*. June 28, 2017. https://knoema.com//GDI2016/democracy-index?country=1001560-libya.

"Derna: An Islamic State Emirate on Egypt's Borders." *Egypt Independent*. October 15, 2014. http://www.egyptindependent.com/derna-islamic-state-emirate-egypt-s-borders/.

Eita, Yasmine. "Libya." *African Economic Outlook*, 2016. June 10, 2017. http://www.africaneconomicoutlook.org/en/country-notes/libya.

Elhag, Asim. "The Sudanese Role in Libya 2011 | Reinventing Peace." June 10, 2017. https://sites.tufts.edu/reinventingpeace/2012/12/17/the-sudanese-role-in-libya-2011/.

Fiddian-Qasmiyeh, Elena. *South-South Educational Migration, Humanitarianism and Development: Views from Cuba, North Africa and the Middle East*, 2015. http://search.ebscohost.com/login.aspx?direct=true&scope=site&db=nlebk&db=nlabk&AN=939446.

"Gaddafi Generals Seek Asylum in Niger." *News24*, September 13, 2011. http://www.news24.com/Africa/News/Gaddafi-generals-seek-asylum-in-Niger-20110913.

Gaddafi, Muammar. *Gaddafi's "The Green Book."* Vol. 2016. CreateSpace Independent Publishing Platform, 2016.

Garland, Landen. *2011 Libyan Civil War*. Delhi: White Word Publications, 2012. http://public.eblib.com/choice/publicfullrecord.aspx?p=841143.

"Global Arab Network | Libyan Ambassador to UN Urges International Community to Stop Genocide | Libya Politics | Politics." June 28, 2017. http://www.english.globalarabnetwork.com/201102219941/Libya-Politics/libyan-ambassador-to-un-urges-international-community-to-stop-genocide.html.

"Groundwater in International Law." June 10, 2017. http://www.fao.org/docrep/008/y5739e/y5739e05.htm.

Haimzadeh, Patrick. *Au Coeur de La Libye de Kadhafi*. Paris: JC Lattès, 2011.

"ICL – Libya – Declaration on the Establishment of the Authority of the People." June 11, 2017. http://www.servat.unibe.ch/icl/ly01000_.html.

"Idris I | King of Libya." *Encyclopedia Britannica*. June 28, 2017. https://www.britannica.com/biography/Idris-I-king-of-Libya.

International Monetary Fund. "Socialist People's Libyan Arab Jamahiriya: Staff Report for the 2004 Article IV Consultation," March 2005. http://www.imf.org/external/pubs/cat/longres.aspx?sk=18109.0.

John, Ronald Bruce St. "LIBYA AND THE UNITED STATES: A FAUSTIAN PACT?" *Middle East Policy* 15, no. 1 (2008): 133–48.

–. "The Changing Libyan Economy: Causes and Consequences." *The Middle East Journal* 62, no. 1 (2008): 75–91.

Kirchick, James. "South Africa Stands With Qaddafi." *The Atlantic.* September 6, 2011. https://www.theatlantic.com/international/archive/2011/09/south-africa-stands-with-qaddafi/244584/.

Lellou, Hamid. "Libya: From All-Seeing Eye to the Evil Eye of Chaos." *Marine Corps Gazette* 100, no. 2 (February 2016): 68–69.

"Libya Inflation Rate | 2004–2017 | Data | Chart | Calendar | Forecast." June 28, 2017. tradingeconomics.com/libya/inflation-cpi.

"Libya: Media on the Frontlines of Revolution – Al Jazeera English." June 10, 2017. http://www.aljazeera.com/programmes/listeningpost/2011/09/2011938838405146.html.

"Libya Protests: Gaddafi's Son Warns of Civil War." *BBC News*, February 21, 2011, sec. Middle East. http://www.bbc.com/news/world-middle-east-12520586.

"Libya Unemployment Rate | 2005–2017 | Data | Chart | Calendar | Forecast." June 28, 2017. https://tradingeconomics.com/libya/unemployment-rate.

"Libya's Economic Outlook- October 2016." Text/HTML. *World Bank*. June 4, 2017. http://www.worldbank.org/en/country/libya/publication/economic-outlook-fall-2016.

"Libya's Unity Government Leaders in Tripoli Power Bid." *BBC News*, March 31, 2016, sec. Africa. http://www.bbc.com/news/world-africa-35929232.

MacAskill, Ewen. "Obama Hails Death of Muammar Gaddafi as Foreign Policy Success." *The Guardian.* October 20, 2011, sec. World news. https://www.theguardian.com/world/2011/oct/20/obama-hails-death-gaddafi.

Mattes, Hanspeter. "Libya since 2011: Political Transformation and Violence." *Middle East Policy* 23, no. 2 (2016): 59–75.

McQuinn, Brian. "Assessing (In) Security after the Arab Spring: The Case of Libya." *PS: Political Science and Politics* 46, no. 4 (2013): 716–20.

"Moro National Liberation Front | Mapping Militant Organizations." June 10, 2017. http://web.stanford.edu/group/mappingmilitants/cgi-bin/groups/view/379.

"Niger, Benin and Togo Recognise Libyan Rebels | Reuters." June 10, 2017. http://www.reuters.com/article/idINIndia-59007720110827.

"Obama Shakes Hands With Libya's Qaddafi | Fox News." June 16, 2017. http://www.foxnews.com/politics/2009/07/09/obama-shakes-hands-libyas-qaddafi.html.

Press, World Trade. *Libya Media, Internet & Telecommunications Complete Profile: This All-Inclusive Profile Includes All Three of Our Communications Reports.* 2;2nd; Book, Whole. Petaluma: World Trade Press, 2010. http://vse.summon.

serialssolutions.com/2.0.0/link/0/eLvHCXMwnV1LS8NAEB58XMSDWl-1CnsSBRPTZJt0vWjxgaBokargpWx2Z7FQ29K0ov4D_7WzSVpaFQ9ed5JhwiwzX2bn2wEIfNdzvsUEaYSJwkhUVCwjJIhNbvdDZSh_cIFoycm1O_F0FdUfLa375I8D1NcEe4eHuqvO0h5LN-v_P9Y5pLXnbpVgFub9CqVuy-h7uBkXXSg087KdgPs7x-hHPE6TzMVS1gySTiKzHdbuh7ZVEpcscdXHz-sb_231MsyjpTiswAx2CrA4MSvhvQClHKK2khe2y6b4I0kBihmdl-UhIWF7-b3V-6vwed2K3yWzRz_ygGWlRhyQkoadtTOlyOrt0Y5BVs9mhrMj1nhuJazWbjsUstpD21U_FqYrGlMxPddHZF3Dbof9b_ax7HciWYP7i_PG6aWTT3pwNH126JhICRmpclyOKGcHUlUrWOWGkoKSOsJqWDaxp7lPMUIbTZgv9qSWMvbiqgxQm2Ad5jrdDm4CI8SGXiwVD7kgqMel8ALFZegbgVxoWYTSpO-bvexSjyaZQei3CBs4vT7yTfrelGTwNpiQbo92TjNVn7fW5mq3_haXYCFrSrCVnW2YG_SHuAOztGe-ADdHBh0.

“Q&A: Libya’s General National Congress Election.” *BBC News*, July 7, 2012, sec. Africa. http://www.bbc.com/news/world-africa-18341022.

“READ QADDAFI’S LETTER TO OBAMA: ‘Our Dear Son, Excellency, Baraka Hussein Abu Oumama’ – Business Insider.” June 16, 2017. http://www.businessinsider.com/qaddafi-obama-letter-2011–4.

Reiter, Dan. *Foreign-Imposed Regime Change*. Oxford University Press, n.d. //politics.oxfordre.com/10.1093/acrefore/9780190228637.001.0001/acrefore-9780190228637-e-335.

Ripley, Tim. “War of Words – Social Media as a Weapon in Libya’s Conflict.” *Jane’s Intelligence Review* 23, no. 9 (September 1, 2011). https://search.proquest.com/docview/885963710?accountid=17203.

Ronald, Bruce St John. “Libya’s Oil & Gas Industry: Blending Old and New.” *The Journal of North African Studies* 12, no. 2 (June 1, 2007): 203–18. doi:10.1080/13629380701220428.

Rosenthal, John. *The Jihadist Plot: The Untold Story of Al-Qaeda and the Libyan Rebellion*. First American edition. New York: Encounter Books, 2013.

Sherwood, Harriet. “Libya Conflict: Journalists Trapped in Tripoli’s Rixos Hotel.” *The Guardian*, August 24, 2011, sec. World news. https://www.theguardian.com/world/2011/aug/24/libya-journalists-trapped-tripoli-hotel.

“S/RES/1973 (2011) | United Nations Security Council Subsidiary Organs.” June 28, 2017. https://www.un.org/sc/suborg/en/s/res/1973-%282011%29.

St. John, Ronald Bruce. *Libya: Continuity and Change*. Contemporary Middle East. Abingdon, Oxon; New York: Routledge, 2011.

Terrill, W. Andrew. “The Libyan Revolution and Its Aftermath.” *Parameters* 45, no. 4 (2015): 93.

“The 38-Year Connection between Irish Republicans and Gaddafi – BBC News.” June 10, 2017. http://www.bbc.com/news/uk-northern-ireland-12539372.

"The World Factbook — Central Intelligence Agency." Accessed June 10, 2017. https://www.cia.gov/library/publications/the-world-factbook/geos/ly.html.

"The World Factbook — Central Intelligence Agency." Accessed June 11, 2017. https://www.cia.gov/library/publications/the-world-factbook/fields/2024.html.

Thorne, John. "In Libya, Media Freedom Isn't Bulletproof." *The Christian Science Monitor*. May 5, 2014. 1520820118. ProQuest Central. https://www.csmonitor.com/World/Middle-East/2014/0505/In-Libya-media-freedom-isn-t-bulletproof.

Tierney, Dominic. "The Libya Intervention: Obama's 'Worst Mistake' as America's Worst Habit." *The Atlantic*, April 15, 2016. https://www.theatlantic.com/international/archive/2016/04/obamas-worst-mistake-libya/478461/.

Times, Military. "Al-Qaida-Linked-Militants-Attack-Is-Affiliate-in-Libya." *Military Times*. June 10, 2017. http://www.militarytimes.com/story/military/2015/06/10/al-qaida-linked-militants-attack-is-affiliate-in-libya/71014000/.

"US AFRICOM Ends Military Operation against IS Radicals in Libya." *Libyan Express – Breaking News and Latest Updates from Libya*, December 21, 2016. http://www.libyanexpress.com/us-africom-ends-military-operation-against-is-radicals-in-libya/.

Vandewalle, Dirk. "After Qaddafi: The Surprising Success of the New Libya." *Foreign Affairs* 91, no. 6 (2012): 8–15.

Wintour, Patrick, and Nicholas Watt. "David Cameron's Libyan War: Why the PM Felt Gaddafi Had to Be Stopped." *The Guardian*, October 2, 2011, sec. Politics. https://www.theguardian.com/politics/2011/oct/02/david-cameron-libyan-war-analysis.

Radka Havlová

Palestine

The following chapter analyses the impact of the Arab Spring on Palestine.[1] Unlike other case studies in this book, Palestine represents a special case, since the simple statute of Palestine as an independent state is not generally recognized.[2] As such, Palestine is by many considered not to be a proper state because it does not fulfil all the conditions of statehood required by international law, which include defined territory, population, independent government with effective authority and international recognition.[3] All these four conditions show significant problems in case of Palestine: 1. the exact borders of the Palestinian territory have not yet been agreed upon due to the missing peace agreement with Israel (and also due to extensive Jewish settlements in the Palestinian territories of the West Bank and around East Jerusalem); 2. a large part of the Palestinian population lives in exile, mostly in refugee camps; 3. there are serious concerns about the ability of the Palestinian government to efficiently perform its functions, in particular after the Hamas-Fatah split following the 2006 elections to the Palestine Legislative Council (PLC); and 4. the number of countries recognizing the Palestinian state is limited and does not include significant world actors such as the United States.

Another significant factor that influences the impact of the Arab Spring on Palestine is the fact that development in Palestine has also been closely linked to development in other Arab countries – in particular Egypt, Jordan and Syria – already since the 1940s. Therefore, it is necessary to briefly discuss the situation

---

1 This case study does not provide in-depth analysis of the Israeli-Palestinian conflict nor does it discuss the Israeli perspective of the conflict resolution. It provides a general overview of the most significant factors influencing the democratization process in Palestine, including discussion of the impact of the Arab Spring on Palestine. For more information about the Israeli-Palestinian conflict see e.g. Tessler, *A History of the Israeli-Palestinian Conflict*; Gilbert, *The Routledge Atlas of the Arab-Israeli Conflict*; Laqueur and Schueftan, *The Israel-Arab Reader: A Documentary History of the Middle East Conflict: Eighth Revised and Updated Edition*.

2 The Palestinian state has so far been recognized by 137 states (i.e. 70.5% of the 193 UN member states) as per January 2017; Al-Arian and Mohsin, 'Palestine: Growing Recognition'.

3 Lauterpacht, 'Recognition of States in International Law', p. 408–414.

in Palestine before the outbreak of the Arab Spring as well as to sum up the main problems Palestine was facing before 2011.

As will be demonstrated in this analysis, the Arab Spring did not really represent a major change for Palestinian society, except for the changed regional context due to the changes in Egypt and Syria. More significant changes within Palestinian society occurred because of the Oslo Accords of 1993, the Second Intifada of 2000 and the Hamas-Fatah split in 2006. This analysis therefore focuses mainly on the Palestinian struggle for independence and full recognition, and discusses the major obstacles which the Palestinians are facing in this process.

1. Internal non-institutional factors

Palestine is composed of two separate territories, the Gaza Strip and the West Bank, whose exact borders have not yet been defined, and whose territories are until now by and large occupied by the State of Israel. The very borders of these territories have been challenged and are not yet officially recognized as no peace treaty between the State of Israel and the Palestinian state has been concluded despite the peace process that started in the 1990s. Any agreement would have to define the exact borders between these two countries, which is rather problematic in the case of the contested West Bank territory and in East Jerusalem because there are significant Jewish settlements in these territories. The question of Jewish settlements as well as the construction of the barrier between the State of Israel and the West Bank territories remain among the most pressing issues in defining the future borders of the Palestinian state.

A further factor which complicates the analysis of the impact of the Arab Spring on Palestine is the fact that development in Gaza and the West Bank has varied significantly since the 2006 Hamas–Fatah split. To understand the contemporary situation in the Palestinian state it is therefore necessary to at least briefly summarize the most significant facts from Palestinian modern history.

The territory of Palestine was inhabited by Jews already in the Biblical period and this Jewish settlement is crucial for today's situation in Palestine, in particular in relation to the question of Jerusalem and the Jewish settlements in the West Bank. Palestinians have been constantly present in the territory of Palestine since the 7th century, bringing Islam to the area. The territory of Palestine has been part of the Ottoman empire since the 16th century, although Palestine as a part of the Ottoman empire was among the least developed territories, and of no special economic importance to the empire. Most of the land was owned by landlords residing outside of Palestine itself. The majority of the population in the territory were Muslims; however, small communities of Jews lived in Palestine, and the relations between Muslims and Jews during the Ottoman empire were mostly peaceful as prior to the Zionist movement in the second half of the 19th century, Jews had no political ambitions in Palestine. Most of the Jews lived around Jewish holy sites, focusing on religious studies and living peacefully with their Muslim neighbours. Jerusalem was a city of special importance not only for Jews and Muslims, but also for Christians and as such enjoyed a special status in the Ottoman empire.

Ottoman rule over Palestine was replaced by the British Mandate administration (1922–1948). British rule was characterized by continuous Jewish immigration to Palestine and rising tensions between Jewish and Arab population in Palestine. The "Palestine question" was finally resolved by the United Nations, which adopted Resolution 181 (II) in November 1947, providing for establishment of three entities in the territory of the British Mandate of Palestine: the Jewish state, the Palestinian state and Jerusalem under international administration. The State of Israel was declared on 14 May 1948, no Palestinian state was declared based on the UN resolution, and the territory of the future Palestinian state was administered by Egypt (Gaza) and Jordan (the West Bank and Jerusalem). Subsequent decades were marked by wars between Israel and the Arab states (fighting also on behalf of the non-existing Palestinian state), of which the 1967 Six Days war is of fundamental importance for the Palestinians, since Israel occupied the territories of Gaza, West Bank and East Jerusalem and introduced military administration of these territories with simultaneous construction of Jewish settlements in these territories. Dissatisfaction with these developments led to the outbreak of the nation-wide Palestinian general uprising (First Intifada) in 1987, which brought the Palestinian question again to the centre of attention of the international public.

The 1990s were a decade of hope as the State of Israel and the Palestine Liberation Organization (PLO) (recognized as the sole representative of the Palestinian people by the Arab Summit in 1974) mutually recognized each other in 1989 and started to engage in peace talks. These became referred to as the "Oslo peace process" (named after the Oslo Accords signed in 1993). The Palestinian Authority was formed from the PLO, and Palestinians were transferred territory and competencies in line with the peace agreements. The PLC was elected in 1996 and Yasser Arafat became the first president of Palestine in 1994. This peaceful decade was terminated by the outbreak of the Second Intifada in September 2000, which had wide implications not only for Israeli-Palestinian relations and security in the territory, but also for the Palestinian autonomy itself. The 2005 Israeli withdrawal from Gaza was of fundamental importance in this period, even though Israel maintained its control over Gaza's borders, territorial waters and air space for security reasons. Nevertheless, the Hamas–Fatah split following the 2006 PLC elections led to a serious deterioration of the situation in both Gaza and the West Bank, with the situation coming close to a civil war. Despite reconciliation efforts, the situation in the Palestinian territories remains tense.

The Arab Spring was nevertheless understood as a chance to change the situation in Palestine. The president of the Palestinian Authority, Mahmud Abbas, called for a "Palestinian Spring" to mobilize the Palestinian public in favour of his effort to win UN recognition.[4] This move resulted in improvement of the status of Palestine within the United Nations after the 2012 voting (see section on political factors), but it did not result in full recognition of the Palestinian state nor in the conclusion of a peace agreement with Israel. This was because the Arab Spring found Palestine rather weak and facing a wide range of economic, political and security problems, of which the split between Fatah and Hamas was among the most crucial. As it will be argued, the internal development in Palestine has been more important than challenges brought by the Arab Spring, except for the changing regional balance to which the Palestinians had to adapt.

1.1 Economic factors

One of the biggest problems of the Palestinian state is the territorial division between the West Bank and Gaza which is also reflected in the political divisions of these two territories (for more details see section on political factors). Disputed territories such as East Jerusalem or territories under Israeli control in the West Bank further complicate the situation, particularly as far as Palestine's economic indicators are concerned. Should all potential territories of the Palestinian state, including the most disputed East Jerusalem, be included, the territory of the Palestinian state would cover 6,020 sq. km.[5]

The Palestinian case is also specific as it is quite complicated to find relevant data on economic and social development in the territories, particularly since parts of the Palestinian territories are still subject to Israeli occupation (the West Bank and East Jerusalem). One of the largest problems when looking at the Palestinian economy therefore results from the fact that many indicators used for characterizing the economic situation in a country are just based on estimates, additionally many have problems with the territorial definition of the Palestinian state. This is for example reflected in the official statistics of the United Nations.[6]

---

4 Aronson, 'The Middle East Conflict after the Arab Spring: The Case of Palestine'.

5 'UN Data State of Palestine'.

6 Ibid.

Another problem is the fact that Palestine is frequently not included in overall indicators referring to economic development. For instance, in the 2017 Index of economic freedom, Palestine is completely missing from the overview.[7]

Based on the data of the Palestinian Central Bureau of Statistics (PCBS) from 2016, the total population of Palestine is approximately 4.8 million people, of whom about 2.9 million people live in the West Bank and 1.9 million in the Gaza Strip.[8] The general census in the Palestinian territories was performed in 1997 and 2007, and the third general census took place in 2017.[9] 7. There is also a large Palestinian diaspora (Palestinian refugees) of approximately 7.5 million Palestinians residing mostly in United Nations Relief and Works Agency for Palestine Refugees in the Near East (UNRWA) operated refugee camps in Lebanon, Syria and other Arab countries.[10] The Palestinian population is in general young: based on the PCBS data for 2016, 39.2% of the population are between 0 and 14 years and 29.9% of population are young people between 15 and 29.[11]

The estimated GDP per capita as of 2014 was $4,300,[12] compared to approximately $10,900,000 for Israel.[13] According to the statement of the Minister of Labour of the Palestinian Authority, Mamoun Abu Shahla, from April 2017 more than 320,000 Palestinian families live below the poverty line.[14] The GINI coefficient illustrating income inequality was 35.5 in 2013, ranking Palestine 107th worldwide.[15] The illiteracy rate for persons above 15 years is, nevertheless, rather low, amounting only to 3.3% in 2015.[16]

---

7 The 2017 Index of economic freedom does not provide only data on economic development, but takes into a large account of factors influencing the economy of the respective territory, such as property rights, government integrity, judicial effectiveness, tax burden, government spending, fiscal health business/labour/monetary/trade/investment or fiscal freedom etc. The index thus provides a good overview of the general situation in the territory. Unfortunately, the organization does not provide data either for Palestine, or the West Bank and Gaza separately ('2017 Index of Economic Freedom').

8 'State of Palestine. Palestinian Central Bureau of Statistics'.

9 "Population, Housing and Institutions General Census 2017 Kicks off."

10 Ma'An News Agency, 'Bureau: Majority of Palestinians Live in Diaspora'.

11 'State of Palestine. Palestinian Central Bureau of Statistics'.

12 The International Center for Not-for-Profit Law, 'Civic Freedom Monitor: Palestine'.

13 The World Bank, 'GDP per Capita (Current US$)'.

14 MEMO Middle East Monitor, 'PA: One Third of Palestinians Live below Poverty Line'.

15 United Nations Development Programme, 'Human Development Reports'.

16 'State of Palestine. Palestinian Central Bureau of Statistics'.

The Palestinian government has been further subject to various restrictions imposed by the State of Israel because of the continuous violence committed by Palestinians. Such restrictions continued to be imposed even after Israel withdrew its settlements in Gaza in 2005, and intensified after the Hamas election victory in 2006. They included Israeli control over border crossings, and control over the air space and territorial waters of the Palestinian state. Under the Egyptian President Mubarak, Israel was also successful in pressing on Egyptian control of the Rafah crossing to Gaza, which was the only point through which goods could be passed to Gaza. Such control led to the creation of a tunnel economy based on construction of secret tunnels under the Egyptian–Palestinian border. These were used for smuggling of not only basic economic goods necessary in Gaza but – as Israel accused the Palestinians – also for smuggling of weapons and other military equipment used by Hamas.[17]

Despite these limitations, one can see significant improvements of the Palestinian economy in the recent years under the Prime Minister Fayyad and his institution-building program, which has been implemented in Gaza since 2007. This strategy, based on good governance, economic growth and enforcing security, was designed to improve Palestinian fiscal policy and reduce unemployment with significant support from the international donor community. The Palestinian economy under this strategy shows increased economic growth. However, as noted below, several severe problems remain unresolved, namely the high level of unemployment, political obstacles of a larger growth imposed by Israel (lack of free movement of goods and people), regional and sectoral inequalities, an insecure investment climate, underdeveloped infrastructure, and lack of domestic production within the Palestinian territories.[18]

Extrapolating from the economic data on Palestine (combining the West Bank and Gaza) provided by the World Bank, the GDP (in current USD) has been increasing steadily since 2000. Nevertheless, the overall level of GDP (12,677 billion USD for 2015) still ranks Palestine among the least developed states.[19] The current data, however, suggest that the GDP of Palestine has been growing steadily since mid-2015, showing a 1.3% growth year-on-year in the fourth quarter of 2016.[20] Based on World Bank indicators, the growth is linked to reconstruction efforts and growth in the construction sector, retail and wholesale trade in Gaza. Further

17 Aronson, 'The Middle East Conflict after the Arab Spring: The Case of Palestine'.
18 Danin et al., 'Palestine: Economic Challenges and Political Implications'.
19 The World Bank, 'West Bank and Gaza'.
20 Trading Economics, 'Palestine GDP Annual Growth Rate'.

growth is, nevertheless, limited by a considerable decline in foreign aid and by the decision of the State of Israel to suspend the transfer of Palestinian taxes in 2015.[21]

The largest problems of the Palestinian economy include a high level of unemployment. According to PCBS data the unemployment level in Palestine amounted to 25.9% in 2015. For the West Bank, it reached 15% of males and 26.7% of females. The numbers were considerably higher for Gaza: 35.9% of males and 59.6% of females over 15 years were unemployed.[22] The generally high level of unemployment is accompanied by an extremely high level of youth unemployment (15–29) which has reached a level of more than 50% in Gaza.[23] Similarly to other countries in which Arab Spring broke out, the unemployment is also very high among university graduates (almost 30%).[24] The problem of unemployment could be solved in cooperation with the State of Israel, and the Quartet[25] has been pressing Israel to issue more work permits to unskilled Palestinian workers. Nevertheless, according to Palestinian representatives, this is only a temporary solution and a long-term solution should be achieved by increased investments into the Palestinian economy.[26]

Further economic problems include a rather high fiscal deficit, amounting to approximately 11.7% of GDP, which results from high governmental expenditures for transfers, goods and services. The debt also results from the decline of foreign aid by almost 30% in 2015 compared to 2014.[27] Inflation, on the contrary, remains rather low, with a figure of around 1.4% in 2015.

The outlook of economic development remains uncertain. Any substantial improvement assumes the Palestinian economy would require a resolution of the Israeli–Palestinian conflict and therewith related removal of restrictions relating to trade and free movement imposed on the Palestinian territories by the State of Israel. Based on World Bank predictions, the growth of the Palestinian economy

21 The World Bank, 'Palestine's Economic Outlook – Spring 2016'.
22 'State of Palestine. Palestinian Central Bureau of Statistics'.
23 The World Bank, 'Palestine's Economic Outlook – Spring 2016'.
24 MEMO Middle East Monitor, 'PA: One Third of Palestinians Live below Poverty Line'.
25 Quartet is the association of the main international actors involved in mediation and resolution of the Israeli–Palestinian conflict, i.e. the United States, Russia, the United Nations and the European Union. They propose peace plans and programs to contribute to de-escalation of violence and final resolution of the Israeli-Palestinian conflict. The most significant proposal of the Quartet was the Road Map of 2003 which set the conditions for final resolution of the Israeli–Palestinian conflict in three stages by 2005.
26 Danin et al., 'Palestine: Economic Challenges and Political Implications'.
27 The World Bank, 'Palestine's Economic Outlook – Spring 2016'.

should continue to be around 3%, provided the violence between Israel and the Palestinian state does not escalate.[28] Economic development in the Palestinian territories will be also significantly influenced by political development and by the ability of the West Bank and Gaza to form a unified government. This would enable implementation of a uniform economic strategy in both territories of the Palestinian state which would need to focus on an export-driven economy (in relation to establishment of a Free Trade Area with other Arab countries, upon simultaneous close cooperation with the State of Israel to remove free trade barriers, restrictions of movement of goods and persons, and foreign investment barriers). Overall economic improvement is therefore clearly linked with improvement of Israeli–Palestinian relations and with the close involvement of the international community in this process.

1.2 Civil society and media

1.2.1 Civil society

The specific situation of Palestine as generally not being a fully recognized state is also reflected in the development of Palestinian civil society, which plays a significant role in the Palestinian territory, frequently replacing the non-existing or non-functioning Palestinian state. The fundamental question which is to be asked is "Can there be a Palestinian civil society without a Palestinian state?" In general there have been three different approaches to this question within Palestinian society: 1. Palestinian society cannot exist before the formation of an independent state, as civil society is defined as organizations independent of a state (and the state itself does not exist); 2. Palestinian society exists even without the existence of a Palestinian state, focusing in particular on provision of missing health, agricultural and educational services; and 3. Palestinian society is in transition and should contribute to a transformation from occupation to independence.[29]

Based on the data of the Palestinian Ministry of the Interior (2015), there are about 2,800 non-governmental organizations (NGOs) active in Palestine today.[30] The Palestinian NGO Network (PNGO), founded in 1993 as an umbrella organization of 92 Palestinian NGOs, focuses primarily on the promotion of the national and developmental roles of the Palestinian NGOs by supporting democracy, civil society, social justice, rule of law and respect of human rights among

28 Ibid.

29 Salem, 'Civil Society in Palestine: Approaches, Historical Context and the Role of the NGOs'.

30 The International Center for Not-for-Profit Law, 'Civic Freedom Monitor: Palestine'.

others. It does this by issuing three major publications, namely the Palestine Monitor, the Palestine Observatory and the Grassroots International Protection for the Palestinian People.[31] Another important NGO with a similar focus on promotion of democratic principles is the Palestinian Center for Human Rights (PCHR), established in Gaza in 1995, which also focuses on monitoring of breaches of Palestinian rights by Israel.[32]

The area of focus of the civil society organisations (CSOs) in Palestine is wide. One of the significant areas on which the CSOs focus in Palestine is freedom of speech and association. Freedom of association is guaranteed in Article 26(2) of the Basic Law (temporary Palestinian constitution, for details see section on judiciary) which was adopted in 1997, signed by Arafat in 2002, and amended in 2003 and 2005. Based on the provisions of this article Palestinians have the right "to form and establish unions, associations, societies, clubs and popular institutions in accordance with the law".[33] Palestine has also signed international and regional agreements focusing on the activities of the NGOs, including the International Covenant on Civil and Political Rights (ICCPR), signed in 2014, and the Arab Charter on Human Rights, signed in 2007. After receiving the non-member observer state status in the United Nations in November 2012, Palestine also acceded to additional international conventions and treaties.[34]

As Palestinians still consider the Israeli occupation to be one of the fundamental problems, many of the civil society campaigns also focus on the boycott of Israeli products (such as the BDS (Boycott, Divestment, Sanctions) campaign) or they target the unlawful actions of Israel (such as the Palestinians Grassroots Anti-Apartheid Wall Campaign ("Stop the Wall" campaign)).

Nevertheless, the continuous Israeli occupation of Palestinian territories and struggles between the Palestinian authorities in the West Bank and Gaza has led to an uneven application of the Palestinian NGO law, in some cases resulting in forced dissolution of Palestinian grassroot organizations or forced changes in organizational structure of the organizations. Such problems remain even after the 2014 Hamas–Fatah reconciliation agreement, which further complicates the efficiency of Palestinian civil society, and does not enable Palestinian NGOs to provide services for the poorest population of Palestine. Palestinian civil society must therefore focus on finding effective tools for dealing with ongoing and new

---

31 NGO Monitor, 'Palestinian NGO Network (PNGO)'.

32 NGO Monitor, 'Palestinian Center for Human Rights (PCHR)'.

33 The International Center for Not-for-Profit Law, 'Civic Freedom Monitor: Palestine'.

34 Ibid.

challenges and meet the real needs of Palestinians, while simultaneously renewing the confidence of Palestinians in civil society.[35]

1.2.2 Media

The media played an important role in the changes promoted by civil societies in the countries in which the Arab Spring took place (see for instance the chapter focusing on Egypt). Looking at the situation of the media in Palestine, one can see that the situation of the media has changed significantly since the Oslo peace agreement. Prior to the 1990s, Palestinians living in the territories occupied by Israel were not allowed to establish independent media or start independent TV or radio stations. Only one newspaper was published in Arabic in East Jerusalem since 1951 (the *al-Quds* newspaper). After the beginning of the peace process Palestinians started to establish independent newspapers, and radio and television stations began to operate in the territory. Currently both traditional and new media operate in Palestine. The Ministry of Information regulates and oversees media in Palestine, and censorship is officially banned in Palestine. Media in Gaza are in general more controlled by Hamas than those in the West Bank by Fatah.[36]

The largest traditional printed newspapers include the *al-Quds*, the *al-Hayat al-Jadidah* and the *al-Ayyam* (all close to the Fatah movement and the Palestinian authority), and three newspapers published in Gaza close to Hamas (*al-Resala, Felesteen,* and *Palestine,* which is published directly by the political wing of Hamas). Independent radio and television stations operate in Palestine as well; however, they frequently cover only the territory of the West Bank. Arabic satellite television channels such as *al-Jazeera* and *al-Arabiya* also broadcast in the territory of Palestine.

New media have been rather influential in Palestine since the beginning of the 21st century. Their impact is, however, limited as Israel still regulates internet access in Palestine,[37] and only about 13% of Palestinians had access to Internet in 2006, mostly in internet cafes.[38] Based on the current data of the PCBS, the

35 Sadiq, 'Civil Society Organizations: Oslo as a Turning Point in Their Work Among the Masses'.

36 Sada, 'Media Landscapes: Palestine'.

37 Israel is also known for control of international press access to the Palestinian territories, which was largely refused for example during Operation Cas Lead in 2008 to 2009. Palestinian media and journalists are also frequently targeted by the Israeli government as a perceived security threat for Israel.

38 Sada, 'Media Landscapes: Palestine'.

number of households which have access to internet increased significantly to 48.3% in 2014.[39]

Nevertheless, the situation of journalists is not easy in Palestine. Although freedom of speech is guaranteed by the Palestinian Basic Law, journalists are frequently subject to various forms of harassment and restrictions of free travel which make their job rather difficult. Conditions have further deteriorated since the outbreak of the Second Intifada and the Hamas–Fatah split, which led to many financial difficulties for media organizations in Palestine.[40]

This is in line with the assessment of general freedom in Palestine[41] provided by Freedom House for 2017. Looking at the scores of Gaza, it is considered to be "not free", with a general score 12 of 100, and freedom rating 5.5 of 7 (political rights score 5 of 7 and civil liberties score 6 of 7).[42, 43] Freedom House ranks the West Bank also as "not free", but the aggregate score is slightly better compared to Gaza (28 of 100). Nevertheless, the freedom rating is 6/7 (5 of 7 for political rights and 7 of 7, i.e. completely not free for political rights which is in particular due to the controversial postponement of municipal elections and restriction of opposition in the territory).[44] A similar assessment is clear from the 2017 World Press Freedom Index prepared by Reporters without Borders, in which Palestine (the West Bank and Gaza combined) ranks 135th and its score is 42.90.[45, 46]

---

39 'State of Palestine. Palestinian Central Bureau of Statistics'.

40 For a detailed analysis of media freedom in Palestine see Birzeit University Media Development Center, 'Assessment of Media Development in Palestine Based on UNESCO's Media Development Indicators'.

41 It is interesting that "Palestine" cannot be found in the ranking as Freedom House provides separate information on the West Bank and Gaza.

42 The overall score ranges from 0 to 100: the higher the score, the freer is the respective society. In contrast, regarding the freedom rating of political rights and civil liberties, the lower the score, the freer is the society. Israel, for comparison, is considered to be a "free" country, with an aggregate score 80 of 100, and a freedom rating 1.5 of 7 (1 of 7 for political rights, 2 of 7 for civil liberties, score "7" is the worst), Freedom House, 'Freedom in the World 2017: Israel'.

43 Freedom House, 'Freedom in the World 2017. Gaza Strip Profile'.

44 Freedom House, 'Freedom in the World 2017. West Bank Profile'.

45 North Korea ranks 180 with a score of 84.89: the higher the score, the less freedom of press and the less freedom of speech in the relevant country. Israel ranks 91st with a score of 31.01. The average score for the Middle East is 50.53 which makes the Middle East and North Africa region the world's most difficult and dangerous region for journalists. Reporters without Borders, '2017 World Press Freedom Index – Tipping Point'.

46 Reporters without Borders, '2017 World Press Freedom Index'.

1.3 Extremism and religion

Lack of political freedom in a country may be also associated with a high influence of extremism and religion in a society. Looking at Palestinian society, it is clear that most Palestinians are ethnically of Arab origin (83%). The Jewish population in the Palestinian territories comprises approximately 17% (Jewish settlers). The major religion is Islam (75%), followed by Judaism (17%) and Christianity (8%).[47] The estimated number of Palestinian Christians in the Palestinian territory is 51,710,[48] living mostly in Bethlehem, Ramallah and Jerusalem. Most Christians are of Eastern Orthodox churches followed by Syrian, Coptic and Armenian Orthodox Churches, and then Catholic churches.[49] Israeli restrictions in the occupied territories are applied equally to Muslims and Christians, and Palestinian Christians are routinely prohibited from travelling to Christian holy places e.g. in Jerusalem.[50] Palestinian Christians, on the other hand, enjoy religious freedom based on the Basic Law which is also recognized by Hamas in Gaza, although Islam is the official religion in Palestine. Even though Islamic institutions receive preferential financial support from the government by law, the government also provides limited financial support to some Christian institutions.[51] Palestinian Christians have also their representatives in the Palestinian Legislative Council.

Extremism in the Palestinian territories is mostly associated with Islamist movements such as Hamas and Islamic Jihad. These organizations are considered terrorist organizations by the United States, European Union and Israel. Some of the tools used by these organizations against the Israeli military, governmental and civil targets are of terrorist nature. Nevertheless, it would be simplistic to link the popularity of these organizations in Palestine only with terrorism and their anti-Israeli attitude. The popularity of these organizations has deeper roots and issues from the past involvement of these organizations in Palestine. This applies mostly to Hamas[52] as the largest and most influential Islamist movement (and a political party) whose popularity in Gaza resulted in its victory in the PLC elections in

47 'Population of Palestine'.

48 Nicolaou-Garcia, 'Christian-Muslim Relations in Palestine'.

49 Ibid.

50 Ibid.

51 Bureau of Democracy, Human Rights and Labor, '2012 Report on International Religious Freedom: Israel and The Occupied Territories – The Occupied Territories'.

52 Hamas was established in Gaza in 1987, having its origins in the Muslim Brotherhood in Egypt. Therefore, Hamas had historically good relations with the Egyptian and Syrian Muslim Brotherhood. These regional alliances changed because of the Arab Spring: for details see section on external factors.

2006 and the subsequent split between Hamas and Fatah (for details see section on political factors). For many Palestinians Hamas represents an uncorrupted viable Islamist alternative to the corrupt Palestinian regime, which has not been able to achieve any significant improvement of the situation of Palestinians vis-à-vis the continuous Israeli occupation of the Palestinian territories. Hamas, however, has long-term experience with provision of relief and social services, including health care and education in the occupied territories. Palmer nevertheless fears that the need for Hamas to act as a responsible government in Gaza after gaining the majority of seats in Gaza in the 2006 elections (followed by international diplomatic isolation, sanctions and boycott) could lead to its rejection by more radical Islamist groups operating in the territory, which could further destabilize the situation in Gaza.[53]

The Arab Spring also had a direct influence on the position of Hamas in Palestine, mostly due to the changes in Egypt and Syria. Because of the changed regional dynamics, Hamas strengthened its ties with Egypt (where the Muslim Brotherhood gained importance during the Morsi presidency), Qatar, Turkey and Saudi Arabia, moving away from its traditional allies such as Syria and Iran[54] (see section on external factors).

2. Internal institutional factors

2.1 Security and defence structures

Security in the Palestinian territories has been among the most significant concerns of Israel since the beginning of the Oslo peace process in the 1990s. Therefore, efforts to establish independent Palestinian security forces have been largely controlled by Israel and the reform of Palestinian security forces came into effect only recently, mostly under US supervision and in line with the Israeli-Palestinian peace process.

The Palestinian Authority Security Force (PASF) was formed in 1994, based on the Cairo Agreement. This called for the establishment of a "strong police force" with a maximum of 9,000 recruits to guarantee "public order and internal security within the jurisdiction of the Palestinian Authority",[55] in line with the Oslo Accords. It also required, from its inception, significant financial assistance from

53 Palmer, 'Trouble in Palestine'.

54 Ezbidi, '"Arab Spring": Weather Forecast for Palestine', p. 99–100.

55 Alaa Tartir, 'The Evolution and Reform of Palestinian Security Forces 1993–2013', *Stability: International Journal of Security and Development* 4, no. 1 (n.d.).

the international community. The main objective of the creation of the PASF was to maintain order, law and stability in the Palestinian territories and to guarantee Israeli security. In the first stage (1993–1999) the PASF faced an identity crisis related to moving from the PLO revolutionary liberation movement (as the PASF was formed around the previous security forces of the PLO leader Yasser Arafat) to the security forces of a civil state. The formation of security forces was accompanied by large scale corruption, lack of inclusiveness (the majority of PASF personnel were linked to Fatah), absence of a uniform security strategy and inability of the PASF to guarantee the security of Palestinians. These factors, together with the fact that Arafat was also strongly directly involved in the security forces, were met with distrust by Israel and Western leaders who doubted that he was dedicated to achieving peace with Israel.[56] Nevertheless, the PASF succeeded in fulfilling obligations set by the Oslo Accords and contributed to protecting Israeli security and dismantling of the Palestinian "infrastructure of terror".[57]

The effectiveness of the PASF further deteriorated after the outbreak of the Second Intifada in 2000 when the PASF was unable to maintain security in the Palestinian territories. The Second Intifada created a security vacuum and chaos in the territory, which in turn led to large-scale destruction of the PASF and security infrastructure.[58] Many security actors, such as the newly established Al-Aqsa Martyrs Brigades, were not under the control of the PASF. Such a security vacuum and the inability of the PASF to maintain order and security in Palestine also led to large public distrust in the PASF. Reform of the PASF was implemented after Arafat's death, upon supervision of the US Security Coordinator for Israel and the Palestinian Authority, with the aim of rebuilding of the PASF into a multi-branch security force. The main motto of the reform ("One law, one gun, one authority") stressed the need for monopolization of violence by the PASF[59] which became increasingly important after the violence escalated following the Hamas–Fatah split in 2006.

---

56 Jeffrey Dean McCoy, 'The Palestinian Security Force: Future Prospects', *Joint Force Quarterly* 84, no. 1 (January 2017), http://ndupress.ndu.edu/JFQ/Joint-Force-Quarterly-84/Article/1038806/the-palestinian-security-force-future-prospects/.

57 Tartir, 'The Evolution and Reform of Palestinian Security Forces 1993–2013'.

58 According to the United Nations Conference on Trade and Development (UNCTAD) data as of 2005 the destruction of physical infrastructure is estimated to have cost the economy $3.5 billion and the World Bank estimated that the destruction of the PA's security apparatus and facilities exceeded $38.5 million in the West Bank and $34.5 million in Gaza up to early 2002. Ibid.

59 Ibid.

The PASF is currently organized into four major services which include the Presidential Guard, National Security Forces, Palestinian Civil Police and Civil Defence directorate. The PASF also includes the Naval Police, whose objective is to protect the Palestinian territorial waters and whose strength is approximately 1,000 men operating mostly in Gaza.[60] Prior to the outbreak of the Second Intifada the PASF also participated in joint patrolling with the Israeli Defence Force (IDF), and even though the practice is currently abolished, the PASF is frequently viewed by Palestinians as the "Israeli sub-contractors for security".[61] This is due to the fact that it frequently has to suppress Palestinian riots in line with the obligation to guarantee security in the Palestinian territories under Israeli pressure, mostly in relation to the security of the Jewish settlements in the West Bank (where the IDF is responsible for security).

2.2 Political factors

The independent Palestinian state was officially declared by a unilateral declaration of independence adopted by the Palestinian National Council in Algeria in November 1988. In line with the Oslo Accords the Palestinians established its legislative, executive and judiciary institutions in the 1990s. The Draft Basic Law for the National Authority in the Transitional Period defining its competencies (adopted in 1997) entered effect in 2002, providing a temporary constitutional framework for the operation of the Palestinian state. The status of Palestine improved significantly after the 2012 UN General Assembly voting which granted Palestine "non-member observer state" status in the United Nations.[62]

The political system in Palestine has been influenced by many historical systems that were incorporated into the Palestinian political system after the Oslo Accords in the 1990s (the Ottoman Empire, the British Mandate system, the Egyptian and Jordanian administration, and the Israeli occupation). The first political movements of the Palestinians started to form in the 1960s. The main political

---

60 TWIP Collective, 'The Security Forces Operating in Palestine. An Overview', n.d., https://thisweekinpalestine.com/wp-content/uploads/2014/07/The-Security-Forces-Operating-in-Palestine.pdf.

61 McCoy, 'The Palestinian Security Force: Future Prospects'.

62 The upgrade of the Palestinian status within the United Nations was supported by 138 UN member states, with 41 states abstaining and 9 states voting against (Canada, the Czech Republic, Israel, the Marshall Islands, the Federated States of Micronesia, Nauru, Panama, Palau, the United States).67th General Assembly of the United Nations, 'General Assembly Votes Overwhelmingly to Accord Palestine "Non-Member Observer State" Status in United Nations'.

forces in Palestine can be divided into secular and Islamist forces. However, there are numerous additional dividing lines within the Palestinian political system, such as the relation to the State of Israel (support of two-state solution vs. support of destruction of Israel), support of the Oslo peace process, reliance on different regional partners for support (e.g. Egypt, Syria, Iran) and full independence of the relevant political party or territorial base of the parties (Palestinian territories vs. neighbouring countries). The most important political parties in Palestine are Fatah, Hamas, Islamic Jihad, the Popular Front for the Liberation of Palestine and the Democratic Front for the Liberation of Palestine.

As Shikaki points out, another significant dividing line is evident in the Palestinian politics since the outbreak of the Second Intifada: the division between the "Old Guard" (former PLO mostly exile leadership such as Yasser Arafat or Mahmud Abbas) and the "Young Guard" (mostly local leaders, frequently leaders of the First Intifada, such as Marwan Barghouti or Husam Khader).[63] This division is becoming more important than the ideological divisions within the Palestinian political parties, as it reflects a completely different approach to leadership and the resolution of the Israeli-Palestinian conflict as the Young Guard intends to push Israel to unilaterally withdraw from the Palestinian territories, and simultaneously replace the weakened Old Guard within the Palestinian leadership.

Probably the most significant dividing line within the Palestinian political spectrum is the competition between nationalists and Islamists which further intensified after the 2006 Hamas election victory in Gaza. However, this competition has deep historical roots and is related not only to the future of Palestinian political system, but also reflects ideological and social divisions within Palestinian society. Islamist movements (Hamas, Islamic Jihad) became popular after the outbreak of the Second Intifada because of the inability of the Palestinian political leadership to find appropriate responses to the increased violence and to promote Palestinian interests vis-à-vis Israel.[64]

63 Shikaki, 'Old Guard, Young Guard: The Palestinian Authority and the Peace Process at Crossroads'.

64 Support for Arafat in July 2000 (after Camp David) was 47% compared to 30% in September 2001 (one year after the outbreak of the Second Intifada). Support for Fatah also declined from 37% in July 2000 to 33% in September 2001, while support for the Islamists rose from 17% in June 2000 to 27% in September 2001, Ibid. The increasing popularity of Islamist parties continues also today, i.e. the 2016 opinion poll carried out by the Palestinian Center for Policy and Survey Research shows that Hamas is still the most popular party (70% public support), compared to 55% support for Fatah, 'Palestinian Public Opinion Poll No (59) – PRESS RELEASE'.

Lack of democracy in the Palestinian political system can be also seen in the absence of regular elections to both legislative bodies and municipal councils. The first legislative and presidential elections in Palestine were held in 1996, while the last legislative elections took place in 2006, demonstrating a significant territorial division within Palestinian society: Fatah received total support of 34% with major support in the West Bank, whereas Hamas was the clear winner of the elections receiving over 56% of total votes.[65] This led to a split between Hamas and Fatah which had fundamental implications on the development of the Palestinian political system, judiciary and security. No additional elections to the PLC have been held since 2006 (elections scheduled originally for 2010 were rejected by Hamas), and the Palestinian parliament has not been able to sit since 2006, which puts "democracy on hold" in Palestine.[66]

Local elections to municipal councils were first held in 2005, in which local councils were elected for a period of four years. Due to the Hamas–Fatah split no further local elections were held in 2010 as the Central Election Commission was unable to operate in Gaza controlled by Hamas, and Fatah was not able to agree on the list of candidates; this postponed the local elections to 2012. A second round of local elections was held in the West Bank in 2012, leading to a Fatah victory after Hamas withdrew from the elections in the West Bank.[67] Hamas did not recognize the election results, and the legitimacy of the polls was also questioned by the Palestinian Centre for Human Rights. Further local elections were scheduled for October 2016; however, they were postponed until May 2017 in the West Bank (and no elections took place in Gaza). Most elected candidates were Fatah (75%), followed by independent candidates (12%).[68]

The main factors which contribute to political instability in Palestine are thus mostly the continuous split between Hamas and Fatah and the inability of the Palestinian authorities to fulfil democratic principles of government. To sum up, the Palestinian political system is facing many challenges. As such it has not been able to fully apply the democratic principles in line with the Oslo Accords. The overall level of political freedom in Palestine, as assessed by the widely accepted Democracy index monitored by the Economist Intelligence Unit, ranks Palestine (West Bank

65 Birringer, 'Results of the Elections of the Palestinian Legislative Council on January 25, 2006'.

66 Palmer, 'Trouble in Palestine'.

67 Greenwood, 'Fatah Claims Palestinian Election Victory'.

68 'The CEC Publishes Detailed Results of the 2017 Local Elections'.

and Gaza combined) as a "hybrid regime" with an overall score of 4.49,[69] which places Palestine 110th worldwide in 2016. It is, nevertheless, quite interesting to see the scores of Palestine in the individual criteria based on which the Democracy index is assessed: in I. (electoral process and pluralism) Palestine scores 4.33; in II. (functioning government) the score is only 2.14; in III. (political participation) Palestine scores very high at 7.78; in IV. (political culture) the score is 4.38; and in V. (civil liberties) the score is only 3.82.[70]

2.3 Rule of law – judicial system

The Palestinian judicial system is yet again influenced by the fact that large parts of the territories of the Palestinian state are under Israeli occupation. The judiciary system in Palestine is rather unique since it is based on a combination of Ottoman law (combining Islam and French law and dating to the Ottoman rule over Palestine from 1516 till 1917), the British common law system (heritage of the British Mandate system from 1922 till 1948), Egyptian and Jordanian law (the result of Gaza administration by Egypt and West Bank administration by Jordan from 1948 till 1967), Israeli law (applied mostly in the form of military orders after the 1967 Six Days War in the occupied territories) and Palestinian law (implemented after the Oslo Accords of 1993). The Palestinian Authority was granted legal authority over the territories under Palestinian administration in accordance with the Oslo Accords of 1993. In his first legal order, the Decree No. 1 concerning the Continuation of the Laws, Regulations and Rules Operative in the Palestinian Territories (West Bank and Gaza Strip) before 5 June 1967, of 20 May 1994, Arafat confirmed the validity of previous laws enacted in the Palestinian territories while abolishing some Israeli military orders.[71]

The PLC, which has legislative and judiciary powers, was elected in January 1996. The PLC adopted the Basic Law in 1997 (it came into force in 2002, and

69 The scores for "hybrid regime" range from 4 to 5.9, which actually brings Palestine close to being an "authoritarian regime" (overall score under 4.0). Should we compare Palestine to Israel, Israel is considered a "flawed democracy", with an overall score of 7.85, which places Israel 29th worldwide, scoring in the individual criteria I. 9.17, II. 7.50, III. 8.89, IV. 7.50 and V. 6.18. Economist Intelligence Unit, 'The Economist Intelligence Unit's Democracy Index'.

70 The Economist Intelligence Unit, 'Democracy Index. Palestine'.

71 Asem Khalil, 'Legislating for Migration: The Anomalous Case of the Palestinian Authority', *European University Institute* 2006 (n.d.), http://cadmus.eui.eu/bitstream/handle/1814/11695/CARIM_ASN_2006_11.pdf?sequence=1. p. 2.

was subsequently amended in 2003 and 2005), which is loosely based on Sharia (by defining Islam as the official religion in Palestine and stating the principles of Islamic Sharia to be the main sources of legislation in Article 4 of the Basic Law). The law stipulated the basic governmental structure of the Palestinian state, including the division of powers between the legislative and judiciary bodies and judiciary independence.

The judiciary system in Palestine has also been significantly influenced by the Hamas–Fatah split of 2006, since different legal systems have been applied in the West Bank and Gaza. Hamas also established an independent Public Prosecutor's Office and Supreme Judicial Council in Gaza, and appointed a new prosecutor, thus completely detaching itself from the judiciary system of the West Bank. The judiciary bodies in Gaza adopted approximately 50 laws since 2006 which apply only in Gaza; in contrast, more than 100 decrees were adopted in the West Bank that apply only to this territory.[72] The reconciliation agreement and formation of the unity government in 2014 failed to unify the legislative and legal systems of the West Bank and Gaza and the dichotomy separating judiciaries in the West Bank and Gaza is growing. This leads to distrust of Palestinians in the legal system, because Gaza's courts refuse to implement the West Bank's courts' decisions in cases such as marriages, divorces or financial matters, and vice versa. Another obstacle to a trustworthy judiciary system of the Palestinian state is represented by the limited Palestinian sovereignty over the Palestinian territories due to the continuous Israeli occupation of the West Bank and East Jerusalem.

3. External factors

External factors are of crucial importance for development in Palestine as it has been closely linked to development in neighbouring Arab countries already since the 1940s.[73] The "Palestinian question" and solidarity with the Palestinian people

72 Balousha, 'Hamas-Fatah Divide Cripples Palestine's Judiciary'.

73 Many external actors (in particular the United States, Russia, the European Union and the United Nations) have been involved in the Israeli-Palestinian conflict since the establishment of the State of Israel in 1948. Due to the limited scope of this study and its focus on Palestine, their involvement is not subject to the analysis in this chapter. Detailed information can be found e.g. in Chomsky, *Fateful Triangle: The United States, Israel, and the Palestinians*; Kurtzer, *Pathways to Peace: America and the Arab-Israeli Conflict*; Persson, *The EU and the Israeli–Palestinian Conflict 1971–2013: In Pursuit of a Just Peace*.

has been an important agenda of the Arab states mostly since the 1967 Israeli occupation of the Palestinian territories, even though the Palestinian communities have been treated with suspicion in various Arab countries.[74]

A significant impact of the Arab Spring on the MENA region, and specifically on Palestine, is the creation of a power vacuum in the region and lack of unity of the Arab states. This is due to the emphasis on domestic changes brought by the Arab Spring, which are more important than focusing on the Palestinian question.[75] Because of the Arab Spring and changes in Syria and Egypt (see case studies in this book), new regional alliances were established in the Middle East as the position of the Egyptian and Syrian governments towards Palestine changed. According to Finkenstein, Rabbani and Stern-Weiner, the intensified regional Cold War[76] has left Palestinians isolated and vulnerable despite the initial expectations that the Arab Spring would strengthen official Arab support for the Palestinian struggle for self-determination.[77]

Due to the limited scope of this study, only the impact of changes in Syria and Egypt on the situation in Palestine is discussed. [78] Egypt is concerned about developments in Gaza. Changes in leadership in Egypt, namely the rise to power of the Muslim Brotherhood which is closely related to Hamas, brought hope to Palestinians as Mubarak had been previously seen as cooperating with Israel on the suppression of Palestinians in Gaza.[79, 80] However, despite the rhetorical

74 Baroud, 'A Post "Arab Spring" Palestine'.

75 Aronson, 'The Middle East Conflict after the Arab Spring: The Case of Palestine'.

76 This regional Cold War led to a situation in which Israel was viewed by many Sunni states as a valuable ally in their fight against Shia Iran, and therefore the Palestinian question was seen as an obstacle to this rapprochement with Israel. Finkelstein, Rabbani, and Stern-Weiner, 'Palestine After the Arab Spring', p. 24.

77 Ibid. p. 23.

78 Changes in Israeli-Palestinian relations will be discussed only briefly in the context of these regional changes, omitting a more in-depth analysis of the impact of the Arab Spring on the Israeli–Palestinian conflict, as this question is too complex and by far exceeds the scope of this analysis.

79 Aronson, 'The Middle East Conflict after the Arab Spring: The Case of Palestine'.

80 After Mubarak was replaced, there were significant worries in Israel about whether the new government would acknowledge the Egypt–Israel 1979 peace treaty, and indeed some Egyptian forces, including the Muslim Brotherhood and the Presidential candidate Amr Moussa, opposed the agreement and called for revision of the treaty. Andrea Dessi, 'Israel and the Palestinians after the Arab Spring: No Time for Peace', *IAI Working Papers 2, Instituto Affari Internazionali*, May 2012, p. 7.

support for Palestinians by the Egyptian government and strong popular support for the Palestinian question in Egypt, the Egyptian government continued to maintain and reinforce Mubarak's approach towards Palestine by maintaining the travel restriction at the Rafah crossing and by supporting the dismantling of tunnels between Gaza and Egypt in particular after the new Egyptian president Morsi banned the Muslim Brotherhood in Egypt.[81] In line with this approach, Gaza and Hamas (in particular) are viewed as security threats. This position has been also confirmed by the Supreme Council of the Armed Forces.[82] Egyptian media also show an unprecedented level of anti-Palestinian hysteria.[83]

The conflict in Syria also had a serious impact on the Palestinian question: the Syrian regime is facing so serious domestic challenges that it virtually neglected the Palestinian question and ceased to pressure Israel to create a Palestinian state. A Palestinian refugee camp has also been targeted by the Syrian forces as a part of their counter-revolutionary operations.[84] Changes in Syria thus posed a dilemma for Hamas, which had been traditionally allied with Hezbollah and the Assad regime in Syria. Due to the civil war in Syria, Hamas was forced to make a choice of alliances: either supporting the Syrian Muslim Brotherhood or the Assad regime. Vis-à-vis the question of more than 450,000 Palestinian refugees in Syria,[85] Hamas chose to support the rebel forces and Muslim Brotherhood in late 2011. This led to the weakening of Hamas' ties with the Syrian government and Iran, and a substantial loss of financial resources from its former allies.[86]

One of the most significant impacts of the Arab Spring on Palestine is that the "Palestinian question" and the Israeli–Palestinian conflict have been overshadowed by rapid and dramatic internal development in the surrounding countries.[87] The long-lasting Israeli–Palestinian conflict has thus almost disappeared from the media agenda and far less attention has been paid to development in the Palestinian territories than prior to the outbreak of the Arab Spring. This leads to the

81 Ezbidi, '"Arab Spring": Weather Forecast for Palestine', p. 101.
82 Aronson, 'The Middle East Conflict after the Arab Spring: The Case of Palestine'.
83 Finkelstein, Rabbani, and Stern-Weiner, 'Palestine After the Arab Spring', p. 24.
84 Aronson, 'The Middle East Conflict after the Arab Spring: The Case of Palestine'.
85 Shabaneh, 'Egypt and Syria's Effect on the Israeli-Palestinian Conflict', p. 6.
86 Ezbidi, '"Arab Spring": Weather Forecast for Palestine', p. 101.
87 Finkelstein, Rabbani, and Stern-Weiner, 'Palestine After the Arab Spring', p. 29.

further regional isolation of the Palestinians[88, 89] and enables continuous Israeli occupation of the Palestinian territories.[90]

4. Conclusion

The Palestinian struggle for independence and full recognition has been more significantly influenced by the domestic problems of Palestine, mainly the lack of unity due to the Hamas–Fatah split than by the challenges posed by the Arab Spring for Palestine. A united Palestinian struggle is still in general absent during the Arab Spring as both Hamas and Fatah are searching for new supporters,[91] and they are unable to overcome their differences and promote the Palestinian cause in the region. Finkenstein, Rabbani and Stern-Weiner compare this to the situation in the late 1980s: the Israeli-Palestinian conflict has been on the agenda for several decades and with the Israeli occupation of the West Bank, Gaza and East Jerusalem lasting for twenty years (without any significant changes), the international media and world powers have started losing interest in Palestine. The situation, nevertheless, changed rapidly due to the outbreak of the First Intifada, which brought the Palestinian question again to the centre of the world's attention, and resulted in significant changes and improvements of the situation in Palestine.[92]

---

88 Ibid. p. 24.

89 Finkenstein, Rabbani and Stern-Weiner demonstrate this regional isolation of Palestinians by e.g. the Kerry initiative of 2013 or the Israeli Operation Protective Edge of 2014, which both clearly document the lack of international support for the Palestinian questions since the outbreak of the Arab Spring. The diplomatic initiative of US Secretary of State John Kerry used the weaknesses of the Palestinians and their disillusionment with their situation to promote the Israeli demands of annexation of Jewish settlements on approximately 10% of the West Bank territories and nullification of the right of return of Palestinian refugees. Operation Protective Edge was launched by Israeli in July 2014 and included almost two months of air strikes and ground assaults on Gaza, with Egypt and Saudi Arabia calling for Hamas removal of power during this operation. The weakness of Palestinians was also reflected in the ceasefire proposed by Egyptian President al-Sisi (and supported by the Arab League), who called among other things for the stabilization of the security situation in Gaza, which could hardly be reached with Hamas in power, Ibid., p. 24–29.

90 Aronson, 'The Middle East Conflict after the Arab Spring: The Case of Palestine'.

91 As a result of regional dynamics and changes in the MENA region Hamas won the support of Egypt (under Morsi) and Tunisia; nevertheless it lost the support of Syria and Iran (Ezbidi, '"Arab Spring": Weather Forecast for Palestine', p. 99).

92 Finkelstein, Rabbani and Stern-Weiner, 'Palestine After the Arab Spring', p. 29.

The question remains if a similar internal process which would lead to renewed interests of the international community in Palestine will happen also as the result of the Arab Spring in Palestine. Should this be the case, it would require large scale changes within the Palestinian government, above all ending the Hamas–Fatah split by a really viable reconciliation agreement, consolidation of power of President Abbas, and legitimization of power in Palestine, for instance by new elections to the PLC, or by new presidential elections to support the real democratization of Palestine. Various campaigns against the Israeli occupation (such as the BDS) could also help to put the "Palestinian question" again on the world agenda.

References

67th General Assembly of the United Nations. 'General Assembly Votes Overwhelmingly to Accord Palestine "Non-Member Observer State" Status in United Nations'. *United Nations*, 29 November 2012. https://www.un.org/press/en/2012/ga11317.doc.htm, access 12 October 2017.

'2017 Index of Economic Freedom', n.d. http://www.heritage.org/index/explore, access 12 October 2017, access 12 October 2017.

Al-Arian, Ali, and Ali Mohsin. 'Palestine: Growing Recognition', 15 January 2017. http://www.aljazeera.com/indepth/interactive/2017/01/palestine-growing-recognition-170115201330185.html, access 12 October 2017.

Aronson, Geoffrey. 'The Middle East Conflict after the Arab Spring: The Case of Palestine'. *European View* 2011, No. 10 (13 November 2011): 215–20.

Balousha, Hazem. 'Hamas-Fatah Divide Cripples Palestine's Judiciary'. *AL Monitor*, n.d. http://www.al-monitor.com/pulse/originals/2015/05/palestine-gaza-west-bank-hamas-fatah-judiciary-legislation.html, access 12 October 2017.

Baroud, Ramzy. 'A Post "Arab Spring" Palestine', 3 July 2012. http://www.ramzybaroud.net/a-post-arab-spring-palestine, access 12 October 2017.

Birringer, Thomas. 'Results of the Elections of the Palestinian Legislative Council on January 25, 2006', n.d. http://www.kas.de/wf/doc/kas_7933-1522-2-30.pdf?130302205726, access 12 October 2017.

Birzeit University Media Development Center. 'Assessment of Media Development in Palestine Based on UNESCO's Media Development Indicators'. *UNESCO IPDC*, 2014. http://unesdoc.unesco.org/images/0022/002277/227784e.pdf, access 12 October 2017.

Bureau of Democracy, Human Rights and Labor. '2012 Report on International Religious Freedom: Israel and The Occupied Territories – The Occupied

Territories'. 2012 Report on International Religious Freedom. U.S. Department of State, 20 May 2013. https://www.state.gov/j/drl/rls/irf/2012/nea/208394.htm, access 12 October 2017.

Chomsky, Noam. *Fateful Triangle: The United States, Israel, and the Palestinians*. South End Press, London, 1999.

Danin, Robert, Oussama Kanaan, Firas Raad, and Marwan Muasher. 'Palestine: Economic Challenges and Political Implications', 27 March 2012. http://carnegieendowment.org/2012/03/27/palestine-economic-challenges-and-political-implications-event-3598, access 12 October 2017.

Dessi, Andrea. 'Israel and the Palestinians after the Arab Spring: No Time for Peace.' *IAI Working Papers 12, Instituto Affari Internazionali*, May 2012. http://www.iai.it/sites/default/files/iaiwp1216.pdf, access 12 October 2017.

Economist Intelligence Unit. 'The Economist Intelligence Unit's Democracy Index', n.d. https://infographics.economist.com/2017/DemocracyIndex/, access 12 October 2017.

Ezbidi, Basem. '"Arab Spring": Weather Forecast for Palestine'. *Middle East Policy* Vol. XX, No. 3, 99–110 (Fall 2013).

Finkelstein, Norman, Mounin Rabbani, and Jamie Stern-Weiner. 'Palestine After the Arab Spring.' *Insight Turkey* Vol. 17, No. 3 (Fall 2013): 86–98.

Freedom House. 'Freedom in the World 2017. Gaza Strip Profile', n.d. https://freedomhouse.org/report/freedom-world/2017/gaza-strip, access 12 October 2017.

–. 'Freedom in the World 2017: Israel', n.d. https://freedomhouse.org/report/freedom-world/2017/israel, access 12 October 2017.

–. 'Freedom in the World 2017. West Bank Profile', n.d. https://freedomhouse.org/report/freedom-world/2017/west-bank, access 12 October 2017.

Gilbert, Martin. *The Routledge Atlas of the Arab-Israeli Conflict*. Routledge, London, 2012.

Greenwood, Phoebe. 'Fatah Claims Palestinian Election Victory'. *The Telegraph*, 16 June 2017. http://www.telegraph.co.uk/news/worldnews/middleeast/palestinianauthority/9624112/Fatah-claims-Palestinian-election-victory.html, access 12 October 2017.

Khalil, Asem. 'Legislating for Migration: The Anomalous Case of the Palestinian Authority'. *European University Institute* 2006 (n.d.). http://cadmus.eui.eu/bitstream/handle/1814/11695/CARIM_ASN_2006_11.pdf?sequence=1, access 12 October 2017.

Kurtzer, Daniel C. *Pathways to Peace: America and the Arab-Israeli Conflict*. Macmillan, London, 2012.

Laqueur, Walter, and Dan Schueftan. *The Israel-Arab Reader: A Documentary History of the Middle East Conflict: Eighth Revised and Updated Edition*. Penguin, London, 2016.

Lauterpacht, H. 'Recognition of States in International Law'. *The Yale Law Journal* Vol. 53, No. 3 (June 1944) (n.d.): 385–458.

Ma'An News Agency. 'Bureau: Majority of Palestinians Live in Diaspora', 13 May 2015. https://www.maannews.com/Content.aspx?id=765378, access 12 October 2017.

McCoy, Jeffrey Dean. 'The Palestinian Security Force: Future Prospects'. *Joint Force Quarterly* 84, No. 1, p. 51–53 (January 2017). http://ndupress.ndu.edu/JFQ/Joint-Force-Quarterly-84/Article/1038806/the-palestinian-security-force-future-prospects/, access 12 October 2017.

MEMO Middle East Monitor. 'PA: One Third of Palestinians Live below Poverty Line', 11 April 2017. https://www.middleeastmonitor.com/20170411-pa-one-third-of-palestinians-live-below-poverty-line/, access 12 October 2017.

NGO Monitor. 'Palestinian Center for Human Rights (PCHR)', 17 January 2017. http://www.ngo-monitor.org/ngos/palestinian_center_for_human_rights_pchr_/, access 12 October 2017.

–. 'Palestinian NGO Network (PNGO)', 2 December 2013. http://www.ngo-monitor.org/ngos/palestinian_ngo_network_pngo_/, access 12 October 2017.

Nicolaou-Garcia, Silvia. 'Christian-Muslim Relations in Palestine'. Briefing Paper. MEMO Middle East Monitor, June 2010. https://www.mapsofworld.com/palestine/information/population.html, access 12 October 2017.

'Palestinian Public Opinion Poll No (59) – PRESS RELEASE'. *Palestinian Center for Policy and Survey Research*, 21 March 2016. http://www.pcpsr.org/en/node/634, access 12 October 2017.

Palmer, Alex. 'Trouble in Palestine'. *Harvard International Review*, 12 January 2012.

Persson, Anders. *The EU and the Israeli–Palestinian Conflict 1971–2013: In Pursuit of a Just Peace*. Lexington Books, New York, 2014.

'Population of Palestine'. *Maps of World*, n.d. https://www.mapsofworld.com/palestine/information/population.html, access 12 October 2017.

Reporters without Borders. '2017 World Press Freedom Index', n.d. https://rsf.org/en/ranking, access 12 October 2017.

Reporters without Borders. '2017 World Press Freedom Index – Tipping Point', 2017. https://rsf.org/en/2017-world-press-freedom-index-tipping-point, access 12 October 2017.

Sada, Abu Fadi. 'Media Landscapes: Palestine'. *European Journalism Centre*, n.d. http://ejc.net/media_landscapes/palestine, access 12 October 2017.

Sadiq, Nancy. 'Civil Society Organizations: Oslo as a Turning Point in Their Work Among the Masses'. *The Palestine-Israel Journal of Politics, Economics and Culture*, Civil Society Challenges, Vol. 18, no. No. 2 and 3 (2012).

Salem, Walid. 'Civil Society in Palestine: Approaches, Historical Context and the Role of the NGOs'. *The Palestine-Israel Journal of Politics, Economics and Culture*, Civil Society Challenges, Vol. 18, No. 2 and 3 (2012). http://www.pij.org/details.php?id=1437, access 12 October 2017.

Shabaneh, Ghassan. 'Egypt and Syria's Effect on the Israeli-Palestinian Conflict.' *Al Jazeera Center for Studies*, 31 October 2013. http://studies.aljazeera.net/mritems/Documents/2013/10/31/2013103110121825273 4Egypt%20and%20Syriat.pdf, access 12 October 2017.

Shikaki, Khalil. 'Old Guard, Young Guard: The Palestinian Authority and the Peace Process at Crossroads'. *Palestinian Center for Policy and Survey Research*, n.d. http://www.pcpsr.org/en/node/267, access 12 October 2017.

'State of Palestine. Palestinian Central Bureau of Statistics', n.d. http://www.pcbs.gov.ps/site/lang__en/881/default.aspx#Population, access 12 October 2017.

Tartir, Alaa. 'The Evolution and Reform of Palestinian Security Forces 1993–2013'. *Stability: International Journal of Security and Development* 4, no. 1 (n.d.): 1–20.

Tessler, Mark. *A History of the Israeli-Palestinian Conflict*. Indiana University Press, Bloomington, 2009.

'The CEC Publishes Detailed Results of the 2017 Local Elections'. *Central Elections Commission – Palestine*, 16 May 2017, http://www.elections.ps/tabid/40/language/en-US/Default.aspx?IDL=681, access 12 October 2017.

The Economist Intelligence Unit. 'Democracy Index. Palestine', n.d. http://country.eiu.com/palestine, access 12 October 2017.

The International Center for Not-for-Profit Law. 'Civic Freedom Monitor: Palestine', n.d. http://www.icnl.org/research/monitor/palestine.html, access 12 October 2017.

The World Bank. 'GDP per Capita (Current US$)', n.d. http://data.worldbank.org/indicator/NY.GDP.PCAP.CD, access 12 October 2017.

–. 'Palestine's Economic Outlook – Spring 2016', n.d. http://www.worldbank.org/en/country/westbankandgaza/publication/economic-outlook-spring-2016, access 12 October 2017.

–. 'West Bank and Gaza', n.d. http://data.worldbank.org/country/west-bank-and-gaza, access 12 October 2017.

Trading Economics. 'Palestine GDP Annual Growth Rate', n.d. http://www.tradingeconomics.com/palestine/gdp-growth-annual, access 12 October 2017.

TWIP Collective. 'The Security Forces Operating in Palestine. An Overview', n.d. https://thisweekinpalestine.com/wp-content/uploads/2014/07/The-Security-Forces-Operating-in-Palestine.pdf, access 12 October 2017.

'UN Data State of Palestine', n.d. http://data.un.org/CountryProfile.aspx?crName=State%20of%20Palestine, access 12 October 2017.

United Nations Development Programme. 'Human Development Reports', n.d. hdr.undp.org, access 12 October 2017.

Jana Samadová

Syria

In the last six years, the situation in Syria has escalated from internal frustration with the regime's economic and social policies to a regional and international engagement unprecedented since the end of the Cold War. The country has witnessed several brutal moments in that period. During the Arab Spring, the democratization attempts in the country turned into a civil war. It was put in the spotlight due to the constant political and security turmoil that is affecting the economic and social life of the Syrian people on a daily basis, in addition to its impact on the whole region.

The civilian Syrian population has been suffering for more than six years as it undergoes losses of life[1], limbs, homes, schools and communities. The regime, as well as other fighters, are using artillery shelling, aerial bombardment, heavy arms and allegedly chemical weapons without distinction between civilians and combatants.[2] In addition, since the beginning of the anti-government protests in March 2011, tens of thousands of arrests, detentions and disappearances have been reported by the Syrian people while pointing at an extensive network of detention facilities and torture centres spread all over the country.[3] As a result, Human Rights Watch requested, in its report in 2012, the UN Security Council to refer the situation in Syria to the International Criminal Court and make the Syrian government open all the detention facilities on its territory to international detention monitors.[4]

The ethnic division, that is happening, is drawing new internal borders that will be very difficult to erase if or when the war ends. Additionally, more than half of the Syrian population has left their homes.[5] Some of them are Internally Displaced Peoples, others have sought refuge in neighbouring countries, such as

1 According to the Syrian Network for Human Rights, almost 207,000 civilian victims were killed between May 2011 and March 2017. Human Rights Watch lists 470,000 as the death toll as of February 2016.

2 'Syria: Civilian Harm and Assistance'.

3 'Torture Archipelago: Arbitrary Arrests, Torture and Enforced Disappearances in Syria's Underground Prisons since March 2011'.

4 'Torture Archipelago: Arbitrary Arrests, Torture and Enforced Disappearances in Syria's Underground Prisons since March 2011', 1–6.

5 Balanche, 'Ethnic Cleansing Threatens Syria's Unity'.

Lebanon, Jordan and Turkey, while others decided to migrate to Europe with hope for a better future. Syria is ethnically and religiously diverse and hence a large portion of Syrians are facing discrimination in terms of a calculated strategy of ethnic cleansing of each faction. Therefore, resettling those people in the future will become a strategic question for all the players involved in the Syrian conflict.[6]

Furthermore, the government is maintaining sieges of civilian areas where armed fighters are hiding, which is causing starvation, inaccessible medical care and basic services. This situation has triggered a humanitarian crisis and an international humanitarian response, in which several international governmental and nongovernmental organizations such as Doctors Without Borders and UN Convoys are trying to help and assist the civilian suffering population. However, under the pretext of security, regime forces sometimes block and deny humanitarian access to some areas. They occasionally attack medical facilities and workers as well (bombing of hospitals, restriction of the inclusion of medical supplies in humanitarian aid deliveries, detaining medical workers and volunteers, etc.).[7]

Taking into consideration that the conflict in Syria is still ongoing, this chapter will focus on the status of democratization before the uprising in 2011 and its evolvement during the war. It presents the details of the war, its actors, its consequences and the position of the international community, along with an analysis of relevant internal and external factors. It also seeks to offer the key events and elements that led to this chaos that has put millions of people out of their homes with huge losses of all kinds and with no vision of a bright foreseeable future of their country that was once homeland to several great civilizations.

1. Internal non-institutional factors

Contemporary Syria represents just a piece of the territory that was historically covered by the Bilad al-Sham under the rule of the Ottoman Empire, also known as "Greater Syria", an era that ended with the beginning of the 20th century. This caused the rise of nationalism and feelings of bitterness towards the West later in history.[8] After the end of the First World War and the fall of the Ottoman Empire, the whole region of the Levant was divided into mandated territories between the French and the British according to the Sykes-Picot agreement of 1916,[9] regardless of the British promise of independence to the Arabs through

---

6 Balanche.

7 'Amnesty International Report 2016/17: The State of the World's Human Rights', 349.

8 Baron, *Histoire de la Syrie, 1918 à nos jours*, 13–14.

9 Dib, *Tarikh Souriya al-Mouaaser*, 37.

the Hussein–McMahon Correspondence of 1915/16.[10] The French held control over Syria and Lebanon under the pretext of guiding and helping them to become self-governing. At that time, Syria was at the rock-bottom of its institutional, economic and political life with no self-rule institutions, no proper implementation of democratic procedures and no politicians experienced in parliamentary and modern civil service. In that political area, France was facing strong nationalism from the Syrian people and decided to empower the minorities, particularly the Alawites, by officially recognizing them and giving them some autonomy, to avoid having a united Sunni opposition[11] (the French mandate in the Middle East was known to be protective of minorities like the Maronites in Lebanon and the Alawites in Syria).[12]

After its independence in 1946 and until the end of the 20th century, Syria went through four essential stages: the period of coups, the period of unification, the rise to power of the Baathist Party and the period of reforms executed by the army under the rule of Hafez al-Assad. First, the Syrians had to develop their own institutions while choosing their leaders, their alliances and the tone of their politics. In the first decade of its independent existence, Syria witnessed a real parliamentary experience regardless of the successive militarily coups that took place, since the French administrations left no functional organization other than the army.[13] Moreover, the coups were carried out by people who tried to implement secular reforms, Western values and democratic elections despite of their undemocratic accession to power.[14]

Second, the period of unification that began in 1955 was characterized by the growing activity of left-wing parties, such as the Syrian Communist Party and the Arab Socialist Baath Party, who achieved significant political gains by attracting the marginalized social classes.[15] In addition to that, the governing parties suggested the establishment of the United Arab Republic with Egypt, which came to life in 1958 and ended in 1961 despite this union seeming very promising in its concept. The United Arab Republic emerged in a period during which the Middle East was dragged into the Cold War through the Baghdad Pact.[16] This course

10 'Husayn-McMahon Correspondence – British-Palestinian History'.

11 Baron, *Histoire de la Syrie, 1918 à nos jours*, 15.

12 Dib, *Tarikh Souriya al-Mouaaser*, 48.

13 John McHugo, *Syria – A History of the Last Hundred Years*.

14 'Souriya min al-istiklal ila hikm al-Assad 1945–2012'.

15 'Souriya min al-istiklal ila hikm al-Assad 1945–2012'.

16 The Baghdad Pact or the Central Treaty Organization was a mutual security organization dating from 1955 to 1979, composed of Turkey, Iran, Pakistan and the United

of action pushed Syria towards Egypt and its president Gamal Abdel Nasser to counter the pro-Western alliance. It also brought Syria closer to the Soviet Union which established strong ties with both Syria and Egypt, including various arms sales and business investments such as the Euphrates Dam.[17] Syria sought in the United Arab Republic the empowerment of pan-Arabism and the reform of the Arab world. The union ended because the Syrian officials realized that they had no chance of imposing their demands on Abdel Nasser.[18] However, this experience weakened and divided Syria between the Baath Party and the Communist Party, which led to the establishment of an authoritarian and repressive regime by the Baath Party that came to power. The Baath party represented the idea of the Arab renaissance and promoted socialism. However, their ideas were different from the communists: a socialism based on Arabism, Islam and nationalism. Moreover, they were also different from the Muslim Brotherhood, which was one of the leading players in Syrian politics, in terms of religion: the Baathists are inspired by Islam as a fundamental source of the Arab culture while the Muslim Brotherhood aims to apply the traditional Islamic rule.[19] This led to the third period of Syrian political life in the 20th century; the Baath Party is nowadays associated with the Alawites, a religious Shia minority that was isolated for many centuries and oppressed by the Sunni majority in Syria for religious reasons, as the Shia religion was considered a heresy.[20]

Finally, Hafez al-Assad, an Alawite, became president in November 1970 and led a very strict internal policy to protect himself and his people from the Sunni majority.[21] On the international level, al-Assad applied an approach of self-interest rather than building allies on the principle of fidelity and loyalty. This explains Syria's relationship with its neighbours and the great powers of the world. After the death of Hafez al-Assad in 2000, his son Bashar took his place,[22] which will be developed further in this chapter (see part 2.2).

Kingdom. It was initiated by the United Kingdom and the United States to counter the threat of the Soviet expansion into vital Middle East oil-producing regions. Source: 'Central Treaty Organization (CENTO)'.

17 Baron, *Histoire de la Syrie, 1918 à nos jours*, 143–52.

18 Baron, 149.

19 Baron, 135–36.

20 Dib, *Tarikh Souriya al-Mouaaser*, 44.

21 Dib, 401.

22 Dib, 405.

1.1 Economic factors

The Arab Spring reached Syria in March 2011 and as it was not just a political uprising it is important to review the Syrian economy over the last two decades. This part will examine the GDP, the unemployment rates, the state of natural resources and the economic reforms made under the rule of Bashar al-Assad.

The GDP of the country in 2010 represented 60,465 million US dollars (2918.1 US dollars per capita)[23] while in 2014 it dropped to 34,184 million US dollars (1821 US dollars per capita)[24]. Taken into consideration that the country is in chaos, economic data are very hard to find. However, symbolically the numbers show the devastating set back by decades in terms of economic, social and human development as the GDP in 2014 is half of what it was before the war. And as the war continues, this situation today could only be worse.[25]

As for the unemployment rate, it is estimated to have reached 13.2% in 2014, while it was 8.4% in 2010.[26] Nevertheless, due to the refugee crisis and the IDPs, it is hard to determine the current unemployment rate. In addition, 3 million Syrians lost their jobs during the conflict and consequently made 12 million Syrians lose their primary source of income.[27] This was reflected in the increase of unemployment to 50% in 2016. [28]

Furthermore, the Syrian population is suffering from poverty, even though al-Assad implemented some neoliberal economic reforms because that benefited a small group of highly ranked people close to the regime.[29] In fact, al-Assad attempted to liberalize the economy at the beginning of his presidency by implementing new laws aiming to encourage private investments and the private banking sector.[30] The economic situation in Syria pushed the regime to privatize some state-owned businesses, particularly in the telecommunication sectors. However, the enterprises were sold to family members and highly ranked party officials, which meant that the reforms did not reach the general population.[31]

23 'Country Profile – Syrian Arab Republic'.
24 'Country Profile – Syrian Arab Republic'.
25 Jeanne Gobat and Kristina Kostial, 'Syria's Conflict Economy'.
26 'Country Profile – Syrian Arab Republic'.
27 'Syria's War'.
28 'The World Factbook – Unemployment Rate'.
29 Adam Coutts, 'Syria's Uprising Could Have Been Avoided through Reform'.
30 Baron, *Histoire de la Syrie, 1918 à nos jours*, 289–90.
31 Moukheiber, 'President Assad And The Syrian Business Elite'.

1.2 Civil society and media

1.2.1 Civil society

Usually, authoritarian regimes tend to ban any political or social opposition and have a discouraging attitude towards the development of independent CSOs with the fear that it may present a counterweight to state power.[32] According to Article 8 of the Syrian Constitution, "*the leading party in the society and the state is the Socialist Arab Baath Party. It leads a patriotic and progressive front seeking to unify the resources of the people's masses and place them at the service of the Arab nation's goals*",[33] which prevents the establishment of any other independent party. Nonetheless, this repression did not stop small groups of intellectuals and critics from trying to express their wish for changes in the country's political system in the new millennium; noting that those are not the efforts that ignited the uprising back in 2011.[34]

Since the insurrection in 2011, after its long absence and the limitation of its role to charitable work, civil society has become significant in the Syrian context. The number of CSOs increased in six years more than it had in a century, reaching more than 1,000 organizations.[35] Furthermore, the reasons of their emergence were various. Some got established with the purpose of reporting the rising violence and the violations and for helping those in need, for example, the Syrian Centre for Democracy and the Syrian Centre for Civil Society and Human Rights Studies, while others were formed to find job opportunities for the frustrated unemployed young population that is fleeing the country[36]. In other words, prior to the uprising, civil society was barely figuring in the public and private life of Syrians because the term civil society was associated with the political opposition which was harshly punished by the regime.[37] Afterwards, the civil society grew in the number of organizations and in the diversity of their objectives. Today, it plays a significant role in helping society while in humanitarian crisis and in life threatening conditions. Many sources claim that it will continue to be a key player in the Syrian question even in post-conflict resolutions and reconstruction.[38]

---

32 Alvarez-Ossorio, 'Syria's Struggling Civil Society'.

33 'The Syrian Constitution – 1973–2012'.

34 Alvarez-Ossorio, 'Syria's Struggling Civil Society'.

35 'Results of the First Phase of Mapping Syrian Civil Society Actors'.

36 Zohbi, 'Mounazamat al-moujtamaa al-madani al-souri'.

37 Khalaf, Ramadan, and Stolleis, 'Activism in Difficult Times – Civil Society Groups in Syria 2011–2014'.

38 Khalaf, Ramadan, and Stolleis.

1.2.2 Media

Nowadays, Syria is in the spotlight of media coverage from all around the world. In addition, the Arab Spring is said[39] to be a social media revolution where information and meetings are being shared among the people as well as with the outside world that is closely following the evolution of the situation in Syria. This part will focus on the condition of the media in Syria and the role of media in the Syrian Arab Spring.

The media in Syria was and is still controlled by the government so the only official news available comes from government sources censored by the regime of Bashar al-Assad.[40] However, the rebels established their own channels, such as the television channel Suria al-Shaab and different Twitter and Facebook accounts, with their own news presentations, since al-Assad lost control over many parts of the country. In addition, rebel-held territories such as places under the control of IS are witnessing a brutal suppression of independent media and public executions of reporters.[41]

According to the Freedom House report for the year 2017, Syria is labelled as a "not free" country in terms of press freedom. It scored 90 points out of 100,[42] knowing that 0 represents the "most free" and 100 the "least free". Furthermore, the report states that the internet penetration rate in Syria is of 30%,[43] which indicates that the population cannot freely access the internet due to the state censorship or has no means to use the internet due to heavy destruction of infrastructure and electric shortages. As the details of the year 2017 have not yet been published, looking at the 2016 report provides a deeper insight into the situation. The legal environment analysis shows that the constitution stands for freedom of press and bans the punishment of journalists, but the government passed a law in 2011 stating that *"the media must respect the freedom of expression by practicing it with awareness and responsibility"*[44] which the regime uses as an excuse to persecute the media. Within those measures, a National Media Council was established to

39 Beaumont, 'The Truth about Twitter, Facebook and the Uprisings in the Arab World'.

40 Salvadoretti, 'The Role of Social Media in the Syrian Crisis'.

41 'Syria – Country Report 2016'.

42 'Syria – Country Report 2017'.

43 'Syria – Country Report 2017'.

44 El Zein, 'The "New" Syrian Media Law Is Nothing New – Committee to Protect Journalists'.

regulate the information sector showing the unwillingness of al-Assad to support a free media environment.[45]

Social media played a pivotal role in the crisis as their essential aim was to shape how the crisis is portrayed and perceived. At the early stages of the uprising, social media were just for information or misinformation. Afterwards, they became a medium to share certain aspects of the revolution that were banned from the mainstream local media.[46] On the other hand, social media gave the people a false hope that dictators can be overthrown with videos of peaceful protests and critical posts.[47] Later, it misled them to think that social media and the openness to the entire world would stop the massacres and the violence in the country. In the case of Syria, social media gave the government the opportunity to prepare for planned protests which made the activists very vulnerable and less resilient to the regime.[48]

1.3 Extremism and religion

As the situation in the Middle East is influenced by religious and ethnic diversity, it is important to explain how this situation is reflected in Syria. Moreover, the Arab Spring in that country took a sharp turn into a religious war.[49] The first part will present the main religious denominations and the ethnic division of Syria. The second part is dedicated to the Islamic State of Iraq and the Levant as one of the major examples of fanaticism and terrorism as well as other extremist organizations.

A person or a regime does not become automatically sectarianist by belonging to a sect but by considering the public affairs, the state's interests and the other constitutions of a society pertinent to a specific sect.[50] Hence, the concept of sectarianism is not only restricted to religious spheres but also to politics, factionalism and ideology. As for Syria, the Baath party that came to power in 1963 began to apply the notion of sectarianism by pushing out the generals and other leaders that were of Nasserist principles with ideas of Pan-Arabism instead of "socialism in one state model".[51] In addition, the Baathists gave the highest military ranks and political positions only to Alawites.[52]

---

45 El Zein.
46 Salvadoretti, 'The Role of Social Media in the Syrian Crisis'.
47 Alkoussa, 'How Facebook Hurt the Syrian Revolution'.
48 Alkoussa.
49 Daniel Bruke, 'Syria Explained'.
50 Kilo, 'Al-Akaliyat Fi Souriya.. Min Al-Assad Ila Al-Thawra'.
51 Adam Garrie, 'An Overview of Competing Ideologies in the Arab World'.
52 Kilo, 'Al-Akaliyat Fi Souriya.. Min Al-Assad Ila Al-Thawra'.

Furthermore, Syria is characterized by a religious diversity. The Sunnis are the largest religious group of the country. They represent 74% of the Syrian population[53] and they are of different ethnical origins: Turkomans, Circassians, Iraqis and Palestinians.[54] As for the Shias, they form 13% of the population including the Alawites.[55] The third largest group (10%) is represented by Christians.[56] They are ethnically diverse – Assyrians, Chaldeans, Syriacs and Armenians. The Druze are a religious minority living primarily in the South of the country and in the Golan Heights, representing around 3% of the population.[57] Lastly, the Jews form a very small minority concentrated in Aleppo and Damascus.[58]

On the other hand, Syria's ethnic diversity consists mainly of Arabs, Kurds and the Yazidis. The Kurds ethnically represent 7 to 10% of the Syrians[59] and are concentrated in the northeast, close to the Turkish borders. Most Kurds are Muslim Sunni and speak a language related to Persian.[60] Finally, the Yazidis are in the Sinjar Mountains, near the Iraqi border. The Yazidis are Kurdish-speaking descendants.[61]

As for extremism in Syria, the Islamic State of Iraq and the Levant (ISIL/IS) is the most famous radical Islamist organization fighting mainly in Syria and Iraq. However, it is far from being the only religious actor in the Syrian scenario: Hezbollah, the Muslim Brotherhood and other Islamist organizations such as Jabhat Fateh al-Sham and the Syrian Islamic Front, also play a role in the Syrian conflict.

The Islamic State of Iraq and the Levant is also known as Daesh, Organization of al-Jihad's Base of Operations in the Land of the Two Rivers, the Islamic Caliphate, and the Islamic State of Iraq and Syria.[62] It is not a newly founded organization but it goes back to the times when Abu Musab al-Zarqawi established an

53 'The World Factbook – Syria'.
54 'Al-Tarkiba Al-Soukaniya Fi Souriya'.
55 'The World Factbook – Syria'.
56 'The World Factbook – Syria'.
57 'The World Factbook – Syria'.
58 'Al-Tarkiba Al-Soukaniya Fi Souriya'.
59 'The Ethnic and Religious Groups of Syria'.
60 'Who Are the Kurds?'
61 Sebastien Maisel, 'Syria's Yezidis in the Kurd Dagh and the Jazıra: Building Identities in a Heterodox Community'.
62 'ISIS'.

affiliation to al-Qaeda in Iraq (AQI) in 2004.[63] In 2006, this organization parted ways with al-Qaeda and became the Islamic state of Iraq (ISI).[64]

ISI already had established ties in Syria as Bashar al-Assad had sent many Syrian jihadists to fight in Iraq the American invasion in 2003. Furthermore, the Syrian regime freed many imprisoned radicals when the uprising started in 2011 to integrate fear among the protesters. ISI expanded its own forces to Syria and declared the creation of ISIL.[65] ISIL gained a significant international attention for its use of military precision, religious ideology and technologic innovations to a point that al-Qaeda feels threatened and is trying to discredit it by criticizing it for the excessive use of violence against civilians and more specifically against the Muslim population.[66]

Moreover, many conspiracies were formed about the real reason behind the rise of ISIL: on one hand, the US and the Zionist movement are doubted to have established this organization for Israel's aim to weaken and destroy Arab countries, on the other hand Iran and Syria are accused of supporting ISIL's ambitions, in order to marginalize the moderated Sunnism.[67] In addition, ISIL has many sources of funding and thus it is hard to defeat. The sources vary from "*illicit proceeds from occupation of territory (theft, extortion and illicit taxation), kidnapping for ransom, donations though non-profit organizations (from Gulf States, from organizations that pledged allegiance to ISIL in the Philippines and Egypt), material support from foreign terrorist fighter and fundraising through modern communication networks*".[68]

The Muslim Brotherhood was assumed to be the strongest opposition of the regime before the uprising in 2011.[69] Its members were exiled by the regime and they co-founded the Syrian National Council (see section 2.2). It was originally established in 1942 as an extension of the Egyptian Muslim Brotherhood (see

---

63 Al-Zarqawi is a Jordanian who in 1999 went to Afghanistan trying to impress al-Qaeda leaders with his revolutionary ideas for the Fertile Crescent (from the Nile River in Egypt to the Tigris and Euphrates rivers in modern Iraq). The collapse of the "Islamic Emirate of Afghanistan" made him leave the country to set roots in Iraq against the US invasion in Iraq in 2003. He was killed by the US forces in 2006 and with his death AQI witnessed a declining period.

64 William McCants, *The ISIS Apocalypse – The History, Strategy, and Doomsday Vision of the Islamic State*.

65 William McCants.

66 Holbrook, 'Al-Qaeda and the Rise of ISIS'.

67 Cheterian, 'ISIS and the Killing Fields of the Middle East'.

68 'Financing of the Terrorist Organisation ISIL'.

69 'The Muslim Brotherhood in Syria'.

chapter about Egypt).[70] They also developed armed militias when they got pushed into the background in the Syrian scenario by the Islamists and radicals.[71] They belong to the Sunni faith and favoured Syria becoming an Islamic state in the political sense, hence their clash with the secular Baath Party.[72]

Finally, Hezbollah is a Lebanese Shia movement affiliated to and sponsored by Iran (see chapter about Lebanon). Its engagement in Syria started under the pretext of protecting the holy places of Shia Muslims such as the shrine of Sayyidah Zaynab to which Shias make pilgrimages, much as Catholics visit the Old City of Jerusalem.[73] Later in the war, Hezbollah's military support was crucial, on several occasions, to the regime's forces in regaining control over rebel-held territories.[74] Hezbollah's engagement in the Syrian question evoked controversial opinions nationally, regionally and internationally as well.

2. Internal institutional factors

2.1 Security and defence structures

Syria is not a member of the 1993 Convention on the Prohibition of the Development, Production, Stockpiling, and Use of Chemical Weapons and on their Destruction but has signed the 1925 Geneva Gas protocol. The use of chemical weapons is also prohibited as a matter of customary international humanitarian law, or the laws of war.[75] This demonstrates the Syrian position on the use of chemical weapons under international law, which means that the confirmed allegations about the government-organised chemical attacks are a serious violation of international law, humanitarian law and even of the laws of war.

The Syrian regime has been allegedly responsible for several chemical attacks since 2013: the attacks on Khan al-Assal on March 19, 2013, on the opposition-controlled Damascus suburbs of Eastern and Western Ghouta on August 21, 2013, and on the rebel-held town of Khan Sheikhoun in north-western Syria on April 4, 2017. There is no hard evidence to support any of the claims on the identity of the offender and therefore it evoked a strong reaction from the international community.

70 'The Muslim Brotherhood in Syria'.
71 Sherlock, 'Muslim Brotherhood Establishes Militia inside Syria'.
72 'The Syrian Muslim Brotherhood'.
73 Reese Erlich, *Inside Syria: The Backstory of Their Civil War and What the World Can Expect*.
74 Marisa Sullivan, 'Hezbollah in Syria'.
75 'Attacks on Ghouta: Analysis of Alleged Use of Chemical Weapons in Syria'.

Finally, as was mentioned above, Syria has witnessed several military coups, hence the importance of the military. The core of the army was formed in 1920, during the French mandate, and was officially established in 1948, after independence.[76] The Syrian military force is one of the essential pillars of the regime, since al-Assad resorted to his armed forces when the demonstrations started in 2011, to repress the protesters demanding the overthrow of the regime.[77] As the uprising progressed, some highly ranked military and security officials started to defect from the army and formed the Free Syrian Army (FSA) that joined the grades of the opposition (see section 2.2). However, the army, in general, is a solid unit and most of the representatives remained loyal to the regime.[78]

2.2 Political factors

After Hafez al-Assad, his son Bashar has become one of the key figures in the politics of Syria particularly and of the Middle East generally. Bashar was not supposed to be the successor to the Syrian presidency. However, his older brother Bassel died in a car accident in 1994 and the political responsibility fell on Bashar.[79] He was elected president on June 10, 2000 after he was approved at the highest levels of the government. As the single candidate for the presidency, chosen by the parliament, he won with 97% of the votes in a referendum.[80]

Moreover, the beginning of the presidency of Bashar al-Assad was considered as a "Damascus' Spring" because he promised in his inaugural speech on July 17, 2000 a variety of reforms that would liberate and modernize the country, including democracy, economic liberation and freedom of speech.[81] He failed to keep those promises for two reasons. First, there was an internal dispute over the methods of execution of those reforms: Bashar wanted a plan backed with hard data and socioeconomic studies while CSOs and the opposition demanded a quick change.[82] Second, external factors such as the second Palestinian Intifada in 2000 and the 9/11 attack in the United States pushed Syria to close up again and fortify its stability. Finally, Syrian politics were forced to change their approach in 2005 when the regime was accused of assassinating the Lebanese prime

76 'Al-Jaysh Al-Souri'.
77 'Al-Jaysh Al-Souri'.
78 'Interactive'.
79 Baron, *Histoire de la Syrie, 1918 à nos jours*, 282.
80 Research Directorate, Immigration and Refugee Board, Canada, 'Refworld | Syria'.
81 Dib, *Tarikh Souriya al-Mouaaser*, 721.
82 'Tarikh Souriya Men Aahed Hafez Al-Assad Ila Al-Harb Al-Souriya'.

minister Rafic Hariri and its soldiers were forced out of the Lebanese territory (see chapter about Lebanon). These factors, along with the devastating situation in Iraq, made the Syrian people support their government in an unprecedented way and the Damascus Spring was pushed aside. However, the first formations of opposition that emerged during the Arab Spring can be traced to this period.[83] This first opposition included many activists that are present in today's conflict such as Michel Kilo (the Committees for the Revival of Civil Society in Syria), Riad Seif (the National Dialogue Forum in 2000) who became a member of the Syrian National Council in 2012, Hussein al-Awdat who is now a member of the National Coordination Body for Democratic Change, etc.[84]

At the beginning of 2011 and following the situation in Tunisia and Egypt (see chapter about Egypt), Bashar al-Assad did not predict that uprisings would take place in Syria.[85] He was convinced that his regime was safe as "*he believed his own public-relations propaganda that Syrians would never rebel against a pan-Arabist, anti-Israel, anti-imperialist fighter like himself. Rarely has a world leader been proven so wrong so quickly*".[86] In addition, the deteriorating economic situation (see section 1.1), along with the dictatorial governance of al-Assad, where criticism meant incarceration, no opposition was allowed and social media were banned,[87] led to the first display of discontent by the population.

The first demonstration of the uprising took place in the provincial city of Daraa in March 2011 where the regime's forces arrested and tortured young boys for spraying anti-regime slogans on the walls. This action made the boys' families protest and demand their release.[88] The police reacted by shooting and killing some of the protesters. Hence, demonstrations started off in other provinces of the country. What distinguishes the uprising in Syria from other countries is that it started in rural areas (the same situation as in Libya) as Bashar had concentrated his repressive apparatus in the main cities.[89] In addition to that, villages were politically and economically marginalized because their populations represented Syria's Sunni majority, which the regime liked to leave on the side-lines. Furthermore, this discrimination was not limited to the village/city differentiation but

---

83 'Tarikh Souriya Men Aahed Hafez Al-Assad Ila Al-Harb Al-Souriya'.

84 'The Damascus Spring'.

85 James L. Gelvin, *The Arab Uprisings: What Everyone Needs to Know.*

86 Reese Erlich, *Inside Syria: The Backstory of Their Civil War and What the World Can Expect.*

87 Reese Erlich.

88 Joe Sterling, 'Daraa'.

89 James L. Gelvin, *The Arab Uprisings: What Everyone Needs to Know.*

demonstrated even within the same city, where there were wide gaps between the rich, the moderate and the poor social classes.[90]

Moreover, the opposition was obliged to escalate its form of demonstration by using arms and violence.[91] At this stage, there was no going back because if protesters eased their position, the regime would have imprisoned them and made any signs of uprising disappear, which would have made the situation in Syria even worse than it was before. Yet, the opposition lacked some political and military organization, and was divided into countless fractions of rebels and militias.

Thus, the civil uprising in Syria started peacefully with demands of reforms and institutional changes. When the regime reacted violently, the opposition did not want any modifications in the same regime but aspired for an entire new government through free elections. Later, the demonstrations became violent in a form of an armed rebellion, political Islam was spotlighted, and what started as an uprising grew into a civil war. Today's conflict in Syria is very chaotic and is very hard to explain. Nonetheless, this part will attempt to list the main actors of the war and describe their role in the ongoing battles.

The Syrian opposition is formed of the National Coordination Body for Democratic Change that was established in 2011 to integrate the opposition and their demands into one non-armed coalition. Next, the Democratic Union Party (YPG) is a Syrian Kurdish party affiliated to the militant Kurdistan Workers' Party PKK (see chapter about Turkey). Their political objectives are to be included in the process of democratization once the war is over to get the rights of the Kurdish people recognized and to gain democratic autonomy.[92]

The third group is the FSA, which was established in 2011 when soldiers and generals deserted the Syrian army and fled to Turkey. Later, it became a part of the Supreme Military Council of the FSA where tens of fronts united to form a strong counterweight to the jihadists.[93] The Syrian Islamic Front is a merger of several Islamist groups following the Salafism ideology (extreme Sunnism), supported by Saudi Arabia.[94] Also, the Syrian National Council was formed in 2011 by the exiled opposition in Turkey, whose activity was weakened by the foreign support of several rebel groups that were in Syria and would help the foreign countries to set their own agendas. Finally, the Local Coordination Committees of Syria is a

90 Balanche, 'Géographie de la révolte syrienne'.
91 Baron, *Histoire de la Syrie, 1918 à nos jours*, 330–31.
92 'The Kurdish Democratic Union Party'.
93 'Guide to the Syrian Rebels'.
94 'The Syrian Islamic Front'.

network of media and civil anti-regime activists since 2011. It initially organised the demonstrations and published information about the uprising.[95]

Further actors include IS (see section 1.3), the Muslim Brotherhood (see section 1.3), Jabhat Fateh al-Sham (formerly Jabhat al-Nusra until 2016 when it broke ties with al-Qaida), Jaysh al-Sham, Fatah al-Islam, Ahrar al-Sham, Martyrs of Syria Brigades, Northern Storm Brigade, Harakat Ahrar al-Sham al-Islamiyya, Jaysh al-Islam, Suqour al-Sham, Ahfad al-Rasoul Brigades and others.[96]

Overall, it is worth noting that the opposition, the rebels and the radicals fight among themselves and have a strategic rivalry for power and territory. They are all supported by different local and foreign parties according to their goals, religious and political aspirations and their capabilities. This causes a serious problem for the Syrian question as there is no united opposition force that can be considered a potential successor to al-Assad's regime.

As for the pro-regime forces, they are as complex as the anti-regime parties. Regardless, the main actors are the regime's forces and militias formed by Syria's official armed forces and the secret services, and are financially and militarily backed by Russia[97], Hezbollah (see sections 1.3 and 3), other Shia militias and foreign aid.

2.3 Rule of law – judiciary system

When the Baath Party came to power in 1970, Hafez al-Assad implemented a new Constitution, which gives the President the power to veto laws and act of his own accord if necessary to protect the nation's interests and national security.[98] In reaction to several attempts of opposition, the regime established different exceptional courts, such as the Economic Security Court in 1977, with the purpose of dealing with financial and economic crimes, but it also had jurisdiction over cases of crimes against the socialist regime. This negates the judicial independence granted by that same Constitution. [99]

Moreover, when Bashar al-Assad was to become president, there was a Constitutional obstacle as the President had to be of the minimum age of 40 while Bashar was only 34. However, this did not constitute any problem, because the

95 'Lijan Al-Tansik Al-Mahaliya Fi Souriya'.
96 'Guide to the Syrian Rebels'.
97 'Who Is Fighting in Syria's Civil War?'
98 Qais Fares, 'The Syrian Constitution'.
99 'ILAC Rule of Law Assessment Report: Syria 2017'.

government changed the mandatory minimum age to 34.[100] This shows how the Constitution and the rule of law in Syria was malleable to fit the regime's needs and always in favour of the governing elite. As for the state of emergency, it has been in place since 1963 and allows the regime to suspend most constitutional protections. It is justified by the state of war with Israel and by the threats posed by militant groups in the country. [101]

Finally, with the uprising in 2011, al-Assad had to initiate some changes and reforms with the thought that satisfying the demands of the opposition will stabilize the situation in Syria. In that matter, he lifted the state of emergency in April 2011[102] and appointed a committee to draft a new Constitution, which was approved in February 2012. The new Constitution was supposed to introduce a multipolar system and multicandidate presidential elections. However, nothing changed and the framework in its core was designed to keep al-Assad and his regime in power.[103]

3. External factors

Syria has swiftly become an international question. As in every international crisis, the various actors of the world had diverging opinions and stood by different sides of the conflict. The world got divided between the supporters of the regime of al-Assad and the supporters of the opposition. However, even on the same side, the international community is not homogenous. For example, despite supporting the opposition against the regime, Turkey and the Gulf States do not back the same groups. It is interesting to observe the behaviour of various states as it has changed along with the circumstances. For instance, the European Union and the United States considered the overthrow of the regime as the only solution to the conflict back in 2011. Later, Bashar became a part of the solution as his regime participates in negotiations such as the Geneva peace talks, and is still a key figure in the Syrian question. This part of the chapter offers a summary of the different reactions of the international community.

The relation between the United States and Syria have been in conflict mainly since the presidency of George W. Bush and his invasion of Iraq in 2003. The American administration accuses the Syrian regime of sponsoring terrorism since

100 Baron, *Histoire de la Syrie, 1918 à nos jours*, 287.
101 'Syria Protests'.
102 'Syria Protests'.
103 Qais Fares, 'The Syrian Constitution'.

1979,[104] hosting Palestinian radicals, having weapons of mass destruction and conspiring against Israel.[105] For that matter, the US imposed sanctions on Syria within the *Syria Accountability and Lebanese Sovereignty Restoration Act* of 2003. This is just one of the many episodes that have isolated Syria from the West and many other countries.

Despite having warned Syria that using chemical weapons would cross a "redline",[106] alleged chemical attacks took place in 2013 (see section 2.1). Obama's decision to intervene militarily was not supported by any of his allies except for France and the United Kingdom which later stepped down. Moreover, a UN resolution backing the intervention was improbable because it would have likely been vetoed by Russia and China[107] (China's foreign policy defends the right of the people to decide their fate without any outside intervention, which can be applied to China's position towards Syria: it keeps its distance from the conflict, without directly meddling in the war, while maintaining good relations with al-Asssad's regime).[108] Surprisingly, the United States and Russia were able to agree on placing Syrian chemical weapons under international control and then destroying them.

Furthermore, the United States had the initiative to support the "moderate" rebels, that are no better than others by any other measures, such as the FSA,[109] claiming that al-Assad is on the wrong side of history. They started financing the Syrian National Council which was in exile and consequently ineffective.[110] Thus, the American administration oriented its effort on helping the opposition fighters inside the country like the FSA,[111] by sending arms and opening training camps in Jordan near the Syrian borders. However, this plan failed because the recruits did not return to the battle fields in Syria or got lured in by extremist organizations.[112] No matter how big of a failure those steps were, Washington was holding back from a military operation after their experience with Libya (see chapter about Libya). Obama's last noteworthy engagement in the Syrian conflict was his decision to combat ISIL in 2015. The operation started first in Iraq and

---

104 'Syria Sanctions'.
105 Baron, *Histoire de la Syrie, 1918 à nos jours*, 299.
106 Kaplan, 'Obama's Way'.
107 Kaplan.
108 Laura Zhou, 'China's Role in Syria's Endless Civil War'.
109 'Syria's "Moderate Rebels" to Form a New Alliance'.
110 Reese Erlich, *Inside Syria: The Backstory of Their Civil War and What the World Can Expect*.
111 Reese Erlich.
112 Tara McKelvey, 'Arming Syrian Rebels: Where the US Went Wrong – BBC News'.

then expanded into Syria. This approach was successful in some zones but its effectiveness could be questioned as it faced massive waves of criticism. Thus, seen that the battles in Syria continues to this day, the fight against ISIL can be overall judged as unsuccessful.[113]

Finally, with the new elections in the United States and the victory of Donald Trump in the fall of 2016, changes in Washington's foreign policy were to be expected. In the matter of the Syrian affairs, Trump indicted that Obama's administration founded the ISIL and created the turmoil that is currently devastating the Middle East.[114] In response to the alleged chemical attacks of April 2017, Trump launched a military strike against the regime's airbase from where the weapons were allegedly deployed. Before that, the Trump administration was fine with al-Assad remaining in power, since then, there is no clear plan of the United States' foreign policy towards Syria.[115]

As for Russia, it expressed its support of the Syrian regime right from the beginning of the uprising in 2011. It provided al-Assad with financial and political support until 2015 when it decided to assist the regime's forces with direct military activities.[116] Moscow offers Syria a diplomatic shield at the Security Council of the UN by blocking any resolution that may harm the regime.[117] However, Putin's interests in Syria surpass loyalty and friendship. Russia has a naval base in Tartus as its only military base in the Mediterranean area and outside of the territory of the former Soviet Union. In addition, Russia is making a statement by intervening in Syria that it is a great power that should be taken into consideration in international politics. Furthermore, Russia faces separatist tendencies in the Muslim region of Chechnya and hence is fighting Islamist groups in Syria fearing that their victory would activate terrorist and Islamist cells in their homeland. Finally, Kremlin is in an economic crisis due to the Western sanctions over Ukraine and the low oil prices; thus, Russia's support of Bashar al-Assad along with selling him weapons and military ammunition boosts the economy and distracts the Russians from their own crisis.[118]

Iran is the biggest supporter and direct ally of Bashar al-Assad for many reasons. First, Syria represents a route for arms and material transport from Iran to Hezbollah in Lebanon which allows Iran to maintain a considerable influence in

113 'Confronting ISIL: Causes and Consequences of America's Strategic Failure'.
114 Charles Dunne, 'The Trump Administration's Complicated Middle East Map'.
115 Ackerman, 'What's Trump's Plan for Syria?'
116 Hasan Selim Özertem, 'Russia's Shifting Strategy in Syria'.
117 'Who Is Fighting in Syria's Civil War?'
118 CNN, 'Syria'.

the region.[119] Plus, it offers a haven for Hezbollah's training camps and arms storages.[120] Second, it is the last country that is openly against Israel besides Lebanon.[121] Third, al-Assad's regime is Alawite, hence if Sunnis came to power it would weaken Iran's position in the region. [122] Overall, the Syrian conflict represents a chance for Iran to fight its enemies: the United States, Israel and the Sunni movements.

The European Union (EU) is one of the actors that is bearing most of the consequences stemming from the Arab Spring. It is mainly influenced by the migration flow heading from the affected countries to the European territory, by the infiltration and the emerging of terrorists in Europe and by the infringement of political and economic ties with many partners entangled in revolutions and wars. It launched far-reaching and advanced sanction plans against the regime in Syria, in May 2015.[123] The sanctions range from the freezing of financial assets to trade and oil embargoes.[124] In addition, the European Council announced, in April 2017, its adoption of an "EU strategy on Syria" aiming to "end the war through a genuine political transition, save lives by addressing the humanitarian needs, promote a meaningful and inclusive transition in Syria, promote democracy, promote accountability for war crimes and support the resilience of the Syrian population".[125] Thus, the EU is trying to play the role of a pacifier by offering neutral ground for negotiations between the regime, the opposition and the different parties involved: the Geneva peace talks on Syria (Geneva I, Geneva II, Geneva III and the most recent Geneva IV). Those negotiations are trying to include the regime as well as the opposition and are convened by the UN. However, as the first three failed to provide a pertinent resolution to the war, the most recent in 2017 were dismissed by the regime for being "irrelevant". [126]

As for Turkey, it has historically close ties with Syria. When Erdogan and his ideologically Islamic party AKP (see chapter about Turkey) came to power in

---

119 Jubin Goodarzi, 'Iran: Syria as the First Line of Defence'.

120 Marisa Sullivan, 'Hezbollah in Syria'.

121 Reese Erlich, *Inside Syria: The Backstory of Their Civil War and What the World Can Expect*.

122 Marwan Kabalan, 'Al-Mas'ala Al-Souriya Wa-Istiktabatiha Al-Iklimiya Wa Al-Douwaliya'.

123 Carla Portela, 'The EU's Sanctions against Syria: Conflict Management by Other Means'.

124 Rosa Balfour, 'Changes and Continuities in EU-Mediterranean Relations after The Arab Spring'.

125 'Council Adopts EU Strategy on Syria'.

126 'Syria War'.

2002, he established with al-Assad the shared perception of a Kurdish threat after the war in Iraq and they went as far as to adopt collective security measures.[127] In terms of economic relations, the two countries were tied by significant trade volumes. In addition, visa requirements were removed in 2009. Afterwards, Turkey warned the Syrian regime to undertake more democratic and liberal reforms when the Arab Spring emerged.[128] Ankara tried to negotiate with al-Assad and when he failed to comply, the Turkish government turned against Syria and started to offer its support to the opposition, such as the Syrian National Council and the FSA.[129] Turkey provided a refuge for the leadership of many opposition groups, and its borders with Syria became a passage for arms and fighters.[130] In brief, Ankara turned against Damascus when the uprising started, it is supporting the Syrian opposition but at the same time is using the chaos in the country to brutally fight the Kurds and weaken their position; noting that the Kurds are being massacred, Turkey is continuingly accused of colluding with ISIL.[131]

Finally, the Gulf States are Sunni and at odds with Iran, which puts them on the side of the Syrian opposition. Thus, within the Arab League, they voted for the suspension of the Syrian membership in this organization.[132] What is quite ironic about those states is that they pretend to support the opposition's demands of freedom and liberation while they are ruled by authoritarian regimes and oppress any hint of revolution in their own countries. Lately, the Gulf States are being accused of financing and supporting Islamist radicals and terrorists, which is of course denied by the authorities.[133] The Gulf States are *"united against Iran, divided over Islamists"*[134]: there is rivalry even among the countries themselves over which opposition groups and rebels to support. However, in general, the Gulf States have major interests in overthrowing the regime of al-Assad to gain a stronger grip over the situation in Iraq and in Lebanon along with pushing Iran out of the equation.

127 Islam, 'Turkey's Akp Foreign Policy Toward Syria'.
128 Islam.
129 Balci, 'Turkey's Relations with the Syrian Opposition'.
130 Nuh Yilmaz, 'Turkey: Goodbye to Zero Problems with Neighbours'.
131 Phillips, 'Research Paper'.
132 David Batty and Jack Shenker, 'Syria Suspended from Arab League'.
133 Reese Erlich, *Inside Syria: The Backstory of Their Civil War and What the World Can Expect.*
134 Hassan Hassan, 'The Gulf States: United against Iran, Divided over Islamists'.

4. The refugee crisis

Beside the humanitarian crisis and the huge number of IDPs (6.6 million people by the beginning of 2016[135]), the Syrian war is also causing a massive flow of refugees to the neighbouring countries and into Europe. Nowadays the biggest obstacle of the common foreign policy of the EU is the refugee crisis as the member countries are not able to decide on where the refugees should go. This is causing problems within the EU as some countries, such as Germany and France, want to impose a quota system to distribute the refugees among the member countries of the Union; while others, like the Visegrád Group (Czech Republic, Hungary, Poland, Slovakia) refuse to comply by those rules.[136] Moreover, Lebanon, Turkey, Jordan, Iraq and Egypt are carrying the heaviest load of this crisis which is causing economic and humanitarian difficulties in those countries.

According to the United Nations High Commissioner for Refugees (UNHCR), the number of registered Syrian refugees has reached 5,056,219[137] in June 2017. Most of them live outside of the camps designated to host them and thus they live primarily in rural and urban areas where they face a high rate of poverty adding to the host nationals that are already in financial difficulties. In addition, the refugee crisis is affecting the economic growth in those countries by presenting demographic, unemployment, social, sanitary, nutritional and many other kinds of problems. Finally, many international governmental and non-governmental organizations are trying to manage the crisis and ease its consequences, for example, the UNHCR, the EU, Doctors Without Borders, the International Red Cross and Red Crescent Movement, etc.[138]; but with the still ongoing conflict in Syria the situation is just getting harder to deal with, taking into consideration the negative effect those conditions are heaving on the psyche of the people who are losing hope of returning to their homeland.[139]

5. Conclusion

It is quite evident that the current situation in Syria is very complex and will not come to an end soon because of the multitude of engaged actors, the economic and political devastation and the international involvement. A resolution will require

135 'Syria IDP Figures Analysis'.
136 'Migrant Crisis'.
137 Refugees (UNHCR), 'UNHCR Syria Regional Refugee Response'.
138 Refugees (UNHCR), 'Complete List of Partners'.
139 'Regional Refugee and Resilience Plan 2017–2018: In Response to the Syria Crisis'.

a tremendous international effort, especially within international, regional and local organizations such as the UN, the Arab League and Syria itself, which will in turn need strong will and exceptional cooperation of all the parties involved in the conflict. This chapter shows that since its independence, Syria was subject to tough politics with a series of coups until Hafez al-Assad rose to power and established an authoritarian regime. His son Bashar took the presidency after his death and continued to practice politics in the same dictatorial tone, despite his promises of change. The demands for reform started well before the civil war but no opposition dared to confront the regime that controlled the media and oppressed Syrian civil society.

Therefore, the Arab Spring motivated the people to rebel against the government of al-Assad who reacted very violently to the first demonstrations. Thus, the uprising turned into a civil war before many Islamists groups and extremists infiltrated the opposition and started their own war. This chapter presents the religious and ethnic diversity in Syria and lists the Islamic State of Syria and the Levant, the Muslim Brotherhood and Hezbollah as religiously oriented actors with an overlap with extremism.

Finally, the Syrian question is evoking the engagement of many actors, such as Russia, the United States, Iran, the EU, the Gulf states and Turkey, but they stand on different grounds as each one of them have different interests and agendas, which is complicating and prolonging the crisis. Some of them support the regime while others condemn it. Hence, while they try to sort out their disagreements, the war in Syria continues, causing a profound economic and social deterioration. A humanitarian crisis and a refugee crisis have broken out since 2011 and the situation is only getting worse with the alleged use of chemical weapons. The democratization process in Syria can be qualified as failing with no clear path of where it is heading. The question remains how and when will this war end and what will happen next.

References

Ackerman, Spencer. 'What's Trump's Plan for Syria? Five Different Policies in Two Weeks'. *The Guardian*, 11 April 2017, sec. US news. https://www.theguardian.com/us-news/2017/apr/11/donald-trump-syria-bashar-al-assad-isis.

'Al-Jaysh Al-Souri'. Al-Jazeera. 19 June 2017. http://www.aljazeera.net/home/Getpage/98de5902-f542-49cc-b509-ceb2273edfdb/58b22715-fa89-4f43-bcc6-2ca1241e7fcc.

'Al-Tarkiba Al-Soukaniya Fi Souriya', 19 April 2011. http://www.aljazeera.net/home/Getpage/f6451603-4dff-4ca1-9c10-122741d17432/4fdec672-b1d2-49a1-9296-40f9539c0898.

Alkoussa, Riham. 'How Facebook Hurt the Syrian Revolution', 4 December 2016. http://www.aljazeera.com/indepth/opinion/2016/12/facebook-hurt-syrian-revolution-161203125951577.html.

Alvarez-Ossorio, Ignacio. 'Syria's Struggling Civil Society'. *Middle East Quarterly* 19, no. 2 (Spring 2012): 23–32.

'Amnesty International Report 2016/17: The State of the World's Human Rights'. United Kingdom: Amnesty International, 2017.

'Attacks on Ghouta: Analysis of Alleged Use of Chemical Weapons in Syria'. USA: Human Rights Watch, September 2013.

Balanche, Fabrice. 'Ethnic Cleansing Threatens Syria's Unity'. The Washington Institute for Near East Policy, 3 December 2015. http://www.washingtoninstitute.org/policy-analysis/view/ethnic-cleansing-threatens-syrias-unity.

–. 'Géographie de la révolte syrienne'. *Outre Terre*, no. 29 (1 October 2011): 437–58.

Balci, Bayram. 'Turkey's Relations with the Syrian Opposition'. Carnegie Endowment for International Peace, 13 April 2012. http://carnegieendowment.org/2012/04/13/turkey-s-relations-with-syrian-opposition-pub-47841.

Balfour, Rosa. 'Changes and Continuities in EU-Mediterranean Relations after The Arab Spring'. In *An Arab Springboard for EU Foreign Policy?*, 27–34. Egmont Paper. Brussels, 54, 2012.

Baron, Xavier. *Histoire de la Syrie, 1918 à nos jours*. Tallandier. Paris, 2014.

Batty, David, and Jack Shenker. 'Syria Suspended from Arab League'. The Guardian, 12 November 2011. https://www.theguardian.com/world/2011/nov/12/syria-suspended-arab-league.

Beaumont, Peter. 'The Truth about Twitter, Facebook and the Uprisings in the Arab World'. *The Guardian*, 25 February 2011, sec. World news. https://www.theguardian.com/world/2011/feb/25/twitter-facebook-uprisings-arab-libya.

Bruke, Daniel. 'Syria Explained: How It Became a Religious War'. *CNN Belief Blog* (blog), 4 September 2013. http://religion.blogs.cnn.com/2013/09/04/syrian-wars-got-religion-and-that-aint-good/.

'Central Treaty Organization (CENTO)'. Encyclopedia Britannica. 17 June 2017. https://www.britannica.com/topic/Central-Treaty-Organization.

Cheterian, Vicken. 'ISIS and the Killing Fields of the Middle East'. *Survival* 57, no. 2 (4 March 2015): 105–18. https://doi.org/10.1080/00396338.2015.1026089.

CNN, Matthew Chance. 'Syria: 5 Things Russia Wants in War'. CNN, 8 February 2016. http://www.cnn.com/2016/02/08/middleeast/syria-aleppo-russia-strategy/index.html.

'Confronting ISIL: Causes and Consequences of America's Strategic Failure'. Arab Center for Research and Policy Studies, July 2015. https://www.dohainstitute.org/en/PoliticalStudies/Pages/Confronting_ISIL_Causes_and_Consequences_of_Americas_Strategic_Failure.aspx

'Council Adopts EU Strategy on Syria'. Council of the European Union, 3 April 2017. http://www.consilium.europa.eu/en/press/press-releases/2017/04/03-fac-conclusions-syria/.

'Country Profile – Syrian Arab Republic'. UNdata. 10 June 2017. http://data.un.org/CountryProfile.aspx?crName=Syrian%20Arab%20Republic#Economic.

Coutts, Adam. 'Syria's Uprising Could Have Been Avoided through Reform'. *The Guardian*, 18 May 2011, sec. Opinion. https://www.theguardian.com/commentisfree/2011/may/18/syria-uprising-reform-bashar-al-assad.

Dib, Kamal. *Tarikh Souriya al-Mouaaser*. Beirut, Lebanon: Dar al-Nahar, 2012.

Dunne, Charles. 'The Trump Administration's Complicated Middle East Map'. Arab Center Washington DC, 12 April 2017.

El Zein, Dahlia. 'The "New" Syrian Media Law Is Nothing New – Committee to Protect Journalists', 7 September 2011. https://cpj.org/blog/2011/09/the-new-syrian-media-law-is-nothing-new.php.

Erlich, Reese. *Inside Syria: The Backstory of Their Civil War and What the World Can Expect*. New York, USA: Prometheus Books, 2014.

Fares, Qais. 'The Syrian Constitution: Assad's Magic Wand'. Carnegie Middle East Center. 20 June 2017. http://carnegie-mec.org/diwan/55541?lang=en.

'Financing of the Terrorist Organisation ISIL'. The Financial Action Task Force, February 2015. http://www.fatf-gafi.org/publications/methodsandtrends/documents/financing-of-terrorist-organisation-isil.html

Garrie, Adam. 'An Overview of Competing Ideologies in the Arab World'. *The Duran* (blog), 20 November 2016. http://theduran.com/an-overview-of-competing-ideologies-in-the-arab-world/.

Gelvin, James L. *The Arab Uprisings: What Everyone Needs to Know*. New York, USA: Oxford University Press, 2012.

Gobat, Jeanne, and Kristina Kostial. 'Syria's Conflict Economy'. IMF Working Paper – Middle East and Central Asia Department, June 2016. http://www.fatf-gafi.org/publications/methodsandtrends/documents/financing-of-terrorist-organisation-isil.html

Goodarzi, Jubin. 'Iran: Syria as the First Line of Defence'. In *The Regional Struggle for Syria*. United Kingdom: European Council on Foreign Relations, 2013.

'Guide to the Syrian Rebels'. *BBC News*, 13 December 2013, sec. Middle East. http://www.bbc.com/news/world-middle-east-24403003.

Hassan, Hassan. 'The Gulf States: United against Iran, Divided over Islamists'. In *The Regional Struggle for Syria*, 17–24. United Kingdom: European Council on Foreign Relations, 2013.

Holbrook, Donald. 'Al-Qaeda and the Rise of ISIS'. *Survival* 57, no. 2 (4 March 2015): 93–104. https://doi.org/10.1080/00396338.2015.1026070.

'Husayn-McMahon Correspondence – British-Palestinian History'. Encyclopedia Britannica. 16 June 2017. https://www.britannica.com/topic/Husayn-McMahon-correspondence.

'ILAC Rule of Law Assessment Report: Syria 2017'. International Legal Assistance Consortium, April 2017. http://www.ilacnet.org/wp-content/uploads/2017/04/Syria2017.pdf

'Interactive: Tracking Syria's Defections'. Al-Jazeera, 30 July 2012. http://www.aljazeera.com/indepth/interactive/syriadefections/2012730840348158.html.

'ISIS'. Counter Extremism Project. 8 June 2017. https://www.counterextremism.com/threat/isis.

Islam, Thowhidul. 'Turkey's Akp Foreign Policy Toward Syria: Shifting Policy During the Arab Spring'. *International Journal on World Peace; New York* 33, no. 1 (March 2016): 7–41.

Kabalan, Marwan. 'Al-Mas'ala Al-Souriya Wa-Istiktabatiha Al-Iklimiya Wa Al-Douwaliya'. Arab Center for Research and Policy Studies, March 2015.

Kaplan, Fred. 'Obama's Way'. *Foreign Affairs*, no. January/February 2016 (7 December 2015): 46–63.

Khalaf, Rana, Oula Ramadan, and Friederike Stolleis. 'Activism in Difficult Times – Civil Society Groups in Syria 2011–2014'. Beirut, Lebanon: Badael Project and Friedrich-Ebert-Stiftung, 2014.

Kilo, Michel. 'Al-Akaliyat Fi Souriya.. Min Al-Assad Ila Al-Thawra', 10 September 2012. http://www.alarabiya.net/articles/2012/09/10/237086.html.

'Lijan Al-Tansik Al-Mahaliya Fi Souriya'. Carnegie Middle East Center. 5 June 2017. http://carnegie-mec.org/syriaincrisis/?fa=50432.

Maisel, Sebastien. 'Syria's Yezidis in the Kurd Dagh and the Jazıra: Building Identities in a Heterodox Community' "The Muslim World" in USA DOI: 10.1111/j.1478–1913.2012.01417.x 103 (January 2013).

McCants, William. *The ISIS Apocalypse – The History, Strategy, and Doomsday Vision of the Islamic State*. New York, USA: St. Martin's Press, 2015.

McHugo, John. *Syria – A History of the Last Hundred Years*. The New Press, New York, USA, 2015.

McKelvey, Tara. 'Arming Syrian Rebels: Where the US Went Wrong – BBC News'. BBC NEWS, 10 October 2015. http://www.bbc.com/news/magazine-33997408.

'Migrant Crisis: Migration to Europe Explained in Seven Charts'. *BBC News*, 4 March 2016, sec. Europe. http://www.bbc.com/news/world-europe-34131911.

Moukheiber, Zina. 'President Assad And The Syrian Business Elite'. Forbes, 30 March 2011. http://www.forbes.com/sites/zinamoukheiber/2011/03/30/president-assad-and-the-syrian-business-elite/.

Phillips, David L. 'Research Paper: ISIS-Turkey Links'. *Huffington Post* (blog), 9 November 2014. http://www.huffingtonpost.com/david-l-phillips/research-paper-isis-turke_b_6128950.html.

Portela, Carla. 'The EU's Sanctions against Syria: Conflict Management by Other Means'. Security Policy Brief. Belgium: Royal Institute for International Relations, September 2012.

Refugees (UNHCR), United Nations High Commissioner for. 'Complete List of Partners'. UNHCR Syria Regional Refugee Response. 19 June 2017. http://data.unhcr.org/syrianrefugees/partnerlist.php.

–. 'UNHCR Syria Regional Refugee Response'. UNHCR Syria Regional Refugee Response. 6 June 2017. http://data.unhcr.org/syrianrefugees/regional.php.

'Regional Refugee and Resilience Plan 2017–2018: In Response to the Syria Crisis'. Regional Strategic Overview. UNHCR, 2017. http://www.unhcr.org/partners/donors/589497237/2017-2018-regional-refugee-resilience-plan-response-syria-crisis-12-december.html.

Research Directorate, Immigration and Refugee Board, Canada. 'Syria: Syrian Presidential Election in 2000; Confirmation of Whether Businessmen And/Or Other Influential People in the Community Were Pressured by Security Officers to Collect Other People's Identity Cards for the Security Officer's Use in the Election (June-July 2001)'. Refworld, UNHCR, 24 March 2003. http://www.refworld.org/docid/3f7d4e22e.html.

'Results of the First Phase of Mapping Syrian Civil Society Actors'. Citizens for Syria. 19 June 2017. https://citizensforsyria.org/mapping-syrian-cs/.

Salvadoretti, Teresa. 'The Role of Social Media in the Syrian Crisis'. *Asfar* (blog), 12 December 2013. http://www.asfar.org.uk/the-role-of-social-media-in-the-syrian-crisis/.

Selim Özertem, Hasan. 'Russia's Shifting Strategy in Syria: Implications for Turkish Foreign Policy', 28 December 2015. http://english.dohainstitute.org//home/getpage/5ea4b31b-155d-4a9f-8f4d-a5b428135cd5/cbf6f7e0-fdf0-4bb7-88b6-d5c925f898d8.

Sherlock, Ruth. 'Muslim Brotherhood Establishes Militia inside Syria', 3 August 2012, sec. World. http://www.telegraph.co.uk/news/worldnews/middleeast/syria/9450587/Muslim-Brotherhood-establishes-militia-inside-Syria.html.

'Souriya min al-istiklal ila hikm al-Assad 1945–2012'. Ahwaz Studies Center. 6 June 2017. http://www.ahwazstudies.org/Article.aspx?aid=282.

Sterling, Joe. 'Daraa: The Spark That Lit the Syrian Flame'. CNN, 1 March 2012. http://www.cnn.com/2012/03/01/world/meast/syria-crisis-beginnings/index.html.

Sullivan, Marisa. 'Hezbollah in Syria'. Middle East Security Report. USA: Institute for the Study of War, April 2014.

'Syria – Country Report 2016'. Freedom House. 6 June 2017. https://freedomhouse.org/report/freedom-press/2016/syria.

'Syria – Country Report 2017'. Freedom House. 6 June 2017. https://freedomhouse.org/report/freedom-press/2017/syria.

'Syria: Civilian Harm and Assistance'. Center for Civilians in conflict, September 2013. https://civiliansinconflict.org/wp-content/uploads/2013/09/Syria_Post-Harm_Brief_Sept_2013.pdf

'Syria IDP Figures Analysis'. Internal Displacement Monitoring Centre. 20 June 2017. http://www.internal-displacement.org/middle-east-and-north-africa/syria/figures-analysis.

'Syria Protests: Assad to Lift State of Emergency'. *BBC News*, 20 April 2011, sec. Middle East. http://www.bbc.com/news/world-middle-east-13134322.

'Syria Sanctions'. U.S. Department of State. 10 June 2017. https://www.state.gov/e/eb/tfs/spi/syria/.

'Syria War: Peace Talks Restart in Geneva'. *BBC News*, 16 May 2017, sec. Middle East. http://www.bbc.com/news/world-middle-east-39934868.

'Syria's "Moderate Rebels" to Form a New Alliance', 6 April 2017. http://www.aljazeera.com/indepth/features/2017/04/syria-moderate-rebels-form-alliance-170403064144285.html.

'Syria's War: 80% in Poverty, Life Expectancy Cut by 20 Years, $200bn Lost'. *The Guardian*, 12 March 2015, sec. World news. https://www.theguardian.com/world/2015/mar/12/syrias-war-80-in-poverty-life-expectancy-cut-by-20-years-200bn-lost.

'Tarikh Souriya Men Aahed Hafez Al-Assad Ila Al-Harb Al-Souriya'. Al Mayadeen, 15 March 2017. http://www.almayadeen.net/books/53902/تاريخ-سوريا-من-عهد-حافظ-الأسد-إلى-الحرب-السورية/.

'The Damascus Spring'. Carnegie Middle East Center, 1 April 2012. http://carnegie-mec.org/diwan/48516?lang=en.

'The Ethnic and Religious Groups of Syria'. *Syrian Civil War Map* (blog). 16 June 2017. http://syriancivilwarmap.com/ethnic-and-religious-groups-of-syria/.

'The Kurdish Democratic Union Party'. Carnegie Middle East Center. 5 June 2017. http://carnegie-mec.org/diwan/48526?lang=en.

'The Muslim Brotherhood in Syria'. Carnegie Middle East Center. 5 June 2017. http://carnegie-mec.org/diwan/48370?lang=en.

'The Syrian Constitution – 1973–2012'. Carnegie Middle East Center, 5 December 2012. http://carnegie-mec.org/diwan/50255?lang=en.

'The Syrian Islamic Front: A New Extremist Force'. 5 June 2017. http://www.washingtoninstitute.org/policy-analysis/view/the-syrian-islamic-front-a-new-extremist-force.

'The Syrian Muslim Brotherhood'. Harvard Divinity School – Religious Literacy Project. 20 June 2017. https://rlp.hds.harvard.edu/faq/syrian-muslim-brotherhood.

'The World Factbook – Syria'. Central Intelligence Agency. 16 June 2017. https://www.cia.gov/library/publications/the-world-factbook/geos/sy.html.

'The World Factbook – Unemployment Rate'. Central Intelligence Agency. 19 June 2017. https://www.cia.gov/library/publications/the-world-factbook/fields/2129.html.

'Torture Archipelago: Arbitrary Arrests, Torture and Enforced Disappearances in Syria's Underground Prisons since March 2011'. USA: Human Rights Watch, 2012.

'Who Are the Kurds?' Washingtonpost.com: Terrorism Report, 1999. http://www.washingtonpost.com/wp-srv/inatl/daily/feb99/kurdprofile.htm.

'Who Is Fighting in Syria's Civil War?' PBS NewsHour. 5 June 2017. http://www.pbs.org/newshour/rundown/fighting-syrias-civil-war/.

Yilmaz, Nuh. 'Turkey: Goodbye to Zero Problems with Neighbours'. In *The Regional Struggle for Syria*, 67–73. United Kingdom: European Council on Foreign Relations, 2013.

Zhou, Laura. 'China's Role in Syria's Endless Civil War'. South China Morning Post, 7 April 2017. http://www.scmp.com/news/china/diplomacy-defence/article/2085779/backgrounder-chinas-role-syrias-endless-civil-war.

Zohbi, Zaydoun. 'Mounazamat al-moujtamaa al-madani al-souri'. Berlin, Germany: Citizens for Syria, 2017.

Kristýna Tamchynová

Turkey

The main focus of this chapter are the reforms undertaken during the rule of the incumbent Adalet ve Kalkınma Partisi (AKP) before the 2017 referendum as these are key for understanding the present Turkey. AKP's governance aimed at ending the old structures imposed under military tutelage and at modernizing the country, the party was praised for its democratizing efforts, inclusive practices and dialogue with previously marginalized groups. This primary trend went hand in hand with efforts to enter the EU, although it is hard to say which was the cause and which the consequence. The concentrated effort to join the EU lasted until 2005.[1] While the pro-EU orientation and reforms continued, more autonomous development and a turn towards the Middle East together with the Zero Problems with Neighbour policy were features of the following period which lasted roughly until 2010 constitutional referendum.

While each of the reformative steps in isolation might have been taken as a step towards democracy, together their result was a distortion of the checks and balances. The power vacuum was gradually filled by President Erdoğan, the AKP and their supporters and since 2010 increasingly authoritarian tendencies have been perceived both within the AKP and in now President Erdoğan's actions.

At the time of writing, the country held a referendum (April 2017) which ended up with yes (although with a narrow margin) to presidential system and changes to constitution providing President Erdoğan with sweeping powers he had already been informally practicing for years (Prime Minister since 2003, President since 2014).[2]

Despite the growing authoritarian tendencies of ruling elites, Turkey's regime was spared the Arab Spring turmoil, although the changes in the region had

1 Alessandri, 'Turkey's Future Reforms and the European Union'. For etapization of Turkish posture towards EU accession cf. Tekin and Güney, 'The Europeanization' of Turkey: Polity and Politics'.

2 The chapter was first written in the time before the referendum and thus it refers to the system in Turkey valid at that time using present tense. A specific subchapter is dedicated to the reforms planed after the referendum yet the changes really adopted since April 2017 are not subject of this chapter. The author is of the opinion that the reforms adopted in the period before the referendum are crucial to understand all what happened after.

repercussions for the situation in Turkey too (such as situation of Kurds).[3] One of the reasons for the continuous support of the AKP, as will be argued further, might be seen in the fact that AKP brought economic prosperity to the country.

Nevertheless, the situation of democracy in Turkey was deteriorating as can be seen also in the Democratic Index, discussed in the first chapter. While Turkey reached 5.76 in 2012 (0 worst, 10 best), its status in the index has decreased ever since, dropping to 5.04 in 2016.[4] That means Turkey was ranked as the 97th most democratic country and put into the "hybrid regime category" (which is ranked as second worst type of regime). For comparison, in 2016 Syria scored 1.43, Egypt 3.31, even Lebanon scored 4,86 and Iraq 4.08 and if we look for a country with comparable level of the index, we can name for example Kyrgyz Republic with 4.93.[5]

The situation in Turkey escalated with the unsuccessful coup of 15 July 2016 and the after-coup purges and reforms, including the referendum on change of constitution on 16 April 2017. The author acknowledges the importance of recent developments, yet she perceives them as the outcome of the more long-term turn towards disputable practices of the ruling elites and of worrying changes to the system to be explained in the following chapter. Yet as the attempted coup and its aftermath are in themselves quite substantial and mark a start of new period of Turkish politics, a separate subchapter will be dedicated to them.

1. Internal non-institutional factors

1.1 Economic factors

One of the key determinants of the AKP's success is the economy. The continued victory of the AKP enabled it to rule the country in relative stability and continue the economic reforms started by its predecessors. The very fact that AKP won the elections in 2002 was to a great extent due to the financial crisis the country was in, which delegitimized several existing parties and opened space for a newcomer.[6] Memories of that crisis also influence the way people perceive the *relative* stability provided by AKP. The GDP growth varied under AKP, yet Turkey managed to achieve a slightly growing GDP even in the turbulent year of 2016.[7]

3 Cook, 'Arab Spring, Turkish Fall'.
4 The Economist Intelligence Unit, 'EIU Democracy Index 2016'.
5 The Economist Intelligence Unit, 'Democracy Index 2016: Revenge of the "Deplorables"'.
6 Karagöl, 'The Turkish Economy During the Justice and Development Party Decade'.
7 World Bank, 'GDP Growth (Annual %) | Data'.

Unemployment stayed relatively high under the AKP (the lowest point between 2002 and 2016 was 8.1% of the total labour force in 2012, while the peak in 2009 was 12.6%). Turkey's unemployment situation was similar to its neighbour Syria's up until 2010 and now is much better than that of its EU neighbour Greece.[8] Youth unemployment has not decreased much under the AKP, either. From 2002 until the last measurement in 2017, it moved between 15.7% (2012) and 22.8% (2009).[9]

While the economy witnessed ups and downs, there was nevertheless continuous improvement in the living conditions of the people. According to the World Bank estimates, the percentage of the population living below the national poverty lines decreased from 30.3% in 2002 (the year when the AKP won the elections) to 1.6% in 2014 – the last year for which data are provided by the World Bank.[10] The improvement is similar for the percentage of the rural population living below the national poverty lines – it decreased from 38.8% in 2002 to 5.1% in 2013.[11]

Furthermore, there was increase in the share of middle class, *"from 18 percent to 41 percent of the population between 1993 and 2010"*.[12] As AKP has governed country since 2002, at least part of it can be perceived as its achievement. It is nevertheless necessary to mention, that AKP's reforms were especially beneficial for the businessmen from parts of Anatolia who were neglected before.[13] This newly risen group, the successful Anatolian businessmen from the pious circles called also Anatolian Tigers emerged as the new elite and constituted for a long time a strong support base of AKP as it represented their interest.[14]

Furthermore, the World Bank praises Turkey for changes made in the aftermath of the financial crisis and inclusive growth. [15] It is crucial to mention, that there has

---

8 World Bank, 'Unemployment, Total (% of Total Labor Force) (Modeled ILO Estimate) | Data'.

9 World Bank, 'Unemployment, Youth Total (% of Total Labor Force Ages 15–24) (National Estimate) | Data'.

10 World Bank, 'Poverty Headcount Ratio at National Poverty Lines (% of Population) | Data'.

11 World Bank, 'Rural Poverty Headcount Ratio at National Poverty Lines (% of Rural Population) | Data'.

12 World Bank, 'New World Bank Report Looks at Turkey's Rise to the Threshold of High-Income Status and the Challenges Remaining'.

13 Jarosiewicz, 'Turkey's Economy'.

14 Taşpınar, 'Turkey'.

15 World Bank, 'New World Bank Report Looks at Turkey's Rise to the Threshold of High-Income Status and the Challenges Remaining'.

also been a boom in expenditures on social assistance under the AKP.[16] Therefore AKP might be seen positively by Turkish citizens as bringing them prosperity.

1.2 Civil society and media

While the economy opened up, the political liberalization was harder to achieve. One of the reasons might be weak civil society. There are many civil society organizations (CSOs) in Turkey *("107,088 associations and 4867 foundations"*[17]) and theoretically, laws regulating the activities of CSOs aren't that restrictive, as the legal situation has significantly improved. The new Association Law from 2004 as well as 2008 Foundations Law brought better conditions for CSOs.[18] Yet reality is often different from the law.[19] Moreover, the situation deteriorated after the 2016 attempted coup. To name only one illustrative example, by a decree from November 2016, 370 NGOs were shut down[20] and further closures followed.

The composition of civil society is another issue; most of the organisations are related to religion or local development.[21] Also, due to existing differences of Turkish society, the different groups struggle to find a common voice.[22] There is also a question of active participation. People used to be "clients" of the state and stayed clients more than citizens.[23] The rather top-down fashion of the Turkish style of ruling and a lack of understanding that seeking compromises is necessary for positive results in the long-run is another problem regarding the civil society.[24]

The famous Gezi park protests in June 2013 were the typical example of problems the civil society is facing. There was obvious government's inability to enter a dialogue. Different segments of Turkish society were also being unable to unite in their opposition for longer time span. To conclude, there was lack of established

---

16 Eder, 'Deepening Neoliberalization and the Changing Welfare Regime in Turkey: Mutations of a Populist "Sub-Optimal" Democracy', 211.

17 Data according to Department of Associations, Number of Active Associations; Directorate General of Foundations, Foundation Records Archive quoted in 2016 in: Doyle, 'State Control of Civil Society Organizations'.

18 The International Center for Not-for-Profit Law, 'Turkey – NGO Law Monitor – Research Center – ICNL'.

19 Kancı and Keyman, 'Democratic Consolidation and Civil Society in Turkey', 147.

20 OHCHR, 'Report of the Special Rapporteur on the Promotion and Protection of the Right to Freedom of Opinion and Expression on His Mission to Turkey'.

21 Kancı and Keyman, 'Democratic Consolidation and Civil Society in Turkey', 146.

22 Park, Modern Turkey, 50.

23 Wiltse, Democratic Reform and Consolidation.

24 Çinar and Sayin, 'Reproducing the Paradigm of Democracy in Turkey'.

channels for voicing discontent, which was also related to the limited press freedom (exemplified by an incident when CNN Türk, one of the main TV channels, replaced Gezi coverage with a programme about penguins[25]).

Freedom of the press is formally anchored in the Turkish constitution, yet with several possible limitations listed.[26] Nevertheless, when we look at the World Press Freedom Index, Turkey scored 50.76 (100 is the worst) and was 151st in the world in 2016 and in 2017 it fell further to 52.98 and 155th place (for comparison, Egypt was 159th in 2016 with 54.45 and in 2017 it scored 55.78 and was 161st).[27] While we can witness detentions of unwanted journalists, especially after the attempted coup in July 2016,[28] the real problem is that in Turkey there are systemic measures limiting press freedom. Those are especially the ownership of big media groups, auto-censorship by the media and allocation of time and space, gag orders, defamation laws, and use of antiterrorism law[29] as well as recurrent bans on social media.[30]

It is no secret that many media are owned by holdings which have close links to the government or are dependent on government contracts.[31] The pressure by the government, together with risk of being fired, also supports the trend towards auto-censorship.[32] Furthermore there is an uneven allocation of time and space in the media concerning the AKP and the opposition.[33] Another instrument of the government is so-called gag orders preventing broadcasting on sensitive issue such as terrorist attacks.[34] When these more "subtle" techniques fail, the government uses arbitrary specific laws, especially ones relating to defamation[35] or antiterrorism. The infamous Turkish antiterrorism law[36] is very broad. Anti-terror legislation has not only been used against those who were perceived to be linked

25 Oktem, 'Why Turkey's Mainstream Media Chose to Show Penguins Rather than Protests | Kerem Oktem | Opinion | The Guardian'.
26 Chapter two, IX., A. Constitution of the Republic Of Turkey (1982 with ammendments).
27 Reporters without borders, 'Media Ownership Monitor'.
28 Amnesty International, 'Turkey', February 2017.
29 Ellis, 'Press Freedom in Turkey's Inter-Election Period'.
30 The Independent, 'Whatsapp, Twitter and Facebook Are Now Blocked in Turkey'.
31 Reporters without borders, 'Media Ownership Monitor'.
32 European Commission quoted in Yesil, 'Press Censorship in Turkey'.
33 Freedom House, 'Turkey | Country Report | Freedom of the Press | 2016'.
34 Alfred, 'Why Turkey Bans News About Terror Bombings | The Huffington Post'.
35 International Press Institute, 'Turkey | Defamation Laws'.
36 Freedom House, 'Turkey | Country Report | Freedom of the Press | 2016'.

to the group led by the self-exiled Islamic cleric Fethullah Gülen[37] but also against Kurdish-related media coverage or against leftist journalists.[38]

The problems with civil rights as well as media freedom are systemic and were present even before the failed coup; yet the situation was aggravated to a great extent afterwards as is obvious also from the Freedom House index, where Turkey scored 4.5 (7 is worst) for year 2016 on the scale of freedom rating and it ended up second (with Gambia) in the list *Largest 10-Year Score Declines* counting decline in aggregate score, in which even Syria ended up much better.[39]

1.3 Extremism and religion

The role of religion in Turkey is complicated and complex. Although the religion in Turkey is seemingly not connected to extremism, the way the so-called Islamic State (IS) appeared in Iraq or Syria, there are jihadist groups active on Turkish soil (again such as IS[40]). Yet rather than talking about extremism, it is necessary to mention the role of religion in Turkey more generally and specifically how the AKP slowly overcame the strict secularism embedded in the Turkish constitution.[41] Secularism was a principle installed by Atatürk and closely observed ever since. Thus AKP was first presented as a conservative party, in the style of the Christian Democrats in Europe.[42] Further on the AKP opened the public space to religious, by among other changes, slowly relaxing the headscarves ban preventing women wearing hijab to for example attend universities.[43] These and other steps bringing Islam back to public life were appreciated especially by prosperous conservative Anatolian businessmen who were thankful that under the AKP they

---

37 (the self-exiled Islamic cleric, head of the loosely-connected Islamic movement active in Turkey and many other countries, focusing largely on educational activities. The movement has long figured as an ally to the AKP until the power contest between the groups arose and ended up with those linked to Güllen being labelled as the orchestrators of the attempted coup. Cağaptay, The New Sultan).

38 Human Rights Watch (Organization), *Silencing Turkey' s Media.*

39 Freedom House, 'Turkey | Country Report | Freedom in the World | 2017'. Furthermore, at time of final proofs to the chapter, March 2018, Turkey's score worsened further and it is listed as 'not free'. Freedom House, 'Turkey | Country Report | Freedom in the World | 2018'.

40 Marks, 'ISIS and Nusra in Turkey Jihadist Recruitment and Ankara's Response'.

41 Constitution of the Republic of Turkey (1982 with ammendments).

42 Demir, 'From Islamic Renaissance to Neo-Fascism in Turkey'.

43 Smith, 'Why Turkey Lifted Its Ban on the Islamic Headscarf'.

finally got their share of power.[44] The Muslim identity played, at least in Erdoğan's mind, even a greater role. He had the presumption, that there can be a Muslim identity, an overarching identity that will surpass ethnic cleavages.[45] The Muslim (Sunni) identity also influenced the foreign policy, especially the initial support for Muslim Brotherhood[46] or the Sunni groups in Syria. Nevertheless, the rising role of Islam which was praised by some at the beginning increasingly causes worries to others as it is disputable how the situation will evolve.

This Muslim identity could have become a means to end the conflict with Kurds – another long term problem plaguing Turkey.[47] Although this idea was proved wrong in the end, there were steps taken in the direction of reconciliation. The problem of the Kurds in Turkey is complex, too, reaching far beyond the questions of extremism and separatism or the limited opinions of the Partiya Karkerên Kurdistan (PKK), Turkish leftist rebel group. The Kurds are actually another systemic determinant impacting all processes within Turkey. As long as its Kurdish issue remains unsolved, a full-fledged democracy can hardly be achieved.

Kurds, Turkey's largest minority population, constitute a significant portion of Turkish citizens (19% according to CIA Factbook[48]). Despite that, they have been oppressed. Apart from restrictions on use of Kurdish language, other disturbing practices include different punishments for criticism of the status quo (for example the mass dismissals of academicians who signed a petition to stop violence in the South-East – the traditionally Kurdish area[49] or targeted arrests of Kurdish politicians accused of links with the terrorist group PKK[50]). There are other human rights violations, especially now after the attempted coup.[51] Furthermore there have been recurrent curfews in the South-East due to the fights of government and the PKK such as the curfew of Cizre (2015/2016).[52] The renewed violence in the South-East also resulted in a high number of internally displaced

44 Cameron-Moore and Butler, 'Special Report'.
45 Aslan, 'Different Faces of Turkish Islamic Nationalism'.
46 Aydın-Düzgit, 'The Seesaw Friendship Between Turkey's AKP and Egypt's Muslim Brotherhood'.
47 Yavuz and Özcan, 'Turkish Democracy and the Kurdish Question'.
48 Central Intelligence Agency, 'Turkey: The World Factbook — Central Intelligence Agency'.
49 Weaver, 'Turkey Rounds up Academics Who Signed Petition Denouncing Attacks on Kurds | World News | The Guardian'.
50 Hurtas, 'Turkey's Top Kurdish Politician Faces up to 143 Years in Jail'.
51 Office of the United Nations High Commissioner for Human Rights, 'Report on the Human Rights Situation in South-East Turkey. July 2015 to December 2016'.
52 Nazish, 'Cizre in Ruins as Turkey Lifts Curfew on Kurdish Towns'.

people[53] and rising casualties.[54] Precise numbers are not mentioned here on purpose, as they differ significantly based on the source and they changed daily. To conclude, the situation is not compatible with a fully functioning democracy. Furthermore, political representation of Kurds is under such conditions close to impossible. For a Kurdish party to cross the 10% threshold for getting into parliament is really hard, thus they for example tended to compete as independents and regroup only when in parliament.[55]

It is nevertheless necessary to stress that AKP attempted to re-start peace talks and find a solution to the Kurdish issue. Yet, old cleavages were hard to bridge.[56] In 2005, Erdoğan stated in his speech that there exists a Kurdish problem and *"more democracy, not more repression, was the answer to the Kurds' long-running grievances"*.[57] Major step in the peace process was the so-called Democratic Opening or Kurdish Initiative declared by Erdoğan in 2009. This included proposal of several reforms ranging from concessions in the area of cultural rights to thoughts about possible changes of definition of citizen in Turkish constitution.[58] Unfortunately, only few from the proposed reforms materialized and in a lasting way.

Part of the rapprochement with Kurds constituted also the secret "Oslo talks". The government initiated these between 2009 and 2011 with the PKK, and also its jailed leader Abdullah Öcalan.[59] Despite his continuous imprisonment and label of terrorist, he is still viewed by some Kurds as their main representative[60] and thus is occasionally sought as a negotiation partner by the government. Nevertheless, due to combination of factors, 2011 saw renewed violence between the PKK and the government.

Another attempt at reconciliation came in 2013, when Öcalan's message was read at the Kurdish New Year's celebration, citing the decision to lay arms down and solve the issue democratically.[61] While attempt to stop the conflict were welcome, as the clashes between government forces and Kurdish insurgents had produced thousands of victims over the years,[62] the violence has again returned.

---

53 Amnesty International, 'Turkey', 6 December 2016.
54 International Crisis Group, 'Turkey's PKK Conflict'.
55 Scott, 'The Kurd Who'd Save Turkey from Erdoğan'.
56 Pope, 'Turkey and Its Rebel Kurds May Want Peace This Time'.
57 The Economist, 'Peace Be unto You | The Economist'.
58 Carnegie Endowment for International Peace, 'The Kurdish Opening in Turkey'.
59 Hess, 'Turkey's PKK Talks'.
60 Peace in Kurdistan, 'Abdullah Öcalan'.
61 'Turkey Kurds: PKK Chief Ocalan Calls for Ceasefire'.
62 UCDP – Uppsala Conflict Data Program, 'Turkey: Kurdistan'.

The ceasefire eventually broke in the wake of the complications following the June 2015 elections in which Kurdish HDP party got into parliament as a party, but in the end did not manage to participate in governing as explained in the section on political factors. The situation has worsened ever since with Kurds being one of the groups targeted by the after-coup repressions. It is also necessary to mention, that further factor in play were the developments in Syria. The rising independence of Kurds in Syria, together with heightened world attention to their fight with IS complicated the matters in Turkey further, pushing both sides of Turkish–Kurdish dispute to more extreme positions.[63]

To sum up the described events, Erdoğan reached out to the Kurds and was praised by some for that, yet he quickly changed his decision when his position seemed threatened, but without a democratic solution to the Kurdish issue, a full-fledged democracy can hardly be achieved at the national level.

2. Internal institutional factors

2.1 Security and defence structures

While blocking democratization, the fight with the Kurds was an important factor providing legitimization to another actor in power – the military.[64] Similarly to other countries in the region, the military has been for decades one of the key players in the Turkish political scene. It was presenting itself as the guarantor of the secularist republican tradition in the so-called system of "military tutelage". As Menderes Cinar wrote multiple times, clearly the military has acted like a political party within the Turkish system.[65]

The military had an influential place among the state structures and it exercised oversight of the civilian part of the state.[66] There has also been lack of oversight from civilian institutions.[67] According to Ahmet T. Kuru, the symbols of the special statute of the military were: financial independence (no-one disapproved of the military expenditures in the state budget); judicial independence; the educational independence of the army (it had its own educational institutions exempted from civilian

63 At the time of the final proofs being made to the chapter, the situation worsened further. Another Turkish operation in Syria targets the Kurdish area in and around the city of Afrin, so far a safe haven, causing new wave of IDPs and rising international tensions.
64 Kuru, 'The Rise and Fall of Military Tutelage in Turkey'.
65 See for example Cinar, 'The Militarization of Secular Opposition in Turkey', 111.
66 Cinar, 'The Militarization of Secular Opposition in Turkey'.
67 UNDP, 'Improvement of Civilian Oversight in Turkey Phase II'; Sooyler, *The Turkish Deep State*.

oversight), and one has to mention also the National Security Council (NSC) and its role.[68] Basically, the NSC was the main organ responsible for long-term planning of the country's priorities and this organ was due to its composition under military control. Its decisions had to be "*prioritised by the Cabinet*".[69] That the position of the NSC increased after 1982 constitution, meant that in questions of national security, it had the main say.[70] Its position changed only in 2003 and 2004 through a series of reforms changing it into a mere advisory body under civilian control.[71]

The role of the army changed with the AKP's coming to power, and the decline of the army's position was perceivable throughout the 2000s. One of the triggering moments was the accession process to the EU.[72] Furthermore, there were several moments of conflict with the ruling AKP out of which the AKP came victorious, such as the failed e-coup in 2007 when the army tried to stop through e-memorandum Abdulah Gül from being nominated and elected president due to his Islamic background yet failed to achieve its goal[73] or the attempt to constitutionally ban the AKP (due to its threat to secularism) in 2008, unsuccessful as well.[74] This moment constituted a breaking point signalling that AKP is gaining control instead of the army and old structures.

Situation escalated further still with the Ergenekon trials.[75] Ergenekon was supposedly a secret organization of ultra nationalist and secularist character planning to take control over the state – an organization in the manner of the "deep state" structures.[76] Processes with its allegedly members, also from military ranks, were widely criticized for their unfairness. Nevertheless, AKP managed later to gain credit even from admitting that the processes were a fabrication – by blaming the Gülenists for orchestrating the processes.[77]

---

68 Kuru, 'The Rise and Fall of Military Tutelage in Turkey'.

69 Wiltse, *Democratic Reform and Consolidation,* 180.

70 Republic of Turkey, Secretariat-General of the National Security Council, 'Secretariat-General of the NSC'.

71 Müftüler Baç, 'Turkey's Political Reforms and the Impact of the European Union'.

72 Müftüler Baç.

73 The Economist, 'Coups Away'.

74 SPIEGEL ONLINE, 'Turkish Verdict'.

75 Jenkins, *Between Fact and Fantasy.*

76 *"networks, known as the "deep state," have been known to do the state's "dirty work," such as targeting terrorist sympathizers with extra-judicial killings; but they have also been known to collude with organized crime and to undermine Turkish democracy"*, Jenkins, Preface.

77 Hüriyet Daily News, 'Turkey's Ergenekon Plot Case Overturned by Top Court of Appeals – CRIME'.

The dissatisfaction with the army strengthened by Ergenekon eventually led to constitutional amendments approved in 2010 referendum which limited army's powers. The visible power of the army (the power it keeps in economy is another matter) was finally broken during the July 2016 attempted coup as it became obvious that the people were strongly against military tutelage when they reacted to President Erdoğan's call and came into the streets to oppose the coup despite the significant danger posed to their lives. Nevertheless, what the eventual outcome will be remains to be seen.

2.2 Political factors

Traditionally, despite the systemic problems depicted above, modern Turkey had been formally until the recent changes to constitution after April 2017 referendum, a secular representative parliamentary democracy, with the president as a head of state with rather limited powers and "*executive power …exercised by the Prime Minister and the Council of Ministers*".[78] The unicameral Grand National Assembly (Turkish parliament) with 550 members had legislative power. It had various powers not strikingly different to other such bodies.[79] The Turkish system has two "peculiarities". The first is that voting is compulsory and the second is that there exists a 10% threshold to enter the parliament; the seats of those not crossing 10% are distributed among the winning parties. This system was of great benefit to the AKP in its first elections in 2002, when it "inherited" a vast amount of seats left empty as the old parties didn't manage to cross the 10% threshold.[80]

Out of the bigger parties, the main party on the Turkish political scene is the presently leading AKP. Its main rival is the CHP (the Republican People's Party), party founded by Atatürk. As it was based on the values of the old republic, it is hard for it to appeal to both the religious and the Kurds despite its recent social agenda. Furthermore, there is the nationalistic MHP (the Nationalist Movement Party) on the far right of the spectrum, supporting some limited rights for minorities, yet opposing the dialogue with the PKK. Last but not least there is the leftist Kurdish HDP (the People's Democratic Party) which tried to overcome its ethnic base and appeal to various minorities unrepresented in Turkey, together with

78 Teachers in Turkey, 'Turkish Political System'.
79 'The Grand National Assembly of Turkey'.
80 Lyons, Kate and Constanze Letsch. 'Why Turkey's Elections Could Upend Its Politics – the Guardian Briefing'. The Guardian'.

focusing on environmental issues.[81] Apart from division along the left-right topics, the secular vs. Islamic divide also plays a role among some of the parties' agenda.

The AKP has been the strongest of all the parties since it came to power in 2002.[82] The only exception to its unproblematic majority rule was the June 2015 elections. During those, the Kurdish HDP managed to cross the 10% threshold needed to enter the parliament by surpassing its ethnic identity and by addressing different minorities – including also LGBT.[83] It gained 80 seats (out of 550) and deprived the AKP (258 seats out of 550)[84] of a clear parliamentary majority and Erdoğan of his wishes for an unproblematic vote on change to the presidential system. These elections were a signal to the ruling party that there is some dissatisfaction among its voters, and also demonstrated that the democratic process was working in Turkey. Yet this image lasted only for a short while. An effort to form a coalition government failed as the opposition remained disunited[85] and the HDP also faced discontent from the PKK, which felt it would lose control over the negotiations with the Kurds.[86] The situation aggravated as the country again witnessed violence between the government and the Kurdish PKK insurgents.[87] Only at this point the voters troubled by insecurity at home as well as behind the borders returned to the "voice of stability" and gave the majority to the AKP in the November 2015[88] snap elections. The result looked like a return to stability at first sight, yet came at the cost of renewed Turkish–Kurdish polarization.[89]

Apart from being *"single party majority rule"*[90] the democratic system in Turkey is also to a great extent influenced by the fact that it was introduced in a top-down fashion rather than being built slowly from bottom up. There exists what Menderes Çinar calls "delegative democracy", where voters invest powers in the party at the ballot box, and that is where their interests and influence end.[91] Another problem

81 Lyons, Kate and Constanze Letsch. 'Why Turkey's Elections Could Upend Its Politics – the Guardian Briefing'
82 Nardelli, 'Turkey Election Results'; Henley and Diyarbakir, 'Turkey Election'.
83 Hüriyet Daily News, 'LGBT Associations Announce Support for HDP Candidate Demirtaş – POLITICS'.
84 Kirişci and Cengiz, 'Turkish Voters Send a Strong Message'.
85 Sayarı, 'Back to a Predominant Party System'.
86 Heinrich Böll Stiftung, 'Turkey's Newest Party'.
87 International Crisis Group, 'A Sisyphean Task?'
88 Sayarı, 'Back to a Predominant Party System'.
89 Yavuz and Özcan, 'Turkish Democracy and the Kurdish Question'.
90 Sayari, 'Towards a New Turkish Party System?'
91 Çinar, 'Explaining the Popular Appeal and Durability of the Justice and Development Party in Turkey'.

is that, as explained in the first chapter, a strong middle class voicing its opinions is a crucial factor in democratization, yet in Turkey a substantial part of that middle class rose to that status under AKP rule, although it is now an *"important player in its own right"*.[92] Last but not least, the issue with the presently governing party is that Erdoğan kept strong ties and influence over the party, which he used as his support base, defying the non-partisan president principle of Turkish politics[93] (a principle proposed to be changed after the April 2017 referendum). Overall, while the level of stability in governing the country enabled the ruling AKP to carry out a set of praised reforms, the long-term coexistence of one party rule with democracy is questionable.[94]

2.3 Rule of law – judiciary system

The AKP has been also especially apt at effectively dismantling the checks and balances system over time, as can be seen also in the reforms in judiciary area. The structure of judiciary is divided both vertically (different instances) and horizontally (into civilian and military sections and those into administrative and ordinary sections).[95] The structure of the judicial system is rather complex. Apart from the courts, there are other notable members of the structure – most importantly the High Council of Judges and Prosecutors (HCoJP, known under its Turkish shortcut HSYK). The HSYK is an independent body tasked also with decisions regarding "*appointments, promotions and assignments of those working under the judge class*".[96] It also has the power to investigate some of the judges, thus being quite a powerful body. Therefore, many of the reforms undertaken seemed as focused on gaining control over it.

Major change to the HSYK came with the constitutional amendments in 2010 aimed at ending the prevailing influence of military and old structures. While the European Union praised the reforms, which should have led to less influence of the executive over the body,[97] after the first election to the HSYK in 2010, it was obvious that pro-government people would rule there.[98] This became a problem especially during the 2013 corruption scandal targeting the very top of the

92 Posch, 'Root Causes and Consequences of the AKP's Victory'.
93 Yetkin, 'What Does a Partisan President Mean for Turkey? – MURAT YETKİN'.
94 Muftuler-Bac M and Fuat Keyman E, 'The Era of Dominant-Party Politics'.
95 Aksel, 'Turkish Judicial System – Bodies, Duties and Officials'.
96 Aksel, 21.
97 Müftüler-Baç, 'Judicial Reform in Turkey and the EU's Political Conditionality (Mis) Fit between Domestic Preferences and EU Demands', 15.
98 Saatçioğlu, 'De-Europeanisation in Turkey'.

ruling elite (including Erdoğan's son). The executive apparently used its powers to exert influence over the judiciary through various means including (but not being limited to) changes in the HSYK which escalated with adoption of Law 6524 adopted on 15 February 2014.[99] The result of the short-lived period of the existence of that law were major personal changes both in the HSYK and subsequently in personnel connected to the case which meant the corruption process was pushed off the table.[100]

The HSYK is also target of further reforms proposed in the constitution-change package approved in the referendum on 16 April 2017 increasing the influence of the president over it further still. There would be 13 instead of 22 members on the HSYK and appointment of six out of these 13 members of the HSYK will be more or less directly controlled by the president, while seven will be nominated by the parliament – again often in hands of the Erdoğan-related AKP.[101] There will be also a change to the constitutional court.[102] Therefore the independent judiciary practically ceases to exist.

The November 2016 report of EU Commission on Turkey quotes several examples of backsliding in the judicial area, such as changes to the structure of courts, replacements and transfers of judges and so on.[103] There are also other, systemic issues regarding the rule of law in Turkey, namely corruption and human rights issues. As the said corruption scandal showed, Turkey has a major problem with corruption, even at the highest levels of the system. It scores 41 (where 0 is worst and 100 best) in the Transparency International 2016 Corruption Perception Index, making it 75th out of 176 states, yet showing a downward trend (in 2013 the score was 50).[104] Any allegations are more hushed up than investigated, as was shown in 2013/2014. Under such circumstances the proper rule of law can hardly be expected.

Omitting for now freedom of speech, other human rights violations are being reported in Turkey, especially in relation to the Kurdish minority and persecution

99 Giegerich, 'Report on the Reform of the High Council of Judges and Public Prosecutors by Law No. 6524 of February 2014'.

100 OECD, 'Phase 3 Report on Implementing the OECD Anti-Bribery Convention in Turkey', 34–35.

101 Chudziak, 'Constitutional Reform in Turkey'.

102 Ekim and Kirişci, 'The Turkish Constitutional Referendum, Explained | Brookings Institution'.

103 European Commission, 'Turkey Report 2016_European Commission.Pdf', 6, 17.

104 Transparency International, 'Corruption Perceptions Index 2016'.

of pro-Kurdish activism as well as persecution of Kurdish politicians,[105] There are also cases of the controversial use of force by police and the military and lack of investigation into such cases.[106] Therefore we can conclude that the rule of law is flawed significantly in Turkey, trend to be probably worsened further still.

3. External factors

One of the strong factors influencing country's development is its international environment. Due to lack of space, let's focus on the lately rather turbulent immediate neighbourhood of Turkey. Viewing the map of neighbouring countries, one can hardly see a good example for Turkey, especially with the latest crisis in Iraq and Syria. The deteriorating situation in both countries impacted Turkey profoundly. What started as a "zero-problems-with-neighbours" policy ended up as *"nothing but problems"*.[107] The positive relationship of Assad and Erdoğan transformed into hatred[108] and the help of Turkish soldiers in Iraq turned into a diplomatic row.[109]

Regarding Syria, the initial support to Sunni Muslim groups in Syria, sometimes of shady background,[110] backfired when IS appeared and eventually started to target Turkish territory as well.[111] The Syrian conflict moreover resulted in a huge migration wave to Turkey, one which is hard for the locals to cope with in the long term, increasing pressure in the border areas. In a Turkish perception survey from 2015, *"84% said that they were worried by refugees coming from Syria"*.[112]

Another, maybe even more important issue influencing Turkey is the rise of Kurds in Syria. As Kurds reached more autonomous position in Syria, as well as received huge international support in their fight with IS, the confidence of PKK was increased as was increased the Turkish fear of intentions of "their" Kurds. The result of the rise of Kurds in Syria was the halt of any possible negotiations with the government and renewed violence (in Turkey).[113] Somewhat surprisingly, the official relations with Kurds in Iraq, who already had autonomy, seemed better

105 Human Rights Watch, 'World Report 2015'.
106 Human Rights Watch.
107 Djavadi, 'Turkey's Foreign Policy'.
108 Hakura, 'Why Turkey Is Increasing Pressure on Assad.
109 'Turkey Says Its Troops to Stay in Iraq until Islamic State Cleared from Mosul'.
110 'Turkey Fury over Islamism Claims in Leaked German Report'.
111 Al-Jazeera, 'Timeline of Attacks in Turkey'.
112 The German Marshall Fund of the United States, 'Turkish Perceptions Survey 2015 – TP Key Findings Report English Final_0.Pdf'.
113 Isik, 'Syrian Kurds and Turkey's Kurdish Question – Al Jazeera English'.

for some time. One factor for that might be the rivalry between the leader of the Iraqi Kurds – Barzani – and Turkish PKK[114] which uses Iraqi territory to hide and regroup. Yet the relations with Iraqi Kurds are strained too, now in the light of the referendum held in Iraqi Kurdistan after the first draft of this chapter was finished, on 25 September 2017.

From the external factors, the relationship which influenced Turkey probably the most was the one with the EU. The EU and the accession negotiations were among the key factors influencing the AKP's reforms. We can safely say that during the period of intense cooperation with the EU (especially by 2005), democratization and liberalisation efforts were undertaken. Yet the causality is not as clear as maybe the proponents of the EU's soft power would like it to seem. Today, there are practically no means of establishing whether the reforms undertaken served only the AKP's interests and whether good relations with the EU were the cherry on the cake of its plans or whether the reforms were truly undertaken because of the negotiations with the EU.

The relationship with the EU has soured, at least at the diplomatic level. After the first draft of this chapter was finished, The European Parliament even voted for the accession to the EU to be stopped (although this call was not heard).[115] Turkey is still seen as an important partner in terms of its geopolitical location and also because of the migration deal, yet the disillusionment with the after-coup purges and constitutional changes proposed in 2017 referendum complicate mutual relations. There exists the opinion that keeping Turkey on a pro-European track has been vital for its democratic development, voiced for example by the Czech Minister of Foreign Affairs Zaorálek.[116] Nevertheless, there is also the opinion that democratization and Europeanization have not been that closely linked in the case of Turkey and there was a chance for Turkey to democratize further along its own lines.[117] The future of Turkey-EU relations is therefore hard to predict.

4. The coup and the referendum

When writing about (de)democratization in Turkey, one cannot omit the attempted coup of July 2016 and the sweeping purges that followed, together with the highly polarized changes to the constitution approved in the criticized referendum on April 16, 2017. The changes that these events brought seem dramatic at first

114 Phillips, *The Battle for Syria*, 112.
115 Reuters, *European Parliament Votes to End Turkey Accession Talks.*
116 lidovky.cz, 'Zaorálek'.
117 Alessandri, 'Turkey's Future Reforms and the European Union'.

sight; nevertheless, under closer scrutiny they are the visible peak of the gradually tightening grip of power by President Erdoğan, the AKP and their loyal elites.

4.1 The failed coup and its aftermath

On July 15, 2016 an attempted coup took place in Turkey. A section of the army tried to capture Erdoğan, attacked parliament and tried to seize power in the country. Yet the plotters failed, Erdoğan survived, appeared in the media and successfully called people to stand up to the rebels. Furthermore, those supportive of democracy condemned the coup irrespective of their opinion on Erdoğan, as it should be the people changing the government, not the army.[118]

While the fact that the coup failed was the final signal that military lost its previous strength and legitimacy as a deal-breaker in politics, massive purges that evolved after the attempted coup shattered the hopes of any positive development. The main target was those suspected of links to Fethullah Gülen's movement (labelled as orchestrator of the coup)[119] but the repercussions extended also the Kurds.[120] Yet the scope of purges has been so great, that the idea to get rid of any possible opposition might be closer to the truth. For one, close to one-fifth of judges were dismissed in the direct aftermath of the coup, which caused grave concerns.[121] Human Rights Watch have reported on continuous human rights violations after the coup.[122] Also, Amnesty International highlighted the strong defects in the rule of law caused by the post-coup state of affairs including the violations of human rights carried out by security personnel in the South-East.[123] Furthermore the Council of Ministers and the President used state of emergency, (repeatedly prolonged and thus still in effect at the time of writing) and governed by decrees, thus bypassing the normal legislative procedure.[124]

118 Cagaptay and Jeffrey, 'Inside Turkey's Failed Coup: What Happened? Why? What Next? – The Washington Institute for Near East Policy'.

119 Weise, 'Long Arm of Turkey's Anti-Gülenist Purge'.

120 Yeginsu and Timur, 'Turkey's Post-Coup Crackdown Targets Kurdish Politicians'.

121 Commissioner for Human Rights, 'Situation in Turkey'.

122 Williamson, Hugh, 'Germany Needs to Pressure Turkey to Stem Post-Coup Abuses'.

123 Amnesty International, 'Amnesty International Report 2016/17: The State of the World's Human Rights'.

124 European Commission, 'Turkey Report 2016_European Commission.Pdf', 8–9.

4.2 The changes proposed to the constitution

The reforms described so far are to be followed by even greater ones proposed and approved in the April 2017 referendum. While the fact that the referendum did indeed take place is a good sign in itself, the fairness of the referendum was disputed by international observers.[125] The opposition to some changes was so fierce that it even led to the split of the MHP party.[126] The fact, that the "yes" campaign got only 51.3%[127] although the media gave space to the "yes" campaign much more and the referendum was heavily influenced by the state of emergency, signalizes the strength of opposition of the other half of Turkish society. Thus, with the referendum done, the society was polarized even further.

What, then, are the proposed changes which stirred so much controversy and polarized the already splintered country even further? The most visible change is that of a presidential instead of a parliamentary system. The function of the prime minister would disappear, while the president would get further powers, such as ruling by decrees, which have to follow the existing legislative (in case of overlap the law gets priority over decree), not breach basic rights, and can be overruled by parliament; yet this last check is very theoretical, as the president doesn't have to be non-partisan anymore and the AKP continues to dominate the parliament.[128] Further *"The president would also have the power to establish and/or abolish ministries, appoint ministers and other senior officials—all of whom ... would be accountable only to the president"*.[129] Therefore position of Erdoğan would be substantially strengthened and the democratization processes harder to achieve.

5. Conclusion

After the complex developments of the last two decades, the country today is totally different from the country it was in 2002 when the AKP came to power. While some reforms undertaken were positive and their effect is still felt (mostly in the economy), other reforms took a backward turn shortly after their introduction, especially in the judiciary. In the first half of their rule, the party and

125 Sachez and Yüksekkaş, 'International Election Observers Deliver Scathing Verdict on Fairness of Turkish Referendum'.

126 Hüriyet Daily News, 'Opposition MHP Dissidents Launch "No" Campaign in Turkey's Referendum'.

127 Shaheen, 'Erdoğan Clinches Victory in Turkish Constitutional Referendum'.

128 Ekim and Kirişci, 'The Turkish Constitutional Referendum, Explained | Brookings Institution'.

129 Ekim and Kirişci.

Erdoğan seemed the true reformists. Nevertheless, more or less after they curbed the secularist-military opposition, their turn to authoritarianism is obvious.

Although the Arab Spring did not take place in Turkey and the developments in the country cannot be accounted to that regional phenomena as such, the Arab Spring played a role as an external factor. Since Syria as well as other countries were plunged into the chaos of Arab Spring and its aftermath, the "zero-problems-with-neighbours" policy of Turkey was no longer feasible, putting another strain on the country's development, as insecurity in region was a good argument for strong rule at home. Especially the Syrian developments and specifically those related to Kurds echoed significantly in Turkey and negatively impacted its peace process with the domestic Kurdish population, thus halting the very significant part of reforms needed for democratization to continue.

While regimes changed in other countries such as Egypt, or fought for survival, such as in Syria, in Turkey throughout the years the power was slowly but steadily concentrated in the hands of Erdoğan, especially after the April 2017 referendum. The checks and balances were dismantled, and the independence of the judiciary distorted. Lately, even the very basics of democracy – the fairness of elections and respect for the results – are not observed. We can safely claim that the democratization of Turkey turned to de-democratization. The attempted July 2016 coup, although not in any way related to coups of Arab Spring could be thus seen as the peak of increasing troublesome developments in Turkey.

While the Turkish system is moving further away from democracy, we have to nevertheless admit there are still masses supporting Erdoğan. One of the main problems Turkey is facing is its extremely weak opposition, leading many to the choice of Erdoğan versus chaos. Yet the question needs to be asked: how much can be placed on the altar of stability?

References

Aksel, Ismail. 'Turkish Judicial System – Bodies, Duties and Officials'. The Ministry of Justice of Turkey, The Department for Strategy Development, 2013, 19 February 2017. http://www.coe.int/t/dghl/cooperation/cepej/profiles/Turkish_judicial_system_en.pdf.

Alessandri, Emiliano. 'Turkey's Future Reforms and the European Union'. *Turkish Policy Quarterly* 10, no. 1 (Spring 2011): 69–78.

Alfred, Charlotte. 'Why Turkey Bans News About Terror Bombings | The Huffington Post', 13 January 2016. http://www.huffingtonpost.com/entry/turkey-media-blackout-istanbul-bombing_us_56957080e4b086bc1cd5a364.

Al-Jazeera. 'Timeline of Attacks in Turkey', 1 January 2017. http://www.aljazeera.com/indepth/interactive/2016/06/timeline-attacks-turkey-160628223800183.html.

Amnesty International. 'Amnesty International Report 2016/17: The State of the World's Human Rights', 22 February 2017. https://www.amnesty.org/en/documents/document/?indexNumber=pol10%2f4800%2f2017&language=en.

–. 'Turkey: Curfews and Crackdown Force Hundreds of Thousands of Kurds from Their Homes', 6 December 2016. https://www.amnesty.org/en/latest/news/2016/12/turkey-curfews-and-crackdown-force-hundreds-of-thousands-of-kurds-from-their-homes/.

–. 'Turkey: Journalism Is Not a Crime', February 2017. https://www.amnesty.org/en/latest/campaigns/2017/02/free-turkey-media/.

Aslan, Senem. 'Different Faces of Turkish Islamic Nationalism'. *Washington Post*, 20 February 2015, sec. Monkey Cage. https://www.washingtonpost.com/news/monkey-cage/wp/2015/02/20/different-faces-of-turkish-islamic-nationalism/.

Aydın-Düzgit, Senem. 'The Seesaw Friendship Between Turkey's AKP and Egypt's Muslim Brotherhood'. Carnegie Endowment for International Peace, 24 July 2014. http://carnegieendowment.org/2014/07/24/seesaw-friendship-between-turkey-s-akp-and-egypt-s-muslim-brotherhood-pub-56243.

Cağaptay, Soner. *The new Sultan: Erdogan and the crisis of Modern Turkey*, London; New York: I.B. Tauris, 2017.

Cagaptay, Soner, and James Jeffrey. 'Inside Turkey's Failed Coup: What Happened? Why? What Next? – The Washington Institute for Near East Policy'. Washington Institute Policy Analysis, 22 July 2016. http://www.washingtoninstitute.org/policy-analysis/view/inside-turkeys-failed-coup-what-happened-why-what-next.

Cameron-Moore, Simon, and Daren Butler. 'Special Report: Erdogan: The Strongest Man in Turkey'. *Reuters*, 8 August 2011. http://www.reuters.com/article/us-turkey-erdogan-idUSTRE7773X420110808.

Carnegie Endowment for International Peace. 'The Kurdish Opening in Turkey: Origins and Future?' Carnegie Endowment for International Peace. 2 October 2017. http://carnegieendowment.org/2009/12/01/kurdish-opening-in-turkey-origins-and-future-event-1494.

Central Intelligence Agency. 'Turkey: The World Factbook — Central Intelligence Agency'. 2 October 2017. https://www.cia.gov/library/publications/the-world-factbook/geos/tu.html.

Chudziak, Mateusz. 'Constitutional Reform in Turkey: The President Takes It All'. *OSW*, 25 January 2017. https://www.osw.waw.pl/en/publikacje/analyses/2017–01-25/constitutional-reform-turkey-president-takes-it-all.

Çinar, Menderes. 'Explaining the Popular Appeal and Durability of the Justice and Development Party in Turkey'. In *Negotiating Political Power in Turkey: Breaking up the Party*, edited by Elise Massicard and Nicole F Watts, Studies in Middle Eastern Politics., 37–54. London: Routledge, 2013.

Cinar, Menderes. 'The Militarization of Secular Opposition in Turkey'. *Insight Turkey* 12, no. 2 (2010): 109–123.

Çinar, Menderes, and Çagkan Sayin. 'Reproducing the Paradigm of Democracy in Turkey: Parochial Democratization in the Decade of Justice and Development Party'. *Turkish Studies* 15, no. 3 (2014): 365–85. https://doi.org/10.1080/14683849.2014.954743.

Cook, Steven A. 'Arab Spring, Turkish Fall'. *Foreign Policy* (blog), 5 May 2011. https://foreignpolicy.com/2011/05/05/arab-spring-turkish-fall-2/.

Commissioner for Human Rights. 'Situation in Turkey'. Commissaire aux droits de l'homme, 20 July 2016. http://www.coe.int/it/web/commissioner/view/-/asset_publisher/ugj3i6qSEkhZ/content/situation-in-turkey.

Constitution of the Republic Of Turkey (1982 with ammendments), 17 June 2017. https://global.tbmm.gov.tr/docs/constitution_en.pdf.

Demir, Firat. 'From Islamic Renaissance to Neo-Fascism in Turkey'. *Review of Middle East Studies* 50, no. 2 (2016): 186–194.

Djavadi, Abbas. 'Turkey's Foreign Policy: From "Zero Problems" To "Nothing But Problems"'. *RadioFreeEurope/RadioLiberty*, 6 June 2016. https://www.rferl.org/a/turkey-foreign-policy-erdogan-zero-problems/27781927.html.

Doyle, Jessica Leigh. 'State Control of Civil Society Organizations: The Case of Turkey'. *Democratization* 24, no. 2 (7 April 2016): 244–64. https://doi.org/10.1080/13510347.2016.1159555.

Eder, Mine. 'Deepening Neoliberalization and the Changing Welfare Regime in Turkey: Mutations of a Populist "Sub-Optimal" Democracy'. In *Turkey's Democratization Process*, edited by Carmen Rodriguez, Antonio Avalos, Hakan Yilmaz, and Ana I. Planet, 195–220, London; and New York: Routledge, 2014.

Ekim, Sinan, and Kemal Kirişci. 'The Turkish Constitutional Referendum, Explained | Brookings Institution'. Brookings, 13 April 2017. https://www.brookings.edu/blog/order-from-chaos/2017/04/13/the-turkish-constitutional-referendum-explained/.

Ellis, Steven M., ed. 'Press Freedom in Turkey's Inter-Election Period'. International Press Institute, October 2015. https://ipi.media/wp-content/uploads/2015/10/IPI_Turkey_Inter-Election_Press_Freedom_Report_-_Final.pdf.

European Commission. 'Turkey Report 2016_European Commission.Pdf', 9 November 2016. https://ec.europa.eu/neighbourhood-enlargement/sites/near/files/pdf/key_documents/2016/20161109_report_turkey.pdf.

Freedom House. 'Turkey | Country Report | Freedom in the World | 2017'. 17 June 2017. https://freedomhouse.org/report/freedom-world/2017/turkey.

–. 'Turkey | Country Report | Freedom in the World | 2018'. 30 March 2018. https://freedomhouse.org/report/freedom-world/2018/turkey.

–. 'Turkey | Country Report | Freedom of the Press | 2016', 2017. https://freedomhouse.org/report/freedom-press/2016/turkey.

Giegerich, Thomas. 'Report on the Reform of the High Council of Judges and Public Prosecutors by Law No. 6524 of February 2014', 18 December 2014. https://www.avrupa.info.tr/fileadmin/Content/Files/File/Docs/Final_TG_Report18122014.pdf.

Hakura, Fadi. 'Why Turkey Is Increasing Pressure on Assad'. *CNN*, 10 February 2012. http://www.cnn.com/2012/02/09/opinion/syria-turkey-oped/index.html.

Henley, Jon, and Kareem Shaheen, Constanze Letsch. 'Turkey Election: Erdoğan and AKP Return to Power with Outright Majority'. *The Guardian*, 2 November 2015, sec. World news. https://www.theguardian.com/world/2015/nov/01/turkish-election-akp-set-for-majority-with-90-of-vote-counted.

Hess, Jake. 'Turkey's PKK Talks'. *Foreign Policy* (blog), 8 January 2013. https://foreignpolicy.com/2013/01/08/turkeys-pkk-talks/.

Human Rights Watch. 'World Report 2015: Turkey'. Human Rights Watch, 29 January 2015. https://www.hrw.org/world-report/2015/country-chapters/turkey.

Human Rights Watch (Organization). *Silencing Turkey's Media: The Government's Deepening Assault on Critical Journalism.*, 2016. https://www.hrw.org/sites/default/files/report_pdf/turkey1216_web.pdf.

Hüriyet Daily News. 'LGBT Associations Announce Support for HDP Candidate Demirtaş – POLITICS'. *Hürriyet Daily News*, 8 August 2014. http://www.hurriyetdailynews.com/lgbt-associations-announce-support-for-hdp-candidate-demirtas-.aspx?nid=70163&pageID=238.

–. 'Opposition MHP Dissidents Launch "No" Campaign in Turkey's Referendum'. *Hürriyet Daily News*, 19 February 2017. http://www.hurriyetdailynews.com/opposition-mhp-dissidents-launch-no-campaign-in-turkeys-referendum.aspx?pageID=238&nID=109914&NewsCatID=338.

–. 'Turkey's Ergenekon Plot Case Overturned by Top Court of Appeals – CRIME'. *Hürriyet Daily News*, 21 April 2016. http://www.hurriyetdailynews.com/turkeys-ergenekon-plot-case-overturned-by-top-court-of-appeals-.aspx?PageID=238&NID=98113&NewsCatID=509.

Hurtas, Sibel. 'Turkey's Top Kurdish Politician Faces up to 143 Years in Jail'. *Al-Monitor: Turkey Pulse*, 8 February 2017. http://www.al-monitor.com/pulse/originals/2017/02/turkey-kurdish-politicians-face-up-143-years-jail.html.

International Crisis Group. 'A Sisyphean Task? Resuming Turkey-PKK Peace Talks'. International Crisis Group, 17 December 2015. https://www.crisisgroup.org/europe-central-asia/western-europemediterranean/turkey/sisyphean-task-resuming-turkey-pkk-peace-talks.

International Crisis Group. 'Turkey's PKK Conflict: The Death Toll | Crisis Group', International Crisis Group, 20 July 2016. http://blog.crisisgroup.org/europe-central-asia/2016/07/20/turkey-s-pkk-conflict-the-rising-toll/.

International Press Institute. 'Turkey | Defamation Laws'. 1 April 2017. http://legaldb.freemedia.at/legal-database/turkey/.

Isik, Ebubekir. 'Syrian Kurds and Turkey's Kurdish Question – Al Jazeera English'. *Al-Jazeera*, 13 February 2016. http://www.aljazeera.com/indepth/opinion/2016/02/syrian-kurds-turkey-kurdish-question-160208132220317.html.

Jarosiewicz, Aleksandra. 'Turkey's Economy: A Story of Success with an Uncertain Future'. *OSW*, 6 November 2013. https://www.osw.waw.pl/en/publikacje/osw-commentary/2013–11-06/turkeys-economy-a-story-success-uncertain-future.

Jenkins, Gareth H. *Between Fact and Fantasy: Turkey's Ergenekon Investigation*. Washington, D.C.: Central Asia-Caucasus Institute & Silk Road Studies Program, 2009. http://xa.yimg.com/kq/groups/19385080/1619728843/name/0908genekon.pdf.

Kancı, Tuba, and E. Fuat Keyman. 'Democratic Consolidation and Civil Society in Turkey'. In *Turkey's Democratization Process*, edited by Carmen Rodriguez, Antonio Avalos, Hakan Yilmaz, and Ana I. Planet, 133–53. London; and New York: Routledge, 2014.

Karagöl, Erdal Tanas. 'The Turkish Economy During the Justice and Development Party Decade'. *Insight Turkey* 15, no. 4 (2013): 115–129.

Kirişci, Kemal, and Melis Cengiz. 'Turkish Voters Send a Strong Message'. *Brookings* (blog), 8 June 2015. https://www.brookings.edu/blog/order-from-chaos/2015/06/08/turkish-voters-send-a-strong-message/.

Kuru, Ahmet T. 'The Rise and Fall of Military Tutelage in Turkey: Fears of Islamism, Kurdism, and Communism'. *Insight Turkey* 14, no. 2 (2012): 37–57.

lidovky.cz. 'Zaorálek: Navzdory Složité Situaci Musíme s Tureckem Dál Udržovat Dialog | Svět'. *Lidovky.Cz*, 25 November 2016. http://www.lidovky.cz/zaoralek-navzdory-slozite-situaci-musime-s-tureckem-dal-udrzovat-dialog-1q7-/zpravy-svet.aspx?c=A161125_123247_ln_zahranici_bri.

Lyons, Kate, and Constanze Letsch. 'Why Turkey's Elections Could Upend Its Politics – the Guardian Briefing'. *The Guardian briefing*, 2 June 2015. https://www.theguardian.com/world/2015/jun/02/sundays-poll-could-upend-turkish-politics-and-weaken-the-parliament.

Marks, Monica. 'ISIS and Nusra in Turkey Jihadist Recruitment and Ankara's Response'. Institute for Strategic Dialogue, 2016. https://www.isdglobal.org/wp-content/uploads/2016/07/ISDJ4677_Turkey_R1_WEB.pdf.

Müftüler Baç, Meltem. 'Turkey's Political Reforms and the Impact of the European Union'. *South European Society and Politics* 10, no. 1 (2005): 17–31. https://doi.org/10.1080/13608740500037916.

Muftuler-Bac M, and Fuat Keyman E. 'The Era of Dominant-Party Politics'. *J. Democr. Journal of Democracy* 23, no. 1 (2012): 85–99.

Müftüler-Baç, Meltem. 'Judicial Reform in Turkey and the EU's Political Conditionality (Mis)Fit between Domestic Preferences and EU Demands'. *MAXCAP Working Paper* 2016, no. 18 (January 2016). http://userpage.fu-berlin.de/kfgeu/maxcap/system/files/maxcap_wp_18.pdf.

Nardelli, Alberto. 'Turkey Election Results: What You Need to Know'. *The Guardian*, 8 June 2015, sec. News. https://www.theguardian.com/news/datablog/2015/jun/08/turkey-election-results-what-you-need-to-know.

Nazish, Kiran. 'Cizre in Ruins as Turkey Lifts Curfew on Kurdish Towns'. *Al-Jazeera*, 13 March 2016. http://www.aljazeera.com/news/2016/03/cizre-ruins-turkey-lifts-curfew-kurdish-towns-160312113030597.html.

OECD. 'Phase 3 Report on Implementing the OECD Anti-Bribery Convention in Turkey', October 2014. http://www.oecd.org/daf/anti-bribery/Turkey-Phase3ReportEN.pdf.

Office of the United Nations High Commissioner for Human Rights. 'Report on the Human Rights Situation in South-East Turkey. July 2015 to December 2016.', February 2017. http://www.ohchr.org/Documents/Countries/TR/OHCHR_South-East_TurkeyReport_10March2017.pdf#sthash.c6fifoZ6.dpuf.

OHCHR. 'Report of the Special Rapporteur on the Promotion and Protection of the Right to Freedom of Opinion and Expression on His Mission to Turkey', 7 June 2017. http://www.ohchr.org/EN/HRBodies/HRC/RegularSessions/Session35/Documents/A_HRC_35_22_Add_3_E.docx.

Oktem, Kerem. 'Why Turkey's Mainstream Media Chose to Show Penguins Rather than Protests | Kerem Oktem | Opinion | The Guardian'. *The Guardian Comment Network*, 9 June 2013. https://www.theguardian.com/commentisfree/2013/jun/09/turkey-mainstream-media-penguins-protests.

Park, Bill. *Modern Turkey: People, State and Foreign Policy in a Globalised World*. London: Routledge, 2012.

Peace in Kurdistan. 'Abdullah Öcalan'. *Peace in Kurdistan* (blog), 15 December 2011. https://peaceinkurdistancampaign.com/resources/abdullah-ocalan/.

Phillips, Christopher. *The Battle for Syria: International Rivalry in the New Middle East*. New Haven; London: Yale University Press, 2016.

Pope, Hugh. 'Turkey and Its Rebel Kurds May Want Peace This Time'. International Crisis Group, 16 January 2013. https://www.crisisgroup.org/europe-central-asia/western-europemediterranean/turkey/turkey-and-its-rebel-kurds-may-want-peace-time.

Posch, Walter. 'Root Causes and Consequences of the AKP's Victory'. European Union Institute for Security Studies, 31 July 2017. http://www.iss.europa.eu/publications/detail/article/root-causes-and-consequences-of-the-akps-victory/.

Reporters without borders. 'Media Ownership Monitor: Government Control over Turkish Media Almost Complete'. RSF, 27 October 2016. https://rsf.org/en/news/media-ownership-monitor-government-control-over-turkish-media-almost-complete.

Republic of Turkey, Secretariat-General of the National Security Council. 'Secretariat-General of the NSC', 2013. https://www.mgk.gov.tr/en/index.php/secretariat-general/about-us.

Reuters, *European Parliament Votes to End Turkey Accession Talks*, 2017. https://www.reuters.com/video/2017/07/06/european-parliament-votes-to-end-turkey?videoId=372041273&videoChannel=13421.

Saatçioğlu, Beken. 'De-Europeanisation in Turkey: The Case of the Rule of Law'. *South European Society and Politics* 21, no. 1 (2016): 133–46. https://doi.org/10.1080/13608746.2016.1147994.

Sachez, Raf, and Burhan Yüksekkaş. 'International Election Observers Deliver Scathing Verdict on Fairness of Turkish Referendum'. *The Telegraph*, 17 April 2017. http://www.telegraph.co.uk/news/2017/04/17/turkish-referendum-opposition-plans-appeal-against-last-minute/.

Sayari, Sabri. 'Towards a New Turkish Party System?' *Turkish Studies* 8, no. 2 (2007): 197–210. https://doi.org/10.1080/14683840701312286.

Sayarı, Sabri. 'Back to a Predominant Party System: The November 2015 Snap Election in Turkey'. *South European Society and Politics* 21, no. 2 (2016): 263–80. https://doi.org/10.1080/13608746.2016.1170254.

Scott, Alev. 'The Kurd Who'd Save Turkey from Erdoğan'. *POLITICO*, 19 May 2015. http://www.politico.eu/article/kurds-to-the-rescue-turkey-erdogan/.

Shaheen, Kareem. 'Erdoğan Clinches Victory in Turkish Constitutional Referendum'. *The Guardian*, 16 April 2017, sec. World news. https://www.theguardian.com/world/2017/apr/16/erdogan-claims-victory-in-turkish-constitutional-referendum.

Smith, Roff,. 'Why Turkey Lifted Its Ban on the Islamic Headscarf'. National Geographic News, 12 October 2013. http://news.nationalgeographic.com/news/2013/10/131011-hijab-ban-turkey-islamic-headscarf-ataturk/.

Sooyler, Mehtap. *The Turkish Deep State: State Consolidation, Civil-Military Relations and Democracy*. 1 edition. London; New York: Routledge, 2015.

SPIEGEL ONLINE. 'Turkish Verdict: Top Court Rejects Ban of Ruling AKP'. *SPIEGEL ONLINE*, 30 July 2008. http://www.spiegel.de/international/world/turkish-verdict-top-court-rejects-ban-of-ruling-akp-a-569147.html.

Stiftung, Heinrich Böll. 'Turkey's Newest Party: Understanding the HDP', 27 October 2015. https://www.boell.de/en/2015/10/27/turkeys-newest-party-understanding-hdp.

Taşpınar, Ömer. 'Turkey: The New Model?' *Brookings* (blog), 30 November 2001. https://www.brookings.edu/research/turkey-the-new-model/.

Teachers in Turkey. 'Turkish Political System'. Teachers in Turkey. 1 April 2017. https://www.teachersinturkey.net/politics-of-turkey.

Tekin, Ali, and Aylin Güney (eds.). *'The Europeanization of Turkey: Polity and Politics.* London: Routledge, 2015.

The Economist. 'Coups Away'. *The Economist*, February 2010. http://www.economist.com/node/15505946.

–. 'Peace Be unto You | The Economist'. *The Economist*, 18 August 2005. http://www.economist.com/node/4300168.

The Economist Intelligence Unit. 'Democracy Index 2016: Revenge of the "Deplorables"'. The Economist Intelligence Unit Limited, 2017. http://www.eiu.com/Handlers/WhitepaperHandler.ashx?fi=Democracy-Index-2016.pdf&mode=wp&campaignid=DemocracyIndex2016.

–. 'EIU Democracy Index 2016'. 23 April 2017. https://infographics.economist.com/2017/DemocracyIndex/.

The German Marshall Fund of the United States. 'Turkish Perceptions Survey 2015 – TP Key Findings Report English Final_0.Pdf', October 2015. http://www.gmfus.org/sites/default/files/TP%20Key%20Findings%20Report%20English%20Final_0.pdf.

'The Grand National Assembly of Turkey'. 1 April 2017. https://global.tbmm.gov.tr/index.php/EN/yd/icerik/13.

The Independent. 'Whatsapp, Twitter and Facebook Are Now Blocked in Turkey'. The Independent, 4 November 2016. http://www.independent.co.uk/news/world/asia/facebook-twitter-whatsapp-turkey-erdogan-blocked-opposition-leaders-arrested-a7396831.html.

The International Center for Not-for-Profit Law. 'Turkey – NGO Law Monitor – Research Center – ICNL', 1 June 2017. http://www.icnl.org/research/monitor/turkey.html.

Transparency International. 'Corruption Perceptions Index 2016'. www.transparency.org. 11 March 2017. https://www.transparency.org/news/feature/corruption_perceptions_index_2016.

'Turkey Fury over Islamism Claims in Leaked German Report'. *BBC News*, 17 August 2016, sec. Europe. http://www.bbc.com/news/world-europe-37109943.

'Turkey Kurds: PKK Chief Ocalan Calls for Ceasefire'. *BBC News*, 21 March 2013, sec. Europe. http://www.bbc.com/news/world-europe-21874427.

'Turkey Says Its Troops to Stay in Iraq until Islamic State Cleared from Mosul'. *Reuters*, 13 October 2016. http://www.reuters.com/article/us-mideast-crisis-iraq-turkey-idUSKCN12C0KF.

UCDP – Uppsala Conflict Data Program. 'Turkey: Kurdistan'. 2 October 2017. http://ucdp.uu.se/#/conflict/354.

UNDP. 'Improvement of Civilian Oversight in Turkey Phase II'. UNDP in Turkey. 18 June 2017. http://www.tr.undp.org/content/turkey/en/home/operations/projects/democratic_governance/improvement_of_civilian_oversight_in_turkey_phase_two.html.

Weaver, Matthew. 'Turkey Rounds up Academics Who Signed Petition Denouncing Attacks on Kurds | World News | The Guardian'. *The Guardian*, 15 January 2016. https://www.theguardian.com/world/2016/jan/15/turkey-rounds-up-academics-who-signed-petition-denouncing-attacks-on-kurds.

Weise, Zia. 'Long Arm of Turkey's Anti-Gülenist Purge'. POLITICO, 21 August 2017. http://www.politico.eu/article/long-arm-of-turkeys-anti-gulenist-purge/.

Williamson, Hugh. 'Germany Needs to Pressure Turkey to Stem Post-Coup Abuses'. Human Rights Watch, 14 November 2016. https://www.hrw.org/news/2016/11/14/germany-needs-pressure-turkey-stem-post-coup-abuses.

Wiltse, Evren Celik. *Democratic Reform and Consolidation.* Colchester: ECPR Press, 2015.

World Bank. 'GDP Growth (Annual %) | Data'. 17 June 2017. http://data.worldbank.org/indicator/NY.GDP.MKTP.KD.ZG?end=2015&locations=TR&start=2002.

–. 'New World Bank Report Looks at Turkey's Rise to the Threshold of High-Income Status and the Challenges Remaining'. Text/HTML. World Bank. 17 June 2017. http://www.worldbank.org/en/news/press-release/2014/12/10/new-world-bank-report-looks-at-turkey-rise-to-threshold-of-high-income-and-challenges-remaining.

–. 'Poverty Headcount Ratio at National Poverty Lines (% of Population) | Data'. 17 June 2017. http://data.worldbank.org/indicator/SI.POV.NAHC?locations=TR.

–. 'Rural Poverty Headcount Ratio at National Poverty Lines (% of Rural Population) | Data'. 17 June 2017. http://data.worldbank.org/indicator/SI.POV.RUHC?locations=TR&year_low_desc=false.

–. 'Unemployment, Total (% of Total Labor Force) (Modeled ILO Estimate) | Data'. 1 October 2017. https://data.worldbank.org/indicator/SL.UEM.TOTL.ZS?end=2016&locations=CZ-GR-TR-SY&start=2002.

–. 'Unemployment, Youth Total (% of Total Labor Force Ages 15–24) (National Estimate) | Data'. 30 March 2018. http://data.worldbank.org/indicator/SL.UEM.1524.NE.ZS?end=2006&locations=TR-SY-EG-GR-CZ-YE&start=1997.

Yavuz, M. Hakan, and Nihat Ali Özcan. 'Turkish Democracy and the Kurdish Question'. *Middle East Policy* 22, no. 4 (2015): 73–87. https://doi.org/10.1111/mepo.12159.

Yeginsu, Ceylan, and Safak Timur. 'Turkey's Post-Coup Crackdown Targets Kurdish Politicians'. *The New York Times*, 4 November 2016, sec. Europe. https://www.nytimes.com/2016/11/05/world/europe/turkey-coup-crackdown-kurdish-politicians.html.

Yesil, Bilge. 'Press Censorship in Turkey: Networks of State Power, Commercial Pressures, and Self-Censorship'. *Communication, Culture & Critique* 7, no. 2 (June 2014): 154–73. https://doi.org/10.1111/cccr.12049.

Yetkin, Murat. 'What Does a Partisan President Mean for Turkey? – MURAT YETKİN'. *Hürriyet Daily News*. 9 April 2017. http://www.hurriyetdailynews.com/what-does-a-partisan-president-mean-for-turkey.aspx?pageID=238&nid=106223&NewsCatID=409.

Aneta Hlavsová

Yemen

In November 2011,[1] when Yemen's former President Saleh agreed to resign and hand over his position to a new regime leader, his deputy Abdrabbuh Mansour Hadi, the Arab Spring was already fully under way in the entire Middle East and the African North. The international community, as well as President Saleh's opposition, welcomed this development as a sign of upcoming democratization and political liberalization. Yet in 2018, Yemen is in a state of chaos – undergoing a civil war with various political and ethnic factions fighting for power, under a foreign military intervention, under a UN sanctions regime, and deep into a severe humanitarian crisis. This chapter focuses on the specifics of Yemen's obstacles to democratization, such as its defiant patronage system, its underperforming and mismanaged economy, the nation-wide addiction to qat chewing, and religious fundamentalists' infiltration of Yemen's rural areas.

1. Internal institutional factors

Yemen's 1990 unification of its northern and southern parts did not produce positive effects for its people. The two Yemens had opposite political- and economy-management experiences, with the North carrying the legacy of the Ottoman Empire, while the South had first a British and later a communist inheritance and "enjoyed more urban characteristics and a better education [system] than the north, despite the similar tribal divisions in the rural areas of both sides."[2] When the now-former President Saleh began his rule over the newly established country, it experienced ongoing conflicts between the two parts which soon resulted in a brief civil war in 1994.[3] Interestingly, even though "the Saudi press and separatist propaganda emphasized cultural differences between North and South, the real divisions were between bureaucracies, armies, and ruling cliques."[4] The possibility of an economic development was therefore crippled almost immediately after unification by this war and its consequences.

1 "Yemen Profile – Timeline."
2 al Tamimi, "Yemen's Crippled Economy."
3 "Yemen Profile – Timeline."
4 Carapico, Civil Society in Yemen: The Political Economy of Activism in Modern Arabia.

1.1 Economic factors

In reaction to the country's dire need of an economic stimulus, in 1996 the IMF approved a $193 million loan[5] which was linked to an intended set of reforms of Yemen's economy (structural reforms of its tax system, civil service, trade liberalization and tariff reform, and widespread privatization); in 2001, the IMF authorized another $121 million loan[6] aimed at poverty reduction. Unfortunately, despite some progress, both of these programs failed at achieving the desired objectives.[7] And while the country's annual growth rate between 2001 and 2009 was relatively stable (or slightly decreasing),[8] Yemen's support of Saddam Hussein's invasion of Kuwait isolated it from the other Gulf countries which traditionally played an important role in the state's finances through economic aid and educational, health, infrastructural, or energy projects[9] – all of which were seized because of Yemen's international stance.

After 1994, the Houthi insurgency further complicated the country's potential for either economic or political development, eventually resulting in the rebels' capture of capital Sanaa in September 2014.[10] The ongoing bloody conflict caused "destruction of infrastructure, disruption of trade, commerce and supplies as well as the displacement of people (about 3 million)."[11] Similarly, the war is reflected in socio-economic and political rankings such as the Fund for Peace's Fragile States Index and Freedom House; in 2017, Yemen ranked as the 4th most fragile state[12] in the world, significantly worsening over the last decade. Freedom House's political assessment of the country had worsened for 2016 as well "due to the collapse of the political system and the effects of an escalating civil war and related Saudi-led military intervention on the civilian population."[13]

The section *Internal economic factors* studies the gravity of Yemen's current economic downturn and the humanitarian catastrophe which engulfs the country. *External economic factors* then analyse the current UN sanctions regime imposed on Yemen and the country's oil sector, which highly significant because it represented "roughly 25% of GDP and [at minimum] 65% of government revenue"[14] in 2014.

5 "Press Release: IMF Approves Stand-By Credit for Yemen."
6 "News Brief: IMF Authorizes US$121 Million in Disbursements to Yemen."
7 al Tamimi, "Yemen's Crippled Economy."
8 "Yemen GDP Annual Growth Rate | 2001–2017 | Data | Chart | Calendar."
9 al Tamimi, "Yemen's Crippled Economy."
10 "Yemen Profile – Timeline."
11 "Yemen's Economic Outlook Fall 2016."
12 "Fragile States Index Annual Report 2017 | Fragile States Index."
13 "Yemen | Country Report | Freedom in the World | 2016."
14 "The World Factbook — Yemen."

1.1.1 Internal economic factors

Yemen is a poor country with an underperforming economy – all economic indicators reviewed have significantly worsened since 2014/2015. For instance, with a population of more than 27 million,[15] GDP per capita in 2015 declined to $774.5[16] (from $1103.8 in 2014); the country's economy stopped growing in 2014 and then in 2015, it contracted by 28.1%.[17] The main economic reason behind such a massive downturn is the cessation of oil and gas exports.[18] Besides the halt to the country's exports, the conflict "pressured the currency's exchange rate, accelerated inflation, severely limited food and fuel imports, and caused widespread damage to infrastructure."[19] Such unwelcomed developments come as no shock given the security situation within the country; however, they illustrate well the primary effects a war has on a country's economic potential.

Given the havoc Yemen is experiencing, some macroeconomic trends are troublesome to track up to the present. For instance, the country's unemployment rate is estimated to have risen since the 27%[20] level in 2014, with numbers ranging between the "modest" estimate of 35% up to 60%[21] in the worst-case scenario. Likewise, the last recorded data concerning Yemen's poverty levels comes from 2014 when 54%[22] of the country's population lived below the poverty line; the Gini coefficient illustrating income inequality was at 37.7[23] in 2013[24] – with all indicators expected to have worsened by 2017.

The humanitarian catastrophe which now paralyzes Yemen is of unprecedented volume and consequences. According to UN sources, more than 10,000 people (mostly civilians) have been killed in the conflict, with about 52,000 injured (as of March 2018). Yemen had severe structural socio-economic and political problems even before the war, including high poverty and unemployment rates (especially the youth unemployment rate), corruption, poor governance and clientelism,

---

15 Ibid.

16 "Yemen GDP per Capita | 1990–2017 | Data | Chart | Calendar | Forecast."

17 "Yemen GDP Annual Growth Rate | 2001–2017 | Data | Chart | Calendar."

18 "Yemen's Economic Outlook Fall 2016."

19 "The World Factbook — Yemen."

20 Ibid.

21 "Yemen Unemployment Rate Forecast 2016–2020."

22 "The World Factbook — Yemen."

23 "Income Gini Coefficient | Human Development Reports."

24 Yemen therefore ranks as 154th worst in the world. For illustration, Palestine ranks as 107th, Iraq as 120th, Lebanon as only 65th, Libya as 55th, Syria as 118th, Egypt as 110th, and Turkey as 69th worst in the world comparison.

secessionism, and environmental degradation. These factors immediately catalysed the consequences of the war and created a massive humanitarian catastrophe.

In March 2017, Stephen O'Brien, the UN's Under-Secretary-General for Humanitarian Affairs and Emergency Relief Coordinator, warned the international community that currently, "two-thirds of the population – 18.8 million people – need assistance and more than 7 million are hungry."[25] As a direct result of the civil war and the Saudi-led coalition's involvement in Yemen which destroyed the country's infrastructure and therefore the supply routes, at least "half of the Yemeni population may be facing food shortages"[26] according to the World Bank. The World Food Programme offers even more upsetting data with 17 million Yemenis being food insecure (with 6.8 of the 17 million severely food insecure).[27] Put bluntly, the civil war which spilled over into a regional conflict, combined with "a Saudi naval blockade preventing food, medicine, and other humanitarian aid from entering the country, resulted in thousands of deaths and widespread destruction."[28]

Additionally, the bloody conflict drove more than 3 million people out of their homes, reaching 3.3 million in spring 2017;[29] including 1 million returnees.[30] In comparison to the Iraqi humanitarian catastrophe during the 1990s, there were over 1 million internally displaced persons (IDPs) in the country[31] before the 2003 US invasion. And while UN officials reprimand[32] the international community for disregarding the Yemeni conflict compared to the attention given to the Syrian–Iraqi struggle against the Islamic State, the number of IDPs in Iraq is more or less comparable to those in Yemen (at 3.3 million in December 2015).[33]

The state of Yemen's health care system and health facilities further exacerbates the gravity of the humanitarian crisis. Not even half of the country's health facilities were functional in November 2016[34] (with "at least 274 health facilities destroyed in the conflict")[35] while there are almost 15 million Yemenis without access to

25 "STATEMENT TO THE SECURITY COUNCIL ON MISSIONS TO YEMEN, SOUTH SUDAN, SOMALIA AND KENYA AND AN UPDATE ON THE OSLO CONFERENCE ON NIGERIA AND THE LAKE CHAD REGION."
26 "Yemen's Economic Outlook Fall 2016."
27 "Yemen Situation Report #27."
28 "Yemen | Country Report | Freedom in the World | 2016."
29 Keane, "Yemen Conflict."
30 "Yemen Situation Report #27."
31 "Iraq IDP Figures Analysis."
32 Keane, "Yemen Conflict."
33 "Iraq IDP Figures Analysis."
34 "Survey Reveals Extent of Damage to Yemen's Health System."
35 "Yemen Conflict."

safe drinking water or sanitation.[36] Such a sinister combination of factors led to a cholera outbreak in October 2016 – the scope of the epidemic described as "unprecedented disaster" by the country's health ministry.[37] By June 2017, the cholera epidemic claimed 1,300 lives with more than 200,000 infected; the rate at which the disease progresses is at 5,000 new cases per day.[38] Distressingly, by December 2017, there were over 1 million people infected with a death toll over 2,200. And then again, in a deadly spiral, the "concurrent difficulties in accessing clean water and sanitation as well as healthcare are likely to cause a sharp uptick in malnutrition"[39] – horrifyingly, the numbers of people with acute lack of food are likely to increase.[40]

Aside from the deep structural economic problems and severe humanitarian crisis, there is another country-specific factor which poses obstacles to the country's development – the nation-wide addiction to qat chewing. Qat is a plant which is indigenous to the region and the chewing of its leaves produces mildly euphoric feelings (even hallucinations).[41] It is also addictive. Already in 2007[42] the rates were at alarming levels, with 72% of males and 33% of women enjoying the drug on a regular basis.[43] It is estimated that qat chewing takes up about 20% of a family's income.[44]

The challenge with a nation addicted to qat is three-fold. Firstly, the most obvious are the health effects on regular or even occasional users; the drugs' side effects not only include cancer, tooth decay, increased blood pressure, but also depression, anxiety, and fatigue; laziness is listed as a perceived effect of qat as well.[45] Secondly,

---

36 "Yemen Crisis."

37 Bendix, "Authorities Declare a State of Emergency in Yemen."

38 "Statement from UNICEF Executive Director Anthony Lake and WHO Director-General Margaret Chan on the Cholera Outbreak in Yemen as Suspected Cases Exceed 200,000."

39 "Yemen's Economic Outlook Fall 2016."

40 At time of this writing, the latest available data comes from July 2017 (WHO) with cholera death toll already at 1885 victims.

41 Kirby, "Yemen's Khat Habit Soaks up Water."

42 Interestingly, the outcomes of a workshop conducted in 2010 by Rachel Jenkins and Nahla Shoja' Aldeen in Yemen on the effects of qat chewing had one peculiar result: "All participants, including policy makers, professionals and NGO leaders, habitually chewed Qat, whether daily or weekly, apart from a single young man who worked for an NGO on mental health promotion."

43 Jenkins and Aldeen, "Qat Consumption in Yemen – Knowledge and Practice of Mental Health Policy Makers and Other Stakeholders."

44 Kramáreková, "Jemen."

45 Jenkins and Aldeen, "Qat Consumption in Yemen – Knowledge and Practice of Mental Health Policy Makers and Other Stakeholders."

there are the socio-economic effects of the drug – the perceived laziness may lead to decreased productivity levels, have a damaging effect on families, and so on. From the macro viewpoint, the demand for qat cultivation has adverse effects on the entire economic system because it is certainly less profitable to grow qat for domestic consumption rather than other crops, such as coffee, which could be exported and therefore the profit margin for the domestic economy would be greater. In other words, every qat field represents forgone profits for the government. In 2011, the drug's production was growing by 10%[46] each year – which ultimately means that the area of arable land used for growing foodstuffs continues to shrink along with the state's revenues. Thirdly, the qat crops have negative environmental consequences – the qat plant is particularly water-demanding and out of Yemen's already "scarce water, 40% goes on irrigating"[47] the qat fields, effectively draining the country.

1.1.2 External economic factors

Historically, several external developments influenced Yemen's economy. Firstly, the construction boom which engulfed the region in the 1970s worked like a miracle for Yemen. Yemeni workers in large numbers took part in Saudi Arabia's booming construction industry and the "remittances sent home from Yemeni labourers raised domestic incomes significantly and reoriented the Yemeni economy towards the importation and distribution of foreign consumer goods."[48] When Saudi Arabia banned Yemeni workers in 1990/1991 as a reaction to Saleh's support of Saddam Hussein's Kuwait invasion and the valuable source of income was therefore cut, the Yemeni economy was transformed into an oil-based one.

Secondly, with Yemen being an oil-producing and oil-exporting country, the fluctuations in the crude oil world price have affected the country's revenues throughout its history. In 1984, the Yemen Hunt Oil Company (a Yemeni–US venture) proclaimed it had discovered oil in Yemen "available in 'commercial' and 'exportable' quantities."[49] What could have been a blessing for the country's development eventually turned into a curse which crippled the economy through reliance on one source of income, as well as reinforcing the crooked political and social mechanisms within the country.

---

46 Ibid.

47 Kirby, "Yemen's Khat Habit Soaks up Water."

48 Schmitz, "Crisis in the Yemeni Economy."

49 Miller, "Yemen Reports Large Oil Discovery."

Not being a member of the Organization of the Petroleum Exporting Countries (OPEC), Yemen is not part of the group of states which dictate world oil prices to their benefit – it can only react and attempt to maximize its own profits. Since the discovery, Yemen's crude oil production has fluctuated between 300 and 400 thousand barrels per day, reaching its historic maximum in February 2001[50] (over 460 thousand barrels per day). Luckily, as Yemen's oil production began to decline, "world oil prices rose steeply and cushioned the economic impact of the decline of Yemen's production,"[51] still operating with rising oil revenues. Nonetheless, with the current security situation of the country, oil exports have come virtually to a halt.[52] This is particularly troubling since between 65 and 70% of the government's revenues come from oil – which represents nearly all the country's exports.[53]

And while ideally the country could rely on its oil exports as a source of revenue for the future, once the security and political situation stabilizes, Yemen acutely needs to diversify its economy and find a new source of income, because the country's "crude oil reserves are expected to be exhausted in the next 10 to 12 years."[54] This World Bank's estimate comes from 2012, therefore, as of 2018, Yemen may have between 5 to 10 years of oil reserves left at its disposal. The need to diversify the country's industries is indeed pressing.

Similarly, even before the war, Yemen already faced food insecurity. The country is heavily dependent on imports of foodstuffs, which was made even more relevant with the current conflict as the humanitarian crisis spread quickly throughout the country. However, even at peace, Yemen's agriculture is not capable of meeting the domestic demand due to a combination of a mismanaged economy and environment which features arable land as a scarce resource. Unfortunately, this is quite unlikely to change because water is a scarce resource in Yemen as well. It was estimated in 2012 that Sanaa, the country's capital, "may become the first city in the world to run out of water in the next 10 years."[55] Combined with the country's addiction to the water-demanding qat plant, the state's food and water security remain seriously challenged.

And finally, as a third external factor, Yemen newly became a subject of UN sanctions. In the beginning of 2014, the UN Security Council adopted Resolution 2140 "*Welcoming Yemen's Peaceful Transition towards New Constitution, General*

50 "Yemen Crude Oil Production | 1994–2017 | Data | Chart | Calendar | Forecast."
51 Schmitz, "Crisis in the Yemeni Economy."
52 "Yemen Crude Oil Production | 1994–2017 | Data | Chart | Calendar | Forecast."
53 Albrecht, "Yemen's Fragile State? Local, National and Regional Dynamics."
54 "Facing the Hard Facts in Yemen."
55 Yammine, "Yemen Running out of Oil and Water."

Elections,"[56] effectively as a reaction to the successful end of the National Dialogue Conferences. The resolution praised members of the conference for their commitment to a peaceful transition of the country towards a more democratized system. The series of National Dialogue Conference concluded in January with a document which outlined Yemen's new constitution, which was supposed to aim for a more federalized regime with more autonomy given to the southern separatist region as well as to the Zaidi Shia region in the north, that is, the Houthis.[57] President Hadi was to remain in office until general elections and oversee the drafting of the new constitution. Acting on the newly reached agreement, "a federation of six regions" was approved in February 2014.[58] At the same time, the Resolution invoked a system of sanctions; specifically, a travel ban and assets freeze of designated individuals, in a reaction to the security situation in the country.[59]

Nonetheless, despite the positive political progress offered by the National Dialogue Conference, the Houthi rebels rejected the proposed solutions, heightened their efforts, and took control of the country's capital in September 2014.[60] They rejected the government's plans for reconciliation and made their move across the country, eventually forcing President Hadi to flee Yemen. It took several more months of fighting before the UN Security Council enacted a more targeted sanctions regime – and that was only after Saudi Arabia commenced their coalitional bombing and after the Islamic State murdered 142 people in Sanaa in March 2015.[61] The April 2015 UN Security Council Resolution 2216[62] invoked a targeted arms embargo on Yemen.

Overall, except for the security and humanitarian crises, Yemen also faces several other challenges for its future – even when (or if) the country stabilizes politically, the road to recovery will be extremely difficult given the state of Yemen's economy. Yemen's leadership will need to solve a range of structural shortcomings in its economy and environment in order to improve its country's food and water security; it will acutely need to find an alternative source of income to replace its oil production; and it will need to do all of this in a post-conflict environment which features a decimated and literally hungry and unhealthy society with a devastated infrastructure.

---

56 "S/RES/2140 (2014)."
57 "Yemen's National Dialogue Conference Concludes with Agreement."
58 "Yemen Crisis."
59 "S/RES/2140 (2014)."
60 "Yemen Crisis."
61 "Yemen Mosque Bombings 'Could Only Be Done by the Enemies of Life' – President."
62 "S/RES/2216 (2015)."

1.2 Civil society and media

Despite all the obstacles, civil society and an independent media do exist in Yemen – and with the worsened security and political environment, their role has become more vital to the functioning of Yemeni society.

1.2.1 Civil society

Given the legal framework which was installed in 1990 in the newly united Yemen, civil society organizations (CSOs) were officially allowed to exist and function. While "the south gained a greater amount of experience in developing CSOs through the socialist-based unions of the 1960s and 1970s", the northern-based CSOs were frequently religion-related charities.[63] Overall, by March 2014 – that is, before the all-out Houthi insurgency – more than 8,300 CSOs existed in the country with "almost a quarter of them springing up since Yemen's transition got underway in 2011." Obviously, the Arab Spring hit Yemen in January 2011 and triggered a bottom-up democratization effort within the Yemeni society "when thousands of demonstrators took to the streets, demanding a change of leadership, with the removal of President Saleh as the head of Yemeni government."[64]

Unfortunately, the CSOs' "ability to operate is restricted in practice"[65] because of the war, with Houthi forces targeting NGOs and journalists who they deem politically dangerous to their cause. Luckily, 21st century technology allows for at least some social activists to continue their work and to appeal to a Western audience – "online advocacy has demonstrated its usefulness and flexibility during this current period of conflict, since Yemen's on-the-ground CSOs are finding it more and more difficult to operate."[66] Importantly, once the security situation stabilizes, the Yemeni CSOs certainly have ground on which to build and continue their work.

In the case of Yemen, the overall functioning of its society is a specific feature of the country's system of governance. Former President Saleh remained in office for more than 30 years, which allowed him to accumulate considerable power. Moreover, "the term 'government' does not refer to the same group of institutions, individuals and political processes that constitute the Yemeni 'regime'."[67] Put differently, President Saleh's way of managing the country was through a network

---

63 al-Sakkaf, "The Tragedy of Yemen's Civil Society."

64 Lewis, Security, Clans and Tribes: Unstable Governance in Somaliland, Yemen and the Gulf of Aden.

65 "Yemen | Country Report | Freedom in the World | 2016."

66 al-Sakkaf, "The Tragedy of Yemen's Civil Society."

67 Phillips, "Al-Qaeda and the Struggle for Yemen."

of clients who would grant their loyalty to the President and expect certain benefits in return. As a consequence, this patronage system "means that the power base of the state is extremely narrow."[68] President Saleh managed to play off the various Yemeni factions and tribes against each other by "paying tribal leaders off or paying one tribe to attack another tribe, thereby weakening both."[69] This divide-and-rule approach was centred on the manufactured resentments which were "exacerbated by resource scarcity and resource competition."[70] Hence, the "regime's exclusionary approach to the creation and distribution of wealth"[71] was reaffirmed by the 1980s oil discovery which poured money into the central government's budget and granted Saleh greater leverage with the tribes.

The patronage system itself poses an obstacle to CSOs' functioning as they tend to "rearticulate the same system of patrimonialism that drives the ruling elite;"[72] in other words, personal connections are the drivers of civil society development because "access to wealth affects the power of the state and the autonomy of civil society."[73] And additionally, because of lack of central synchronization, there is an "evident concern with working through CSOs" which is the "lack of coordination of activities and oversight."[74] This may be detrimental to future development of the country's civil society when post-conflict reconstruction begins and foreign donors become reluctant to work with the local CSOs – which is crucial in the case of Yemen because any Western input without the "legitimization" of local CSOs could be viewed as a form of imperialism or colonialism and therefore the input's effect would be (at best) only marginal.

Another related feature of Yemen's society is the role and position of tribes. Tribes are a significant actor in Yemeni politics because "a large portion of Yemenis interpret their socio-political circumstances through the lens of their tribe."[75] However, arguably it is not the tribes having substantial power in the country's governance which weakens the central system, but quite the opposite: "the strong presence of tribes in Yemen is due to the corruption and weakness of the state

68 Albrecht, "Yemen's Fragile State? Local, National and Regional Dynamics."
69 Ibid.
70 Lewis, Security, Clans and Tribes: Unstable Governance in Somaliland, Yemen and the Gulf of Aden.
71 Phillips, "Al-Qaeda and the Struggle for Yemen."
72 Albrecht, "Yemen's Fragile State? Local, National and Regional Dynamics."
73 Carapico, Civil Society in Yemen: The Political Economy of Activism in Modern Arabia.
74 Albrecht, "Yemen's Fragile State? Local, National and Regional Dynamics."
75 Phillips, "Al-Qaeda and the Struggle for Yemen."

institutions there."[76] In a country with weak central governance and an inadequate redistribution system and service provision, it is "the role the tribal system plays, particularly in terms of resolving conflicts, preserving order, and providing safety nets"[77] which has held the entire system and its society afloat. In other words, despite the current conflict, Yemeni tribes contributed to the country's security and stability more than the central government, which relies on "methods of crisis-creation and divide-and-rule to maintain power."[78]

1.2.2 Media

In addition to Yemen's problematic civil society, the war also put the country's media and independent journalism under severe pressure. While all sides to the conflict attempt to skew information in their favour, the biggest threat comes from the Houthi insurgency as "the Houthis have systematically persecuted journalists and attempted to manipulate media coverage of their activities."[79] According to Reporters Without Borders, the Houthis, in their fight against the free press, rank as the second most dangerous threat to independent journalism, right after the Islamic State.[80] By the end of 2016, there were 15 journalists reported missing or detained by the Houthi forces; their other tactics include threats or confiscations of materials. On the other hand, the massive propaganda from the Houthi-held areas makes media sources a target of the pro-Hadi coalition.[81]

In fact, there are deeper issues stemming from the regional war in relation to Yemen's media. Firstly, the information which is received by Yemenis is strongly polarized on all sides of the conflict as the media "instigates regionalism, antagonism, and violence by humanizing one side and dehumanizing the other."[82] However, not only Yemenis suffer from a lack of free and unbiased information about their war: the international community also does not have access to quality information or sources since foreign journalists do not have access to the country. Similarly, the Houthis eliminate any journalism which does not adhere to their propagandist direction. However, the regionalization of the conflict has allowed Saudi Arabia to employ their massive funds for "buying media silence along with

---

76 al-Dawsari, "Tribal Governance and Stability in Yemen."

77 Ibid.

78 Phillips, "Al-Qaeda and the Struggle for Yemen."

79 "Yemen | Country Report | Freedom in the World | 2016."

80 "Worldwide Round-Up of Journalists Who Are Detained, Held Hostage or Missing 2016."

81 "Yemen | Country Report | Freedom in the World | 2016."

82 Nasser, "The Yemen War, Media, and Propaganda."

hiring PR companies to polish its image in media"[83] which further explains the lack of headlines about Yemen in Western media.

Nonetheless, in conclusion, even with the extremely dysfunctional state of the country's media, the wave of Arab Spring popular youth protests "demonstrated that Yemen does have an active political culture,"[84] which is a necessary requirement for a successful post-conflict reconstruction of the country – if it shall be towards a more democratized system of governance.

1.3 Extremism and religion

Yemen is a Muslim country of more than 27 million people – the majority of them Sunni. Between 35 and 40% of the population is designated as Zaidi Shia with a particular set of beliefs which "causes them to align closer to Sunni practices."[85] Despite the fact that the Houthis represent this Zaidi Shia branch of Islam, the conflict should be not simplified into a Sunni–Shia struggle because religious differences are not a focal factor of the insurgency. "The Houthis' demands have been primarily economic and political in nature,"[86] rather than calls for an imamate.

Still, the Houthis have opposed President Saleh's government on numerous occasions ever since the early 2000s[87] – the primary trigger being Saleh's approval of the US-led Iraqi invasion in 2003. They periodically clashed with the government's forces and by 2009 Saudi Arabia[88] became openly entangled in the conflict out of fear that the insurgency would spill over the northern Yemeni border; Saudi Arabia carried out *Operation Scorched Earth* in 2009/2010 "after rumours of clandestine Saudi military operations on the border against Houthi rebels."[89] When the Arab Spring triggered mass demonstrations against Saleh's regime, the Houthis were already considered the most dangerous anti-government force.

Yet their actual potential was demonstrated in 2014 when they managed to gain broader popular support by organizing protests against the Hadi government. As part of the UN-supported transition process, the new government lifted fuel subsidies[90] in order to take the strain off the central budget. Nonetheless, the

---

83 Ibid.

84 Lewis, Security, Clans and Tribes: Unstable Governance in Somaliland, Yemen and the Gulf of Aden.

85 "5 Facts You Need to Know about Yemen and Its Conflicts."

86 "Key Facts about the War in Yemen."

87 Laub, "Yemen in Crisis."

88 Kramáreková, "Jemen."

89 Boucek, War in Saada.

90 Laub, "Yemen in Crisis."

substantial increase in price levels generated the dissatisfaction of the Yemenis which played out well for the Houthis, who then managed to take control of the capital Sanaa[91] by September 2014. They further consolidated their power base by pushing south and controlling significant parts of the country – this time, with the support of former President Saleh,[92] who was ousted in 2011 by popular protests, and who retains considerable political power and opposes the new Hadi government.

Importantly, the Houthis created a regional conflict out of a local civil war – with Saudi Arabia and Iran involved in Yemen in what has been described as a proxy war between the two Middle Eastern rivals.[93] Saudi Arabia fears the Houthis' agenda and therefore supports the central government's fight against the insurgency while Iran was accused of supporting the rebels through financial and military infusions. While it would be beneficial to Iran to strengthen its influence next to Saudi Arabia's southern border,[94] officially the country's leaders deny such involvement.[95] However, when the US Navy intercepted shipments of weapons from Iran in the Arabian Sea, the US statement claimed that the weapons were "likely" en route to Houthi-held areas[96] since the "Houthi rebels continue to rely on Iranian arms."[97]

While the Houthi insurgency is the most massive opposition to Yemeni government and it lured in outside actors, thereby regionalizing the conflict, there are other extremist movements operating in Yemen. The spread of Al-Qaeda throughout the country is an important feature of the country's war with itself.

Yemen's experience with modern day terrorists began in the early 1990s when fighters against the Soviet invasion in Afghanistan returned to their home countries – in Yemen, they sometimes enjoyed political prestige through becoming part of the patronage regime under President Saleh.[98] Predating the events of 9/11 by almost a year, terrorists struck the US aircraft carrier USS Cole[99] in October 2000, killing 17, when the ship was in port in Aden in the south of Yemen. In January

---

91 "Yemen Profile – Timeline."

92 "Key Facts about the War in Yemen."

93 Instances of Syrian and Izraeli involvement in Yemen have been reported as well.

94 Kramáreková, "Jemen."

95 "Key Facts about the War in Yemen."

96 "U.S. Navy Says It Seized Weapons from Iran Likely Bound for Houthis in Yemen."

97 Lamothe, "Iranian Weapons Keep Getting Smuggled at Sea. Stopping Them Isn't Easy for the Navy."

98 Kramáreková, "Jemen."

99 "USS Cole Bombing Fast Facts."

2009, the terrorists regrouped and formed the so-called AQAP (Al-Qaeda in the Arabian Peninsula), quickly drawing the attention of the international community by December of the same year when they attempted to bomb an American passenger jet.[100] This prompted the still-ongoing US drone strikes in response, further increasing the number of countries involved in the Yemeni war.

The many problems the central government caused for its population created a space which Al-Qaeda attempted to fill. The regime's way of conducting business left too many people in poverty, without political representation, and without access to basic services or education, creating frustrated and unemployed strata of society, with the various tribes often (at best) distrusting each other as well. Al-Qaeda therefore intended to lure in followers through capitalizing on the government's inefficiency – "AQAP's narrative displays an awareness that the group's survival depends on its ability to appeal to ordinary Yemenis and to tailor its arguments to the grievances of a Yemeni audience."[101]

Following the Arab Spring protests, Al-Qaeda was one of the groups which managed to employ "the growing chaos and insecurity in Sanaa" and opportunistically seized control of several cities in the south of the country.[102] Still, despite some undeniable success, the Yemenis are a traditional conservative society and Al-Qaeda's appeal does not find too fertile ground.[103] The terrorists' "arbitrary violence that endangers civilians and the incitement of sectarianism is highly objectionable to the Yemeni population.[104] The tribes are fearful of the terrorists as they realize that they "seek to replace tribal culture and social structure with new leaders and agendas."[105] Nonetheless, Al-Qaeda is highly operational in Yemen, especially in some of the southern provinces of the country, and moreover, it is supplemented by the so-called Islamic State's Yemeni branch which "operates training camps in some areas of the south and takes credit for attacks on Houthi-linked targets."[106] IS in Yemen finally drew the attention of the wider international community in March 2015 – killing 142 people in Sanaa[107]; and then again in

---

100 Kramáreková, "Jemen."
101 Phillips, "Al-Qaeda and the Struggle for Yemen."
102 Lewis, Security, Clans and Tribes: Unstable Governance in Somaliland, Yemen and the Gulf of Aden.
103 Kramáreková, "Jemen."
104 Phillips, "Al-Qaeda and the Struggle for Yemen."
105 al-Dawsari, "Tribal Governance and Stability in Yemen."
106 "Mapping the Yemen Conflict."
107 "Yemen Mosque Bombings 'Could Only Be Done by the Enemies of Life' – President."

December 2016[108] when it claimed responsibility for two bombings in Aden, killing at least 100 people.[109]

Additionally, there are more participants in the bloody Yemeni conflict. Technically, the biggest opposition party was the Yemeni Congregation for Reform (al-Islah Party), which is a movement organized right after unification of the country in 1990; as leaders of the opposition, the movement "disavowed violence as a political strategy in domestic politics."[110] Al-Islah is a Yemeni offshoot of Muslim Brotherhood and therefore has religious roots; in fact, "the party combines tribal influences along with those of the Yemeni Muslim Brotherhood and more radical Salafi groups,"[111] which often leads to internal struggles within the party. In general, they seek political and socio-economic reforms of all aspects of life in order to Islamize Yemeni society.

The role al-Islah played within the Yemeni conflict was quite particular – even though they were the main opposition party to the government, they were not at the heart of Arab Spring protests and yet they managed to come out as winners from the ensuing chaos: "Yemen's Muslim Brotherhood was not the primary driver of mobilization, but did secure a substantial share of power in the transition process."[112] However, members of the party soon became targets of the Houthi insurgency as "Houthi forces systematically persecuted their associates"[113] because of the group's support for the foreign intervention. By 2015 already, "much of Islah's senior leadership [was] in exile along with other members of the transitional regime."[114]

2. International institutional factors

2.1 Security and defence structures

It has long been assumed that the country's central government's capacity does not go far beyond the capital's outskirts. Except for the threat to security in the form of religious or ideological extremism (that is, the Zaidi Shia Houthi insurgency,

108 There were also other terrorist attack committed by the IS in Yemen besides the ones listed here.
109 Al-batati, "ISIS Suicide Attack Kills 48 in Southern Yemen."
110 Yadav, "Yemen's Muslim Brotherhood and the Perils of Powersharing."
111 Hamzawy, "Between Government and Opposition: The Case of the Yemeni Congregation for Reform."
112 Yadav, "Yemen's Muslim Brotherhood and the Perils of Powersharing."
113 "Yemen | Country Report | Freedom in the World | 2016."
114 Yadav, "Yemen's Muslim Brotherhood and the Perils of Powersharing."

AQAP, the Islamic State, and the non-violent Islamist al-Islah movement), Yemen's security situation has been affected by other influences as well.

In particular, Yemen's security has been undermined by the South's secessionist tendencies. After the 1990 unification, the newly established regime quickly experienced tensions between leaders of the two countries since "high inflation, inefficiency in running the state's fiscals, centralization of state bureaucracy and the accompanied marginalization of Southern administrative centres formed the bases of dissatisfaction."[115] It eventually degenerated into a civil war in 1994 – decisively won by the North.[116] President Saleh then implemented a set of policies which did indeed prevent another civil war; nonetheless, they were perceived by some as forms of colonialism imposed by the North on their southern neighbours. Important posts were replaced by northern officials in order to ensure loyalty to the central government; "simultaneously, 'an estimated 100,000 military and civil employees' were also 'forcibly retired.'"[117] Economic domination of the North is facilitated through YECO (the Yemen Economic Corporation) which "was the main beneficiary of the post-civil-war privatization drive" and it "continues to receive considerable allotments of public land free of charge."[118]

In other words, the southern grievances with the central government all share a similar theme – that the funds are not being redistributed equitably between North and South even though the majority of natural resources are to be found in the south of the country. In any case, President Saleh's failure to address the southern demands and complaints effectively sowed "the seeds of what would become a flourishing secessionist movement."[119]

Hence, by 2007, the southern "dissent started to culminate in public demonstrations"[120] and the ideas of the movement were quickly gaining supporters for the cause.[121] Eventually, the various groups united and formed the Southern Mobility Movement in 2009 (the al Hiraak),[122] which became particularly popular

115 Dahlgren, "The Southern Movement in Yemen."
116 Kramáreková, "Jemen."
117 Lewis, Security, Clans and Tribes: Unstable Governance in Somaliland, Yemen and the Gulf of Aden.
118 Phillips, "Al-Qaeda and the Struggle for Yemen."
119 Lewis, Security, Clans and Tribes: Unstable Governance in Somaliland, Yemen and the Gulf of Aden.
120 Dahlgren, "The Southern Movement in Yemen."
121 Kramáreková, "Jemen."
122 Lewis, Security, Clans and Tribes: Unstable Governance in Somaliland, Yemen and the Gulf of Aden.

in the oil-rich region of Hadhramaut[123] in the east of the country – reflecting the southerners' dissatisfaction with funds redistribution within the country.

When the Arab Spring spread throughout the Middle East and Northern Africa, the Southern Movement was well-known for its secessionist demands. They participated in the anti-government demonstrations as the movement "exploded from its hiding places to stand proudly and defiantly against the ailing President."[124] In fact, despite internal dissonance, the movement "benefited from the backing given by Gulf states to anti-Houthi factions" making it a significant fighting force.[125] As the movement gained strength during the post-2011 chaos, the 2014 National Dialogue Conference's final document granted the South more independence – aiming for a federalized system of governance of the country. Nonetheless, the implementation of the document's objectives was hindered by the Houthi insurgency and the ensuing war.

Moreover, the ongoing conflict deepened Yemen's problem of organized crime. Yemen, with its unique geostrategic position between the Middle East and the Horn of Africa, gradually earned itself the reputation of a "transit country" – "organized crime in Yemen is mainly linked to human smuggling and trafficking,"[126] and additionally, qat is being smuggled from Yemen into African countries where the growing of this plant is banned by law. Unfortunately, the "war increased the risk of human trafficking in Yemen,"[127] crime being a sort of last resort of the local population which is plagued by high unemployment, particularly youth unemployment. Interestingly, Saudi Arabia's reaction to increased human trafficking and the worsened security situation in Yemen, especially in terms of terrorism, was to invest in building a wall along the shared border.[128]

2.2 Political factors

Politically, Yemen is experiencing a peculiar situation in which two presidents fight for power. The current president of the country, Abdrabbuh Mansour Hadi, who was supposed to lead the country out of the Arab Spring turmoil, soon found himself in the position of the leader of a country in the middle of a civil war which

123 Dahlgren, "The Southern Movement in Yemen."
124 "Is South Yemen Preparing to Declare Independence?"
125 "Mapping the Yemen Conflict."
126 Lewis, Security, Clans and Tribes: Unstable Governance in Somaliland, Yemen and the Gulf of Aden.
127 "Yemen | Country Report | Freedom in the World | 2016."
128 Lewis, Security, Clans and Tribes: Unstable Governance in Somaliland, Yemen and the Gulf of Aden.

had spilled over into a regional conflict. Hadi was even forced to resign in January 2015 when the Houthi rebels tightened their grip on Sanaa.[129] Nevertheless, with the support of forces loyal to him, he managed to "come back" and assume leadership about a month later – this time setting up new camp in Aden in the south of the country.[130] Hadi is recognized by the international community as a legitimate leader of the country and receives support from the Saudi-led coalition in his fight against the Houthis and the various terrorists groups which operate in Yemen.

On the other hand, former President Saleh refuses to give up power and forces loyal to him fight alongside the Houthis against the current establishment as well as against the Saudi intervention (while ironically, the Houthis were quite a sore point for Saleh during his presidency). Nonetheless, the international community did not recognize their joint National Salvation Government.[131] Still, Saleh's patronage system of governance was evidently effective enough for him to secure support even after popular protests forced his resignation.

Saudi Arabia – supporting Hadi against Saleh – has been more or less openly intervening in Yemeni affairs for decades. The two countries clearly have an unbalanced relationship: Saudi Arabia is a rich Wahhabist country that acts as a hegemon of the region; on its southern borders there is Yemen – an endemically poor country with a crippled governance system and several groups periodically fighting for autonomy from the central government. Yemen financially depends on Saudi Arabia (along with the rest of the Gulf countries) – either through remittances which Yemeni workers send home, through direct investment into development projects, or through the world oil prices which Saudi Arabia as an OPEC country controls.

In fact, Saudi Arabia used a range of instruments for influencing the developments in Yemen – they did not hesitate to ban Yemeni workers from the country when they did not agree with Saleh's support of Saddam Hussein in 1990/1991. Recently, the Saudis conducted a renewed campaign of Yemeni workers' deportation between 2013 and 2015.[132] They also established a set of their own patronage contacts, a network parallel to the one of Saleh's, and used it to achieve their own goals through tribal pressure on the central government.[133]

Saudi Arabia is the world's top arms importer, heavily supported in this mission by the US and the EU, and since the commencement of *Operation Decisive Storm*

129 "Yemen President Quits amid Worsening Crisis."
130 Al-batati, "Hadi's Comeback a Game Changer in Yemen."
131 al-Deen, "How Long Can Yemen's Houthi-Saleh Alliance Last?"
132 Black, "Saudi Arabia Expels Thousands of Yemeni Workers."
133 Kramáreková, "Jemen."

in March 2015 it has committed numerous breaches of international law, including war crimes. The Saudis bombed hospitals, markets, schools, weddings, and even funerals.[134] Through arms supplies or logistical support, countries such as the US, the UK, France, or Germany – leaders of the Western democratic world – de facto allowed these inhumane crimes to take place and should bear responsibility for the horrific situation in today's Yemen.

Evidently, the new US administration has decided to continue the massive support for the Saudi-led intervention in Yemen as Donald Trump announced additional arms deal worth $110 billion[135] in May 2017. The US involvement in Yemen also has another feature – drone strikes. As part of the war on terror, the US has been carrying out drone strikes in Yemen against terrorist targets ever since 2002; nonetheless, their input has had negative consequences as well. Apart from killing civilians in the process, the strikes raised the Yemeni population's feelings of anti-Americanism and in fact helped groups such as Al-Qaeda to recruit new members.[136]

So far, there is no evidence that foreign intervention would have democratizing effects on Yemen – on the contrary, the conflict is being dragged on with more people every day becoming affected. Even historically, regardless of the current conflict, "foreign influence has hardly promoted democratization: the British did not do so in Aden or the protectorates; the USSR and other donors did not do so during the cold war; [and] regional donors are explicitly anti-republican and anti-democratic."[137] In other words, through the vicious cycle of poverty and malgovernance, Yemen has been dependent on foreign powers for funds; however, the foreign influence has almost never had a positive effect on the country's internal developments.

In fact, there is barely any chance the foreign Saudi intervention will have positive development effects on Yemen, to put it mildly. The international community can hardly expect a democratizing effect through military operations in Yemen, a country which scores 2.07 points[138] according to the Economist Intelligence Unit.

---

134 "Yemen."

135 "Trump Signs $110 Billion Saudi Arms Deal."

136 Kramáreková, "Jemen."

137 Carapico, Civil Society in Yemen: The Political Economy of Activism in Modern Arabia.

138 Yemen scores 2.07 according to The Economist Intelligence Unit's Democracy Index, which measures countries on a scale between 0 and 10 (10 being the best possible result).

How could possibly Saudi Arabia – whose score is even worse with 1.93 points – have a positive effect on Yemen's development?

2.3 Rule of law – judiciary system

In terms of Yemen's judiciary system and rule of law, the country, given its colonial history, features a mixture of English common law, Napoleonic, customary, and Islamic law.[139] While the judiciary system is by law independent, Yemen lacks "an effective court system"[140] as the country's legal system has been distorted, similarly to other socio-political institutions, by the deep network of patronage and clientelism. Yemen's judiciary is plagued by corruption, interference from the powerful executive, and lack of resources.[141] Therefore, the largely-absent state's judiciary system is often substituted by Yemen's "tribal laws and procedures, as these constitute the most widespread and applied informal justice system(s)" in the country.[142]

Additionally, an even more pressing issue concerning Yemen's judiciary might arise with the end of the civil war, as tribunals may be set up in order to settle war grievances and the many breaches of military and humanitarian law.

3. External factors

This section summarizes the external factors which have an effect on the democratization process in Yemen, since they have all already been debated above.

The role of neighbouring countries[143] in Yemen's existential struggle has been thoroughly analysed; especially the role Saudi Arabia has played in the country's development process. Additionally, for the detrimental role that Saudi Arabia plays, Yemen has a particular geostrategic location which makes it the more vulnerable to negative influences as "the Gulf of Aden and its surrounding countries comprise one of the most dangerous regions in the world, being home to multiple terrorist, insurgency, criminal and pirate organizations."[144]

---

139 "The World Factbook — Yemen."
140 "Yemen | Country Report | Freedom in the World | 2016."
141 "Yemen Corruption Report."
142 al-Zwaini, "State and Non-State Justice in Yemen."
143 For more information about Saudi Arabia's role in Yemen, see parts 1.3 Extremism and Religion and 2.2 Political Factors.
144 Lewis, Security, Clans and Tribes: Unstable Governance in Somaliland, Yemen and the Gulf of Aden.

Regarding international shocks which could have affected Yemen's democratization process, there have been several in history. Before the country's unification, the discovery of oil in the 1980s and the resulting dependency on oil exports (with volatile world oil price levels) could be interpreted as an international shock. Then, as part of the collapsing system of Soviet satellites, Yemen was able to reunify and follow its own course. A serious shock came with the 2010 Arab Spring – a popular movement which did not originate in Yemen, but which, however, had far-reaching consequences for the country: namely, a new president, an old one who refuses to give up power completely, an insurgency in the north, a foreign intervention, a secessionist movement in the south, and Al-Qaeda with the IS anywhere in between.

Yemen's modern experience is full of systemic wars – most importantly, the southern struggle for independence stems from a history of divisions and the central government's treatment of the south's post-independence. What resulted in a brief civil war in 1994 is still relevant to the Southern Movement's current demands. Still, the southern secessionist movement might have been appeased, albeit with major reservations, by the federalist proposal of the National Dialogue Conference – nonetheless, the Houthi insurgency, which has been operational ever since the early 2000s, poses a greater threat to Yemeni unity.

4. Conclusion

Yemen's obstacles to democratization are indeed manifold – from its devastated and dysfunctional economy full of structural shortcomings, a severe humanitarian crisis, to a civil war which features several domestic actors fighting for power and a foreign military intervention.

In terms of Yemen's economy, the country has been plagued by widespread poverty, high unemployment, inflation, and the population's addiction to qat chewing, which not only negatively affects the country's agriculture, but also poses additional dangers to water and environmental security. Yemen has always been dependent on foodstuffs imports and the current conflict makes 17 million people food insecure. Moreover, the country has been historically dependent on oil exports and aid coming from the Gulf countries. With the regional situation volatile and Yemen's oil reserves running out, the country needs to acutely find other sources of income for its future development. Still, Yemen's post-conflict reconstruction will be hindered by the war's consequences: the destroyed infrastructure, the humanitarian crisis with its enormous toll on the civilian population rendering it unhealthy and hungry, and destroyed health facilities all over the country due to Saudi Arabia's bombings.

Overall, there are several domestic and outside actors partaking in the war. Former President Saleh joined ranks with the Houthi insurgency and together they oppose the current (internationally-recognized and supported) government of President Hadi as well as the Saudi-led coalition. The coalitional bombings and blockades are in turn leveraged by most of international community, that is, the US and the EU, through arms sales and logistical or intelligence support. It is necessary to emphasize that it is the international intervention which put millions of Yemenis in immediate danger, in large part being responsible for the humanitarian disaster plaguing the country. Then, additionally, the US has been involved in Yemen since early 2000s through its war on terror and drone strikes.

Al-Qaeda and the IS's Yemeni branch have found a sort of safe haven in Yemen, controlling parts of the South and running terrorist training camps. The South has been periodically striving for more autonomy; nonetheless, they are ready to accept the federalizing solution proposed by the National Dialogue Conference, albeit with reservations. The Muslim Brotherhood, in the form of the non-violent political al-Islah, needs to be taken into account, as their pro-Islamizing agenda will certainly reappear during the post-reconstruction process after the war.

Yemeni civil society, despite all the obstacles, does indeed exist. Nonetheless, its on-the-ground operations during times of war are severely limited and there are reservations about Yemeni CSOs functioning (in terms of lack of central coordination of efforts, etc.). Most importantly, even the CSOs have been crippled by the country's vast patronage system as the network of clients and loyalties is apparently the Yemeni way of "getting things done". Still, the international community can remain hopeful as Yemen's society has proved it features sparks of democracy, and once the civil war concludes there is ground to build on.

References

"5 Facts You Need to Know about Yemen and Its Conflicts." *RT International*, March 27, 2015. https://www.rt.com/news/244325-facts-about-yemen-crisis/.

Al-batati, Saeed. "Hadi's Comeback a Game Changer in Yemen." *Al Jazeera English*, February 22, 2015. http://www.aljazeera.com/news/2015/02/hadi-comeback-game-changer-yemen-150222104412745.html.

–. "ISIS Suicide Attack Kills 48 in Southern Yemen." *The New York Times*, December 18, 2016. https://www.nytimes.com/2016/12/18/world/middleeast/isis-suicide-attack-kills-48-in-southern-yemen.html.

Albrecht, Peter Alexander. "Yemen's Fragile State? Local, National and Regional Dynamics." In *How the Local Matters: Democratization in Libya, Pakistan,*

Yemen and Palestine, 65–81. Copenhagen: Danish Institute for International Studies, DIIS, 2013.

Bendix, Aria. "Authorities Declare a State of Emergency in Yemen." *The Atlantic*, May 15, 2017. https://www.theatlantic.com/news/archive/2017/05/chlorea-outbreak-state-of-emergency-yemen-capital/526776/.

Black, Ian. "Saudi Arabia Expels Thousands of Yemeni Workers." *The Guardian*, April 2, 2013, sec. World news. https://www.theguardian.com/world/2013/apr/02/saudi-arabia-expels-yemeni-workers.

Boucek, Christopher. *War in Saada: From Local Insurrection to National Challenge*. Washington DC, Moscow, Beijing, Beirut, Brussels: Carnegie Endowment for International Peace, 2010.

Carapico, Sheila. *Civil Society in Yemen: The Political Economy of Activism in Modern Arabia*. Cambridge and New York: Cambridge University Press, 1998.

Dahlgren, Susanne. "The Southern Movement in Yemen." *ISIM Review, 50–51*, 2008.

Dawsari, Nadwa al-. "Tribal Governance and Stability in Yemen." *Carnegie Endowment for International Peace*, April 2012. http://carnegieendowment.org/2012/04/24/tribal-governance-and-stability-in-yemen-pub-47838.

Deen, Maysaa Shuja al-. "How Long Can Yemen's Houthi-Saleh Alliance Last?" *Al-Monitor*, January 4, 2017. http://www.al-monitor.com/pulse/originals/2017/01/yemen-houthis-saleh-government-relations.html.

"Facing the Hard Facts in Yemen." *World Bank*, September 26, 2012. http://www.worldbank.org/en/news/feature/2012/09/26/yemen-talking-points.

"Fragile States Index Annual Report 2017 | Fragile States Index." Fund for Peace, May 10, 2017. http://fundforpeace.org/fsi/2017/05/14/fragile-states-index-2017-annual-report/951171705-fragile-states-index-annual-report-2017/.

Hamzawy, Amr. "Between Government and Opposition: The Case of the Yemeni Congregation for Reform." *Carnegie Endowment for International Peace*, 1–25, November 2009.

"Income Gini Coefficient | Human Development Reports." *United Nations Development Programme*, 2013. http://hdr.undp.org/en/content/income-gini-coefficient.

"Iraq IDP Figures Analysis." *iDMC Internal Displacement Monitoring Centre*. May 20, 2017. http://www.internal-displacement.org/middle-east-and-north-africa/iraq/figures-analysis/.

"Is South Yemen Preparing to Declare Independence?" *Time*, July 8, 2011. http://content.time.com/time/world/article/0,8599,2081756,00.html.

Jenkins, Rachel, and Nahla Shoja' Aldeen. "Qat Consumption in Yemen – Knowledge and Practice of Mental Health Policy Makers and Other Stakeholders." *Journal of Public Mental Health*, 110–114, 2011.

Keane, Fergal. "Yemen Conflict: UN Official Accuses World of Ignoring Crisis." *BBC News*, December 6, 2016, sec. Middle East. http://www.bbc.com/news/world-middle-east-38220785.

"Key Facts about the War in Yemen." *Al Jazeera*, August 1, 2016. http://www.aljazeera.com/news/2016/06/key-facts-war-yemen-160607112342462.html.

Kirby, Alex. "Yemen's Khat Habit Soaks up Water." *BBC News*, April 7, 2007. http://news.bbc.co.uk/2/hi/programmes/from_our_own_correspondent/6530453.stm.

Kramáreková, Veronika. "Jemen." In *Arabské Jaro – Příčiny, Průběh, Důsledky: II. Díl Sýrie a Arabský Poloostrov*. Západočeská univerzita v Plzni, 2014.

Lamothe, Dan. "Iranian Weapons Keep Getting Smuggled at Sea. Stopping Them Isn't Easy for the Navy." *Washington Post*, April 5, 2016. https://www.washingtonpost.com/news/checkpoint/wp/2016/04/05/iranian-weapons-keep-getting-smuggled-at-sea-stopping-them-isnt-easy-for-the-navy/.

Laub, Zachary. "Yemen in Crisis." *Council on Foreign Relations*, April 19, 2016. https://www.cfr.org/backgrounder/yemen-crisis.

Lewis, Alexandra. *Security, Clans and Tribes: Unstable Governance in Somaliland, Yemen and the Gulf of Aden*. Basingstoke: Palgrave Macmillan, 2015.

"Mapping the Yemen Conflict." *European Council on Foreign Relations*. May 29, 2017. http://www.ecfr.eu/mena/yemen.

Miller, Judith. "Yemen Reports Large Oil Discovery." *The New York Times*, December 21, 1984, sec. Business. http://www.nytimes.com/1984/12/21/business/yemen-reports-large-oil-discovery.html.

Nasser, Afrah. "The Yemen War, Media, and Propaganda." *Atlantic Council*, May 3, 2017. http://www.atlanticcouncil.org/blogs/menasource/the-yemen-war-media-and-propaganda.

"News Brief: IMF Authorizes US$121 Million in Disbursements to Yemen." International Monetary Fund, October 24, 2001. http://www.imf.org/external/np/sec/nb/2001/nb01105.htm.

Phillips, Sarah. "Al-Qaeda and the Struggle for Yemen." *Survival*, 95–120, March 2011.

"Press Release: IMF Approves Stand-By Credit for Yemen." International Monetary Fund, March 20, 1996. http://www.imf.org/external/np/sec/pr/1996/pr9611.htm.

Sakkaf, Nadia al-. "The Tragedy of Yemen's Civil Society." *The Washington Institute*, February 19, 2016. http://www.washingtoninstitute.org/policy-analysis/view/the-tragedy-of-yemens-civil-society.

Schmitz, Charles. "Crisis in the Yemeni Economy: A Troubled Transition to Post-Hydrocarbon Growth." Middle East Institute, January 13, 2012. http://www.mei.edu/content/crisis-yemeni-economy-troubled-transition-post-hydrocarbon-growth.

"Statement from UNICEF Executive Director Anthony Lake and WHO Director-General Margaret Chan on the Cholera Outbreak in Yemen as Suspected Cases Exceed 200,000." *UNICEF*, June 24, 2017. https://www.unicef.org/media/media_96544.html.

"STATEMENT TO THE SECURITY COUNCIL ON MISSIONS TO YEMEN, SOUTH SUDAN, SOMALIA AND KENYA AND AN UPDATE ON THE OSLO CONFERENCE ON NIGERIA AND THE LAKE CHAD REGION." UNICEF, March 10, 2017. http://reliefweb.int/sites/reliefweb.int/files/resources/ERC_USG%20Stephen%20O%27Brien%20Statement%20to%20the%20SecCo%20on%20Missions%20to%20Yemen%2C%20South%20Sudan%2C%20Somalia%20and%20Kenya%2C%20and%20update%20on%20Oslo%20Conference%20-%2010%20March%202017.pdf.

"Survey Reveals Extent of Damage to Yemen's Health System." World Health Organization, November 6, 2016. http://www.emro.who.int/media/news/survey-reveals-extent-of-damage-to-yemens-health-system.html.

Tamimi, Amer Daib al. "Yemen's Crippled Economy." *Al-Monitor*, March 6, 2015. http://www.al-monitor.com/pulse/business/2015/03/yemen-crippled-economy-political-security-solution.html.

"The World Factbook — Yemen." Central Intelligence Agency, May 1, 2017. https://www.cia.gov/library/publications/the-world-factbook/geos/ym.html.

"Trump Signs $110 Billion Saudi Arms Deal." *Reuters*, May 20, 2017. http://www.reuters.com/video/2017/05/20/trump-signs-110-billion-saudi-arms-deal?videoId=371718495&videoChannel=13421.

"UN SC Res. 2216 (2015)." United Nations Security Council, April 14, 2015. http://www.securitycouncilreport.org/atf/cf/%7B65BFCF9B-6D27-4E9C-8CD3-CF6E4FF96FF9%7D/s_res_2216.pdf.

"UN SC Resolution 2140 (2014)." United Nations Security Council, February 26, 2014. http://www.un.org/ga/search/view_doc.asp?symbol=S/RES/2140%20(2014).

"U.S. Navy Says It Seized Weapons from Iran Likely Bound for Houthis in Yemen." *Reuters*, April 4, 2016. http://www.reuters.com/article/us-iran-usa-yemen-arms-idUSKCN0X12DB.

"USS Cole Bombing Fast Facts." *CNN*, October 6, 2016. http://www.cnn.com/2013/09/18/world/meast/uss-cole-bombing-fast-facts/index.html.

"Worldwide Round-Up of Journalists Who Are Detained, Held Hostage or Missing 2016." Reporters Without Borders, December 9, 2016. https://rsf.org/sites/default/files/rsf_2016-en_0.pdf.

Yadav, Stacey Philbrick. "Yemen's Muslim Brotherhood and the Perils of Powersharing." Brookings, August 2015. https://www.brookings.edu/wp-content/uploads/2016/07/Yemen_Yadav-FINALE.pdf.

Yammine, Denise. "Yemen Running out of Oil and Water." *Al-Monitor*, February 17, 2012. http://www.al-monitor.com/pulse/business/2012/02/the-economic-horrors-of-yemen-oi.html.

"Yemen's Economic Outlook Fall 2016." World Bank, Fall 2016. http://pubdocs.worldbank.org/en/941121475773070794/Yemen-MEM-Fall2016-ENG.pdf.

"Yemen | Country Report | Freedom in the World | 2016." *Freedom House*, 2016. https://freedomhouse.org/report/freedom-world/2016/yemen.

"Yemen Conflict: How Bad Is the Humanitarian Crisis?" *BBC News*, March 28, 2017, sec. Middle East. http://www.bbc.com/news/world-middle-east-34011187.

"Yemen Corruption Report." *GAN Business Anti-Corruption Portal*, August 2016. http://www.business-anti-corruption.com/country-profiles/yemen.

"Yemen Crisis: Who Is Fighting Whom?" *BBC News*, March 28, 2017, sec. Middle East. http://www.bbc.com/news/world-middle-east-29319423.

"Yemen Crude Oil Production | 1994–2017 | Data | Chart | Calendar | Forecast." *Trading Economics*, 2017. www.tradingeconomics.com/yemen/crude-oil-production.

"Yemen GDP Annual Growth Rate | 2001–2017 | Data | Chart | Calendar." *Trading Economics*, 2017. www.tradingeconomics.com/yemen/gdp-growth-annual.

"Yemen GDP per Capita | 1990–2017 | Data | Chart | Calendar | Forecast." *Trading Economics*. May 20, 2017. www.tradingeconomics.com/yemen/gdp-per-capita.

"Yemen Mosque Bombings 'Could Only Be Done by the Enemies of Life' – President." *The Guardian*, March 21, 2015, sec. World news. https://www.theguardian.com/world/2015/mar/21/yemen-mosque-bombings-enemies-of-life-president-abedrabbo-mansour-hadi-houthi-isis-al-qaida.

"Yemen President Quits amid Worsening Crisis." *Al Jazeera English*, January 22, 2015. http://www.aljazeera.com/news/middleeast/2015/01/yemen-president-resigns-amid-political-crisis-2015122135030512445.html.

"Yemen Profile – Timeline." *BBC News*, March 1, 2017, sec. Middle East. http://www.bbc.com/news/world-middle-east-14704951.

"Yemen: Saudi-Led Funeral Attack Apparent War Crime." *Human Rights Watch*, October 13, 2016. https://www.hrw.org/news/2016/10/13/yemen-saudi-led-funeral-attack-apparent-war-crime.

"Yemen Situation Report #27." World Food Programme, March 15, 2017. http://reliefweb.int/sites/reliefweb.int/files/resources/WFP%20Yemen%20Situation%20Report%20%2327%2C%2015%20March%202017.pdf.

"Yemen Unemployment Rate Forecast 2016–2020." *Trading Economics*, 2017. www.tradingeconomics.com/yemen/unemployment-rate/forecast.

"Yemen's National Dialogue Conference Concludes with Agreement." *BBC News*, January 21, 2014, sec. Middle East. http://www.bbc.com/news/world-middle-east-25835721.

Zwaini, Laila al-. "State and Non-State Justice in Yemen." Kabul, Afghanistan: United States Institute of Peace, 2006. https://www.usip.org/sites/default/files/ROL/al_zwaini_paper.pdf.

Radka Havlová

Conclusion

The so-called Arab Spring has been widely discussed in recent years (see for example Inbar, 2013; Danahar, 2013; Altomonte & Ferrara, 2014; Yusuf, 2014). As pointed out in the introduction of this volume there are numerous problems related to the analysis of "crises and democratization of the MENA region," ranging from the lack of a universally acknowledged definition of democratization to the fact that the Middle East and North Africa (MENA) region is defined differently by various authors. However, the authors neither wish to provide the reader with a comprehensive theoretical analysis of the MENA region nor with the theoretical analysis of the process of democratization. This volume is intended to demonstrate that the outcomes of the Arab Spring in the individual countries varied significantly, mostly due to the difference of the historical, political, economic, security or religious conditions in the relevant countries.

The introductory theoretical chapter clearly defined the factors which the authors consider fundamental for the analysis of the democratization processes in the case studies, even though the extent of the influence of the individual factors in the various states has fluctuated substantially. The authors see a set of common features of democratization that have an impact on the process of transition to democracy in the MENA region. These include non-institutional factors such as economic indicators, the role of civil society and media, and the role of religion and extremism; further aspects of each country's institutions related to security structures, political factors and the rule of law and the judicial system; and last, but not least external factors influencing development in the respective countries.

As demonstrated in the case studies, history is of fundamental importance for understanding the current situation in the respective countries. It is virtually impossible to understand the course and outcomes of the Arab Spring in the individual countries without having a good general knowledge of the modern history and recent developments in the countries. However, this volume did not intend to provide a detailed overview of the history of the individual states as this would be far beyond the scope of the analysis. Only the most relevant events in their modern history have been emphasized.

Economic factors are very important in many of the analysed case studies. Unemployment in general, and youth unemployment among university graduates in particular were the source of discontent leading to demonstrations calling for democratization in many countries of the MENA region (e.g. Egypt). Many of the countries, such as Iraq or Libya, were also affected by changes in the oil price, which had a fundamental impact on their economies. In particular, in Iraq, the plummeting price of oil in the world market, combined with the country's indebtedness, led to Saddam Hussein's fateful decision to invade neighbouring Kuwait.

Egypt, Lebanon and other case studies in this volume clearly demonstrate the importance of civil society in the democratization effort of the relevant countries. In Egypt, civil society was strong enough to unite and overthrow Mubarak; nevertheless, it was not operational enough to counter the military rule and preserve the newly gained democracy. Similarly, in Turkey, the political situation is very much influenced by the weak civil society and disunited opposition.

Another factor which can be seen as a direct result of the democratization efforts in selected MENA countries is the rise of the role of religion and extremism. This is clearly illustrated in the case of Egypt, which went through some democratization changes, as free elections took place and Mubarak was removed from power. However, both parliamentary and presidential elections were won by Islamists, and one year after assuming office, the elected president Mohammed Morsi was ousted by the army. This change was widely supported by the Egyptian people, many of whom feared that Egypt was heading towards theocracy. The rise of extremism is also clearly visible in Syria, Iraq and Yemen where religious extremism translated into massive conquests by the so-called Islamic State, growing sectarianism, and al-Qaeda proliferation. Even in Turkey, while yet far from extremism, the rise of Islam in public life as well as in politics is clearly visible.

The role of security forces has been crucial in the development of some MENA countries; for instance, the extraordinary power of the military in Egypt, which has been on the rise since the revolution, further impedes the democratic potential of the country. The security forces also play an important role in countries such as Syria, Iraq or Yemen where the central governments have lost the power monopoly over their territories.

Strong leaders and personalities also significantly influence the development in the analysed countries. It is unimaginable to understand contemporary Libya without comprehending the heritage of Muammar Gaddafi, or to understand modern Palestine without taking account of the influence of Yasser Arafat. Similar influence of strong leaders can be seen in the case of Egypt and Hosni Mubarak, Syria and Bashar al-Assad, Iraq and Saddam Hussein, as well as Recep Tayyip Erdoğan and contemporary Turkey. These leaders are not just historical figures since in most cases their methods of country management have had a wide impact on the current situation of the countries, because they introduced or promoted significant changes in the economic, political or religious structures.

As was clearly demonstrated by this volume, the development in the individual countries has been also influenced by the surrounding countries. This is evident in the case of Egypt, where the protests were inspired by the successful revolution in Tunisia, and further served as a source of inspiration for revolts in other countries. The crisis in Syria also significantly influenced the situation in the neighbouring countries, as the crisis generated hundreds of thousands of refugees in Turkey and Lebanon. This had a fundamental impact on the security, political and economic situation in these two countries.

Foreign intervention also frequently contributed to instability in the countries. In the case of Libya, where regime change was imposed to be swift and with no back-up plan concerning what was going to happen with the country when Gaddafi was gone, foreign-imposed regime change did not lead to democratization, but to a civil war. In Iraq, the 2003 US-led invasion, coupled with several unfortunate policy decisions by the newly installed government, led to increased sectarianism and social disintegration which eventually paved the way for Islamic State (IS.)

The results of the Arab Spring, which was interpreted as a hope for a larger democratization of the MENA region, does not provide much ground for optimism. Libya, Syria and Yemen are in a state of civil war, with different parts of the territories controlled by governmental and opposition forces. Yemen and Libya have two governments fighting for power and searching for different sources of recognition. Syria is being torn apart by dozens of groups fighting for territorial control. Concerning Palestine, it can be argued that the impact of the Arab Spring was detrimental, as the Palestinian question almost disappeared from the international agenda, being overrun by more pressing regional issues such as the Syrian civil war.

The Middle East is struggling to restore its historical glory and renew its peace. The different rulers of the countries are trying to maintain their power no matter the costs, while the civil population is fighting to survive on a daily basis. There is a tremendous potential lost in those countries, from human and natural resources to the strategic position of a region that can be used as a cultural and economic link between Asia, Europe and Africa. As if the internal chaos in each of the states is not enough, foreign actors are intervening and manipulating the events to implement their own agendas, regardless of the people that are losing their lives, their families and their dignities. What is the destiny of the rising generations that are deprived of a promising future in their own homeland? What will become of the children who have witnessed nothing but war, fear and violence?

INTERNATIONAL RELATIONS IN ASIA, AFRICA AND THE AMERICAS

Edited by Andrzej Mania & Marcin Grabowski

Band 1 Olga Barbasiewicz (ed.): Postwar Reconciliation in Central Europe and East Asia. 2018

Band 2 Adam Novis: A Short Guide to the New Silk Road. 2018

Band 3 Radka Havlová (ed.): Untangling the Mayhem: Crises and Prospects of the Middle East. 2018

www.peterlang.com

www.ingramcontent.com/pod-product-compliance
Ingram Content Group UK Ltd.
Pitfield, Milton Keynes, MK11 3LW, UK
UKHW011005120926
8556IPUK00027B/51

9 783631 740927